Equity and Inclusion in Physical Education and Sport

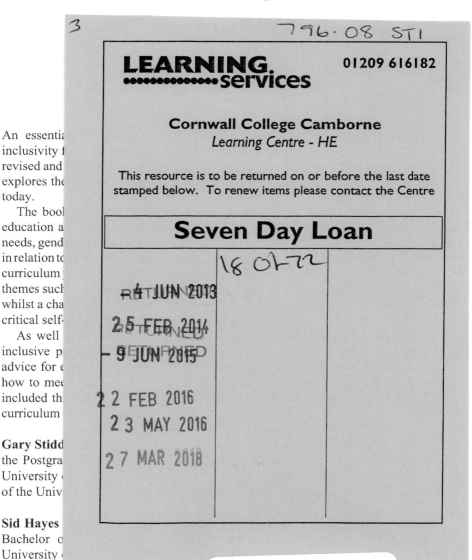
An essenti
inclusivity f
revised and
explores the
today.

The bool
education a
needs, gend
in relation to
curriculum
themes such
whilst a cha
critical self-

As well
inclusive p
advice for e
how to mee
included th
curriculum

Gary Stidd
the Postgra
University
of the Univ

Sid Hayes
Bachelor o
University

Equity and Inclusion in Physical Education and Sport

Second edition

Edited by Gary Stidder and Sid Hayes

LONDON AND NEW YORK

First edition published 2003
by Routledge

This second edition published 2013
by Routledge
2 Park Square, Milton Park, Abingdon, Oxon OX14 4RN

Simultaneously published in the USA and Canada
by Routledge
711 Third Avenue, New York, NY 10017

*Routledge is an imprint of the Taylor & Francis Group, an informa
business*

British Library Cataloguing in Publication Data
A catalogue record for this book is available from the British Library.

Library of Congress Cataloging in Publication Data
Equity and inclusion in physical education and sport / edited by Gary
Stidder and Sid Hayes. -- 2nd ed.
p. cm.
Includes bibliographical references and index.
1. Physical education and training--Study and teaching--Great Britain.
2. Physical education and training--Curricula--Great Britain. 3. Inclusive
education--Great Britain. I. Stidder, Gary, 1962- II. Hayes, Sid, 1964-
GV363.E78 2012
613.7'071041--dc23
2012011135

ISBN: 978-0-415-67060-9 (hbk)
ISBN: 978-0-415-67061-6 (pbk)
ISBN: 978-0-203-13284-5 (ebk)

Typeset in Times New Roman
by Saxon Graphics Ltd, Derby

MIX
Paper from
responsible sources
FSC
www.fsc.org   FSC® C004839   Printed and bound in Great Britain by the MPG Books Group

Personal dedication

This book is dedicated in memory of Tom Tranter (1940–2005). Tom Tranter retired in July 2002 after 34 years' service at Brunel University and its constituent colleges. He joined the then Borough Road College in 1968 and, following mergers, worked for West London Institute, Brunel University College and then the University. Following his retirement from full-time teaching in 1997, he continued to work part-time in the Department of Sport Sciences. Tommy was my lecturer, tutor and mentor from 1982–1986 when I studied for a Bachelor of Education degree in Physical Education and English. In 2003, following his retirement, Brunel University made him an honorary fellow. It has since introduced a Tom Tranter award for final year sports and Physical Education students who have triumphed despite adversity and achieved against the odds.

Gary Stidder

Contents

A new survey by the Women's Sports and Fitness Foundation has found that more than half of Britain's schoolgirls find PE lessons so excruciating that it puts them off sport altogether. Almost half said that they felt "forced" into team sports such as hockey and netball, and one in five just felt embarrassed about her body.

I can't say that I'm too surprised. It sounds like not much has changed since I was at school. My own inability to play any sort of team sport at school was a great shock and disappointment to my mother, who looked fabulous in a short white skirt and was captain of all her sports teams.

I, on the other hand, was hopelessly short-sighted, woefully uncoordinated and thoroughly uncompetitive. I was quite a good swimmer, being strong and broad-shouldered, but my faulty eye-sight made it nigh on impossible for me to compete (corrective goggles had not yet been invented or, if they had been, we couldn't afford a pair). The moment I took off my glasses the pool became a blur of disorientating splashes and shouts, and I was paralysed by fear.

But the real problem started around the age of 13. Bosoms. While all the other girls in my class were stuffing loo paper down their shirts, I was struggling to see my feet. And there is nothing more excruciating for a short-sighted 13-year-old girl than having a bunch of spotty, leery boys rolling their eyes and making rude gestures at you behind the teacher's back as you do star jumps.

Luckily, the bosoms were swiftly followed by periods, and so I became something of a medical phenomenon in the school: the only girl in my class to have her period once, sometimes twice a week. While everyone else was thundering up and down some sodden pitch waving sticks at each other, or thrashing about in the chlorine cultivating a lovely crop of verrucas, I was in the warmth of the head's outside office, reading a book or doing extra homework. Bliss.

Why I hated PE
Sarah Vine
The Times (2) Thursday May 3rd 2012: 2

Figures

Tables

Notes on contributors

Lincoln Allison: Former reader in Politics, University of Warwick and visiting professor in the politics of sport at University of Brighton's Cheslea School of Sport.

Alan Bairner: Professor of Sport and Social Theory within the school of sport, exercise and health sciences at Loughborough University.

Daniel Burdsey: Principal lecturer in the Sociology of Sport, Leisure and Popular Culture at the University of Brighton's Chelsea School of Sport.

Gill Clarke: Former reader in Auto/Biographical Studies in the school of Education, University of Southampton. Currently convener of the British Sociological Association Study Group on Auto/Biography.

John Evans: Professor of Sociology of Education and Physical Education in the school of Sport, Exercise and Health Sciences at Loughborough University.

Gerald Griggs: Senior lecturer in Physical Education and Sports Studies within the school of Sport and Performing Arts at the University of Wolverhampton.

Sid Hayes: Principal lecturer in Physical Education at the University of Brighton's Chelsea School of Sport and course leader for the Bachelor of Arts Physical Education Degree programme with Qualified Teacher Status.

Marc Keech: Principal lecturer in Sport and Leisure Studies at the University of Brighton. Co-editor, *Issues and Values in Sport and Leisure Cultures* (Aachen: Meyer and Meyer).

Saul Keyworth: Senior lecturer specialising in Dance Education and Socio-cultural studies in the department of Physical Education and Sports Studies, University of Bedfordshire.

Gill Lines: Principal lecturer and Assistant Head of School at the Chelsea School of Sport, University of Brighton.

Nico Schulenkorf: Lecturer for Sport Management at the University of Technology, Sydney (UTS), Australia.

Gary Stidder: Principal lecturer in Physical Education at the University of Brighton's Chelsea School of Sport and pathway leader for the Postgraduate Certificate of Education (Physical Education).

John Sugden: Professor in the Sociology of Sport at the University of Brighton's Chelsea School of Sport.

Andrew Theodoulides: Principal lecturer in Physical Education and programme leader for Physical Education and Dance at the University of Brighton's Chelsea School of Sport.

Alan Tomlinson: Professor of Leisure Studies at the University of Brighton's Chelsea School of Sport. Director of Research at the Chelsea School's Centre for Sport Research.

Philip Vickerman: Professor of Inclusive Education and Learning and Director of Academic Delivery in the Faculty of Education, Community and Leisure at Liverpool John Moores University.

James Wallis: Senior lecturer in Physical Education and course leader for the Sport Coaching and Development Degree at the University of Brighton's Chelsea School of Sport.

Foreword

Everybody remembers something about their Physical Education (PE) lessons at school, and in the genre of the memoir the PE teacher is an unforgettable presence, for both those who loved their games and PE, and those did all they could to get out of those lessons. The author Salman Rushdie, on BBC 4's gentle confessional show *Desert Island Discs*, recalled how life as a precocious black intellectual was difficult enough at one of England's most élite public schools. Being clever and black was tough enough. But even worse, he was bad at games.

No-one who ever saw the football lesson scene in Ken Loach's 1969 movie *Kes* could ever forget Brian Glover's brilliant portrayal of the bullying, crude and selfish games' teacher who brushed aside scraggy boys in his personal fantasy of being the top football star of the day. Any fan of Roald Dahl's *Matilda* (1988) will grin, or grimace, at the mention of Miss Agatha Trunchbull, headmistress of Crunchem Hall Primary School, and her demonic PT (Physical Training) lessons. Here, in the foreword to the second edition of this influential and important book, we think back to our boyhoods in post-war Lancashire, when equity and inclusion were far from the minds of our teachers, whether they were champions of OG (Organised Games), PT instructors from the old military school, or missionaries of the still relatively new male-PE profession.

Lancaster Royal Grammar School 1957–1964 (Lincoln Allison): It was only years later that we discovered that 'Egghead' Holborn had been a 'pretty decent fly-half' in his day; we didn't really associate him with games. He was 'PT' rather than 'OG' and he was called Egghead not because he was a government advisor on nuclear physics nor a legendary quizzer, but because he had a head like an egg. He was bald, small, old and bespectacled, but he was also impressively muscular and fit. Our favourite Egghead moment was when he divided us into teams of four: the four shirts and the four skins. As if that wasn't funny enough he had a slight speech impediment so it came out as 'fourthkins'.

When you are young you take on board the existing social arrangements and work with them, only later realising how bizarre they were; there is a kind of social osmosis that tells you that whatever is, must be. PT was 'physical training'; during my time it changed to PE – 'physical education' though we didn't notice any change in content. OG was 'organised games', primarily cricket and rugby. It was what gave meaning and purpose to life. We played games more or less all the time whereas PT was an irksome chore which occurred twice a week. The idea that they could be merged and called 'sport' or 'sports' did not occur to us.

The two activities were sharply distinguished in status. OG was coached by senior masters, men of Oxford and Cambridge, and also by visiting stars from the firmaments of cricket and rugby. PT was poor old Egghead who had been to some kind of 'training' college and was on a par with the woodwork master; boys understand status. The two activities had entirely different origins. OG came from the endless rule-making debates of the boys on the Close at Rugby School and places like it, the only people with the time and space to invent games. PT came from the state grafting 'fitness' onto its system of compulsory education due to competition from the newly unified German Empire.

Lancaster Royal Grammar School, where I boarded, was (and remains) a school which straddles two educational worlds. There were boarders and houses and very fancy fixture lists which pitted the school only against the grandest schools in Northern England. In several quite detailed respects procedures were a direct imitation of Rugby. On the other hand, in the financial hierarchy it was (and is) no more than a 'voluntary aided' school principally funded by Lancashire County Council.

Like most of my friends I disliked PT and the gym. Rope climbing and wallbars were OK, but you got bored with them after a few minutes. Medicine balls were fine, but we were rarely allowed to use them for what we regarded as their proper purpose, which was 'murderball'. But I loathed the vaulting equipment. In summer I liked the long jump and even the high jump (to which I was less well suited). I voluntarily practised athletics on my own for many hours. But leaping over a 'horse' with bars sticking out of it was something I could not give myself to. Creatures with testicles are reluctant to fly over things legs akimbo: note that most steeplechasers are geldings!

Of course, the solution – with Egghead's connivance – was to subvert PT into forms of OG. There would be a few warm-up exercises on the equipment and then we would play five-a-side football, volleyball, basketball or 'murderball'. In summer, when the pool was open, there would be water polo. The older and bigger (and more dangerous) we became, the shorter were the exercises. Only the 'weeds' were left on the equipment.

We lived through all this without really understanding it and only more recently have books like this one begun to offer an analytical understanding of the physical aspects of education. I sometimes wonder how frustrating Egghead must have found all this. And how good a fly-half he had been.

Burnley Grammar School 1961–67 (Alan Tomlinson): At my own grammar school in the 1960s the PE lesson given over to outdoor games was simple. The best boys played a football game against each other. You might combine the best defence with the second best attack, or vice versa, in a mix of trialling and coaching. Those who didn't make it into any of these line-ups were tossed a worn-out casey (a leather football, flaking and battered), and dispatched to the swamp in the corner of the playing-fields on the unforgettable command 'Remnants over there'. Those of us who represented the school were not permitted to play against the local secondary-modern school or technical high school and could not compete in the town's school cup, whose final was played at Turf Moor, the ground of Burnley Football Club, recent champions of the English Football League and European trailblazers of the day. Instead, we travelled around the county and the region to other grammar schools, on roundtrips of up to 160 miles, in a comical parody of public school networking. In one game of a particularly competitive nature I conceded a freekick and the teacher-in-charge (who might be the physics or the history master – the status of running the school side was often considered too precious to give to the lowly PE teacher) commented that it was 'the worst foul I've ever seen in schoolboy football'. He'd barked this, but then he smiled: 'Well done Tomlinson. That showed them'. So much for the character-building virtues of OG and the school PE lesson.

One of the legendary PE teachers of my grammar school days was not known for the sophistication of his lesson plans, as he forced boys to heave themselves up the rope to the roof of the gym, thighs reddening on each tortuous pull. We liked it when we could play Pirates on the last day of term, but most of the time most of us wanted to be out on the playing fields competing for the House, or against a grammar-school rival. The PE teacher was, though, as son of the local Member of Parliament, a minor celebrity, and liked to flaunt his physique in and out of the gymnasium. And he was sunburnt every summer term, stripped down to his shorts for much of the day and lazing on the edge of the playing field. Taffy Jones, as we predictably called him, wouldn't have liked this book, encouraging as it does personal reflection on one's professional role, and a contextual awareness of the social, cultural, and political influences shaping school-based Physical Education.

This valuable collection is a well-respected source for the professional development of contemporary physical educationalists whose professional prowess is a world apart from the worlds of Egghead and Taffy Jones. The book is both a professional manual and a critical, reflexive analysis. At the heart of the book is a plea for and exemplification of professional reflection, linked to potentially transformative practice. The contributions champion the value of experientially rooted, modestly conceived but analytically focused research for the professional development of the physical educator.

It is pleasing and a source of pride to write the foreword for this new edition of *Equity and Inclusion in Physical Education and Sport*, a book that is anchored in the commitment and professional practice of teachers and scholars at the Chelsea School of Sport, University of Brighton. Since the end of the nineteenth century, Chelsea has trained generations of physical educators, and engaged in debate, development and research concerning the value and future directions of physical education and sport. This book maintains that tradition, and has proved an invaluable resource for those entering the modern profession and continuing to challenge and supersede the stereotypes that emerged from our real-life cases of Taffy and Egghead.

Professor Lincoln Allison, Visiting Professor (Politics of Sport)
Professor Alan Tomlinson, Professor of Leisure Studies and
Director of Research Centre for Sport Research,
Chelsea School of Sport, University of Brighton

Professional acknowledgements

We would like to thank Professor Jo Doust, Head of the Chelsea School of Sport at the University of Brighton, for his encouragement in pursuing this venture. An edited book is dependent on its contributors and to this end we would like to thank all of the authors for their chapters.

Personal acknowledgements

Gary Stidder

I would like to thank Richard Evans and George Gibson (they know why) and my wife Karen for her encouragement and support. Also, to my children Megan, Oliver and Lily who have provided the inspiration and impetus for pursuing my academic endeavours and writing.

Sid Hayes

Elaine and Ethan, you are my inspiration and I would like to thank you for all the support you give me.

Abbreviations

AfL	Assessment for Learning
AfPE	Association for Physical Education
AoL	Assessment of Learning
ASA	Amateur Swimming Association
BBC	British Broadcasting Corporation
BISI	Badminton Into Schools Initiative
BTEC	Business and Technology Education Council
CCPR	Central Council for Physical Recreation
CCSP	Cross Community Sport Partnerships
CPD	Continued Professional Development
CSE	Certificate of Secondary Education
CSLA	Community Sports Leader Award
DCFS	Department for Children, Families and Schools
DCMS	Department for Culture, Media and Sport
DES	Department of Education and Science
DfE	Department for Education
DfEE	Department for Education and Employment
DfES	Department for Education and Skills
DIPPY	Department of Inclusive Policies and Practices
DNH	Department of National Heritage
EAL	English as an Additional Language
EBD	Emotional and Behavioural Difficulty
ECM	Every Child Matters
ECPE	Extra-Curricular Physical Education
EFDS	English Federation of Disability Sport
ESAPLD	English Sports Association for People with Learning Disabilities
ETTA	English Table Tennis Association
F4P	Football 4 Peace
FIFA	*Federation Internationale de Football Association*
GCSE	General Certificate of Secondary Education
GECO	Gender Equity Compliance Officers
GIRES	Gender Identity Research and Education Society
GNVQ	General and National Vocational Qualification

HEI	Higher Education Institution
HSLA	Higher Sports Leader Award
IDF	Israeli Defence Forces
ITT	Initial Teacher Training
JCGQ	Joint Council for General Qualifications
JSLA	Junior Sports Leader Award
KS	Key Stage
LGBT	Lesbian, Gay, Bi-Sexual and Transgender
LOGOC	Legal Office for Gender Order and Compliance
NCPE	National Curriculum for Physical Education
NDTA	National Dance Teachers' Association
NGB	National Governing Body
NGBA	National Governing Body Award
OCR	Oxford Cambridge and RSA Examinations
OFSTED	Office for Standards in Education
PE	Physical Education
PE(TE)	Physical Education (Teacher Education)
PEA UK	Physical Education Association (UK)
PEGP	Physical Education Gender Police
PESSCL	Physical Education School Sport Club Links
PESSYP	Physical Education and Sport Strategy for Young People
PESS	Physical Education and School Sport
QCA	Qualifications and Curriculum Authority
QCDA	Qualifications and Curriculum Development Authority
QTS	Qualified Teacher Status
RLSS	The Royal Life Saving Society
SCAAT	School and College Achievement and Attainment Tables
SEND	Special Educational Needs and Disabilities
SENDA	Special Educational Needs and Disability Act (2001)
SEU	Social Exclusion Unit
SLA	Sports Leader Award
SSCo	School Sport Coordinator
SSP	Schools Sport Partnership

1 Equity and inclusion in physical education

Themes and perspectives for practitioners

Gary Stidder and Sid Hayes

Now if you were good at football or netball, you were fine ... if you weren't then you were screwed. Fortunately I am pretty tall so I had a natural advantage for netball, but many people didn't ... and because our school focused on netball a lot, we went to (and won) many competitions, so a lot of our PE lessons were basically training sessions for the A & B teams, with the rest of the year sort of thrown together as what became known as the 'reject team' to play against us and get shouted at ... I dropped out of the netball team asap because I was basically forced into the team by my fearsome headmistress (who coached the teams) and nobody could understand the fact that I liked the sport but didn't want to play because I wanted to play because I chose to, not because I had to (if that makes sense). And of course the teachers would always have their favourites – the kids who were natural athletes who did the whole lesson and didn't break into a sweat and wanted to do more etc. ... I hated them!

http://www.digitalspy.co.uk/forums/showthread.php?t=798976&page=6
Accessed 25 August 2009

During the mid-1980s we were both training to become physical education teachers at different institutions in England. For both of us this was an aspiration that we shared from a very early age and was influenced by our passion for and achievements in competitive team sport. During our secondary school years neither of us had paid much attention to the ways in which we were taught physical education and it was not until we were exposed to the pedagogical process during our undergraduate training that we began to realise and appreciate ways in which physical education could be an alienating experience for some pupils. Much of our understanding of and interest in this particular aspect of education was informed by Richard Peters (1973) and Ronald Morgan (1974) but inspired by the edited work of John Evans (1986) and subsequently by other related publications (Evans 1988; Evans 1993). This influenced us to pursue our own postgraduate studies during the nineties (Hayes 1994; Stidder 1998) and ultimately led to the publication of 'Equity and Inclusion in Physical Education and Sport' (Hayes and Stidder 2003).

Twenty five years since the writing of these texts we believe that the physical education profession still has work to do with regards to inclusive practice and like our predecessors we contend that the teaching of physical education in some secondary schools still *'fosters rather than contests sexism, racism and élitism'* (Evans and Davies 1993: 21). Moreover, it remains the case that the values of those who define physical education programmes in schools needs to be confronted if a commitment to equity and inclusion *'is to be more than a façade behind which old habits hide'* (ibid. 21*)*. Despite the seminal work of Evans (1986; 1988; 1993), the types of practices witnessed over a quarter of century ago still exist in some schools today whereby ability, performance-related outcomes and sex-differentiated provision in separate male and female physical education departments work against a *'same for all thrust'* (Evans and Davies 1993: 19). Penney and Evans (1999) initially prompted us to reconsider the rhetoric and reality of policy whilst Ken Green's excellent publication *Understanding Physical Education* (2008) has led us to re-examine our own stance on matters related to inclusion in physical education and has provided the impetus for us to proceed with a second edition of our initial publication.

At this point we are keen to establish what inclusive physical education is and, more importantly, what is not. Our use of the term 'physical education' rather than the abbreviation 'PE' relates specifically to the 76 hours (or 5%) of formal curriculum time devoted to the teaching and learning of physical education to all pupils in an academic year.[1] Whilst we accept that there might be a tenuous link between the structured learning that takes place in the physical education curriculum and the extended school sport programme, we would like to make it clear that physical education has broader educational objectives and learning outcomes. In this context, the teaching and learning of physical education has little or no relationship to the provision of competitive school sport, as these experiences are usually for élite performers often in sex-segregated teams which have performance-related outcomes. As we have stated in one of our previous publications

> The term 'school sport' has been increasingly used in government policy documents alongside 'physical education' in the title of the subject thus giving the impression that school sport is synonymous with physical education. We believe that to refer to 'school sport' alongside 'physical education' is potentially misleading and may cause some confusion amongst our readers. Our use of the term 'physical education', therefore, refers specifically to the UK government's intended offer of at least two hours of high quality physical education in the curriculum to all 7 to 14-year old pupils.
>
> (Stidder and Hayes 2011: xix)

We are also keen to emphasise the fact that sport and carefully managed competition can be a valuable educational experience for all pupils but by the same token should not be at the expense of their overall holistic development. In this respect, we believe that all pupils irrespective of social categorisation are entitled to engage with all aspects of a broad, balanced and relevant physical education curriculum. This book is, therefore, our attempt to emphasise a child-centred approach to the teaching and learning of physical education in schools and to dispel the myth and any misconceptions that physical education teachers just coach sport!

The writing of the first edition of this book began at a time when the physical education profession in the UK was entering a period of transition and significant change. Ironically, the writing of the second edition of 'Equity and Inclusion in Physical Education and Sport' also began as physical education teachers in the UK prepared for yet another major policy change under the Labour government with the introduction of a fourth version of a national curriculum for physical education implemented in September 2008 alongside a 'Physical Education and Sport Strategy for Young People' PESSYP (DCFS 2008). This text has, therefore, been both hindered and helped by the speed of change in the educational world and (metaphorically speaking) the '*moving of goalposts*' with regards to physical education, UK government policy and yet another anticipated National Curriculum for Physical Education due for implementation in 2014.

The election of a UK coalition government in May 2010 resulted in further change of education policy and the re-emergence of competitive school sport as a major area of policy development, in order to reverse a decline in competitive sport brought about by left-wing councils that scorned it as 'élitist' and insisted on politically correct activities with no winners or losers. During the course of our work, voices from within educational circles in the UK began to drive the place of competitive school sport and physical education onto the political agenda, particularly since London achieved the rights to hosts the 2012 Olympic Games. In June 2010 the UK coalition government announced plans for the introduction of a 'schools Olympics' and endorsing this particular initiative education secretary of state Michael Gove said: '*We need to revive competitive sport in our schools. Fewer than a third of school pupils take part in regular competitive sport within schools and fewer than one in five take part in regular competition between schools*',[2] echoing his previous sentiments at the Conservative Party conference in October 2007 when he pledged to make it easier once more for children to do 'proper' competitive team sports in schools. In our opinion, this comment only served to misinform the general public about the perceived demise of competitive activities in schools and was nothing more than an ill-informed doctrine about the place of competition in physical education.

Michael Gove's 'one-size-fits-all' policy received a luke warm reception and his subsequent public letter to Baroness Campbell at the Youth Sport Trust dated 20 October 2010 was, in our view, a nail in the coffin for physical education in schools. In his correspondence Michael Gove confirmed that '*The Coalition Government will encourage more competitive sport, which should be a vibrant part of the life and ethos of all schools through the creation of an annual Olympic-style school sport competition*'. In our opinion, this was a sad indictment of the way in which physical education was viewed by policymakers reflected by Michael Gove's use of the term 'sport' 32 times compared to physical education once and the abbreviated term 'PE' on five occasions. In her response dated 29

October 2010, Baroness Campbell referred to the change of government policy as 'deeply disappointing' and would potentially exclude pupils with special needs, disaffected teenage girls, pupils on the verge of exclusion and those where sport is not culturally embedded. Whilst offering support for competitive sport, Baroness Campbell also stressed her commitment to ensuring that young people who do not enjoy team sports are provided with opportunities to engage in an activity that they can pursue throughout their lifetime. Eileen Marchant, chair of the Association for Physical Education also corresponded with the Secretary of State for Education on 2 November 2010 expressing concern about the impact of the intended policy on the teaching and learning of physical education in schools.

> I know that the National Curriculum is shortly to be reviewed and AfPE is very much committed to keeping physical education as a statutory subject. We are aware that competition will feature strongly in the revised curriculum but without an effective grounding in a high quality physical education curriculum competition will suffer at all levels.

Despite a recognition by academics that boys and girls could not be categorised as one homogeneous group (Penney and Evans 2002), Michael Gove proceeded without due regard for the dynamics and inter-relationship between gender, ethnicity, ability, sexuality, age, religion, culture and disability. His only public acknowledgement of the effect of social diversity upon British school children was when he publically acclaimed to the Commons Education Select Committee on 27 July 2010 that '*Rich thick kids will always do better than clever poor ones*',[3] a reference to the 'yawning gap' which had formed between the attainment of poor children and their richer counterparts.

On 24 November 2010 the UK government's White Paper 'The Importance of Teaching' was announced in the House of Commons signalling the beginning of a radical overhaul of the education system in England. In terms of physical education it was clear that the vision for physical education was firmly embedded in competitive team sport as a means of providing pupils in school with moral fibre and personal toughness.

> 4.28 Children need access to high-quality physical education, so we will ensure the requirement to provide PE in all maintained schools is retained and we will provide new support to encourage a much wider take-up of competitive team sports. With only one child in five regularly taking part in competitive activities against another school, we need a new approach to help entrench the character building qualities of team sport.

(DfE 2010: 45)

On the same day as announcing the government reforms to teaching, Prime Minister David Cameron attempted to justify the government's decision to axe the school sport partnership programme along with £162 million of previously ring-fenced funding on the basis that it was a poor use of public money. Whilst accurately claiming that the numbers of schools offering the traditional team sports of netball, rugby and hockey had fallen under the previous government, the Prime Minister failed to acknowledge the unprecedented numbers of young people who had actually rejected these types of competitive team sports in favour of other individual, alternative or lifestyle activities and the increasing numbers of schools who were making these types of provision available through the school sport partnership.

David Walsh, *The Sunday Times* chief sports writer implied that the government's decision to cut school sport funding was contradictory and full of double standards citing the fact that it was young people that had actually helped London (and Sebastian Coe) to achieve the rights to host the 2012 Olympic games during the bidding and lobbying process in Singapore in 2005. In return, funding for school sports partnerships would be slashed.

> Five years on and one feels nothing but disgust at the way young people were used and are now being abused ... Sport and young people are being exploited for political purposes, used by any amount of careerists for their own ends and it asks a serious question about Coe's sincerity when he said that the London games would be about inspiring young people.
>
> (Walsh 2010: 20)

Physical education and school sport were literally being kicked about like a political football. It was clear that the UK Coalition government intended to restructure the interface of physical education in schools and emphasise competitive sport as the vehicle to engage more young people in physical activity whilst overlooking the significance of lifestyle activities. In this respect, physical education was regarded as no more than a '*conveyor belt for élite level sport, showcasing able and talented youth with potential to succeed*' (Green 2010: xiv) whilst ignoring the individual needs of those pupils who had rejected competitive team sport in favour of alternative team games and non-competitive lifestyle activities. It was in effect an invitation to a small proportion of 'gifted and talented' pupils into what Brown (1997) described as the 'inner sanctum of the physically able and keen young male athletes of the school'.

As the 2012 London Olympic Games approached, the vision held by politicians was for physical education to '*serve as a vehicle for the flow of talented athletes into top-level representative sport*' (Green 2010: 4) even though the percentage of pupils in schools aged between 9 and 16 who were defined as gifted and talented was only seven per cent of the total population of pupils in schools (Quick *et al.* 2008 cited in Green 2010: 4). Even the Queen's 2010 Christmas broadcast contained references to the belief that competitive sports could contribute to the formation of a nation's character and may have been reminiscent of David Cameron's experiences as a former Etonion schoolboy. After all, it is reputed that the Duke of Wellington once said that '*the Battle of Waterloo was won on the playing fields of Eton*'. Subsequently, the revised policy for physical education in schools had the potential to stigmatize the vast majority of pupils who did not have advanced physical skills, as inferior. Such was the level of public and professional outrage to the planned reforms, the UK Coalition government announced a minor U-turn on their intentions to remove all funding from the existing school sport partnerships and instead cut the funding by 87 per cent enabling this to continue over three years.

In our opinion, the UK coalition government's vision for physical education in schools represented a retrograde step and signified the advent of more performance-related outcomes and a greater emphasis on sex-segregated team sport which would have little or no relevance to a large proportion of young people in schools. For us, it was a blatant attempt to re-affirm the gendered and élitist nature of the 'PE ritual' (Hargreaves 2000). Indeed, it was tantamount to legitimizing the dominant hegemonic forms of masculinity that had historically prevailed throughout the development of physical education, robustly defended as natural and desirable by politicians in the past (Brown and Evans 2004: 49). Needless to say, the UK coalition government's generic education reforms received considerable criticism from opposition politicians but also had equal relevance to the world of physical education. In spite of all this, the intended reforms to school physical education did receive some support. Eleanor Mills wrote in *The Sunday Times* (17 July 2011: 4) that a sporting education should be every child's birthright:

> Competitive sport, for too long a dirty word in state schools, needs to be put back centre stage. All kids need tough, competitive sport – and lots of it. Michael Gove, the education secretary, is shaking up our schools and making lots of the right noises; let's all ensure that sport is at the heart of his reforms.
> Eleanor Mills, *The Sunday Times* (17 July 2011: 4)

It was becoming increasingly clear that physical education was being used as a euphemism for competitive school sport and that sport was considered to be the main focal point of government policy whereby the ability and achievements of physical education teachers and their respective departments was not to be judged on their achievements inside the formal physical education curriculum but more on the accolades and trophies won on the sports field. It appeared to us that physical education teachers were being encouraged to promote the achievements of *their* school teams, to proudly display silver trophies in glass cabinets as the centre piece of the school's main reception area and to compete for overall bragging rights over other schools in their local communities. This has hardly been surprising given that Green (2008) has highlighted the contradictions that physical education teachers face when implementing physical education policy into practice.

> The goals of (UK) government policy towards PE, rhetorically at least, continue to be varied, and tend to include health promotion, academic attainment, and social inclusion alongside the development of sport and sports performance; goals which are by no means compatible.
> Green (2008: 40)

For us working in physical education teacher training institutions we were questioning whether the UK coalition government's intentions meant that we should be training sports coaches rather than specialist teachers of physical education? Were we being asked to condone the type of practice where physical education lessons were just an arena for the selection of school teams, or representation at the annual school sports day, swimming gala or inter-school sport competitions? Was physical education simply being used as a guise for promoting élitist competitive school sport? Would an over-emphasis on sex-stereotyped team games leave the vast majority of pupils in secondary schools disillusioned and disaffected? As such this posed other vexed questions with regards the content of the physical education curriculum.

Why was the UK coalition government privileging the place of 'proper' competitive team sport at the expense of other types of activities? Did this contradict Ofsted (2011; 2009) evidence suggesting that pupils were participating in an ever-increasing range of physical activities, rejecting traditional team games and turning instead to yoga, skateboarding, martial arts and cheerleading? Was this neglecting the needs and interests of young people in schools today? If competitive sport was putting children off exercise how would this address the UK national obesity problem amongst children with experts estimating that one-in-ten children would be obese by 2015 and almost 50 per cent of adults and one-quarter of children by 2050? Would this address the UK Department for Health's physical activity guidelines for 5–18 year olds (Department for Health 2011) and the recommendation that all children and young people should engage in moderate to vigorous intensity physical activity for at least 60 minutes every day? Was this undermining the government's own policy to tackle and curb the UK's increasing record of teenage obesity? Would the 'fast-tracking' of ex-servicemen and women into the physical education profession provide a solution to the lack of physical fitness amongst pupils in schools? Why were 50 per cent of all primary school pupils being denied the opportunity to take part in two hours of school physical education per week as highlighted by Eileen Marchant during the BBC 'You and Yours' Radio Four broadcast on 15 December 2011? Would mandatory physical literacy tests in schools, alongside reading and maths, provide the silver bullet solution as suggested by a leading sports medicine specialist? Did this comply with the statutory statement for social inclusion in schools? If the government was serious about winning gold medals in cycling and swimming at the London Olympics then why were there no velodromes or very few swimming pools in our schools and if mountain biking and swimming were as popular out of school as we were led to believe (Quick *et al.* 2009) how much cycling or swimming was actually being taught to pupils as part of their formal physical education curriculum?

Following the UK coalition government's White Paper 'The Importance of Teaching', a systematic and comprehensive review of the primary and secondary National Curriculum in England for 5–16 year olds was announced. The remit stated that the first phase of the review will 'set out a clearer expectation that all pupils should play competitive sport by 2013 and retain an expectation that all children learn to swim as well as consider the merits of providing schools with guidance about the allocation of time to outdoor physical activities' (DfE 2011: 15: 3). To us, the government's shifting focus away from physical education to school sport only served to increase the existing misgivings amongst the physical education profession about the place of competitive team games. Our concern was that this would simply provide the green light for 'dinosaur' games teachers bearing one ball and a bag of bibs to continue with the types of practices undertaken for most of their teaching careers. In essence, we believed that it was a deliberate attempt to stabilise the types of physical education that had existed for the past three decades despite research that had shown that a broad, more diverse physical education curriculum might be more usefully employed thus challenging the legitimization of a certain type of 'maleness' in terms of what it is to be a successful heterosexual male in Western culture (Brown and Evans 2004; 49).

In effect, we believed that the politicians had dug their own grave by rejecting quality physical education in favour of a defunct model trialled in the 1950s, and as you will hear from other contributors to this book, caused many to suffer injury and pain. The intended policy was in direct contrast with the definition of quality physical education given by the World Summit on Physical Education (1999)[4] and evidence from schools visited by Ofsted in consecutive years (2002–11). Ofsted consistently found that a disproportionate amount of the curriculum time available to physical education is devoted to competitive team games. In 2006 Ofsted reported that six out of twelve schools were judged to have good curriculum provision overall in physical education and in the best schools there was 'a broad and balanced curriculum, sufficiently flexible to incorporate more aesthetic and individual opportunities to meet the wider needs of all learners' (Ofsted 2006: 12). Moreover, good provision in physical education was often tailored to attract pupils previously uninterested or disenchanted by introducing an increasing number of leisure-based clubs and contemporary sporting activities which had encouraged more pupils to become involved in physical education (ibid. 12). The 2009 report suggested that, increasingly, pupils were being offered a much wider experience of physical education and sport. Golf, skateboarding, mountain biking and cycling, yoga, archery, cheerleading, martial arts and problem-solving challenges were being taught alongside more traditional activities, often at pupils' requests. This not only enriched the provision but provided creative solutions when facilities were limited or the programme of traditional team activities was proving unpopular. This had reduced disaffection and improved engagement, particularly among vulnerable groups (Ofsted 2009: 38). Moreover, Ofsted (2011: 7) highlighted the fact that where secondary schools had provided a wider range of games, performing arts and alternative sports this had increased participation in after school clubs by pupils of all ages, interests and abilities including those that had special educational needs and/or disabilities and had a significant impact on improving pupils confidence, self-esteem and attitudes towards learning in other subjects.

We believed that the UK coalition government's vision contained many mixed messages and were full of contradictions. In essence, they had shot themselves in the foot and scored a political own-goal. This was at odds with what we believed to be the most effective and inclusive means of engaging all pupils in physical activities and contradicted our own understanding of the nature and purpose of physical education in schools. If the proportion of pupils playing competitive school sport regularly had remained disappointingly low with only around two in every five pupils playing competitive sport regularly within their own school, and only one-in-five playing regularly against other schools were they suggesting that the failure of the English national football team at the FIFA World Cup finals in South Africa was the fault of the physical education profession? If this was the case then do we blame our Science or Mathematics teachers if we fail to win Nobel prizes? Do we blame our English teachers if we fail to win Booker prizes? Do we blame our Drama teachers if we fail to win Oscars or our Art teachers if we fail to win Turner Prizes? Do we blame our Food Technology teachers for the alarming rate at which teenage obesity levels have continued to rise? Do we blame our Music teachers when we fail to win International Music awards? And as highlighted in other chapters of this book (Evans and Bairner) do we cast aspersions on our Religious Education teachers for the diminishing numbers of young people attending a church, mosque or synagogue on a regular basis?

Through our analysis this book modestly attempts to identify past, present and future changes in education policy and examine the relationship between physical education and social inclusion and its impact upon the teaching of physical education to secondary-aged pupils. Examples of inclusive practice are examined in the hope of identifying common themes in physical education and issues in policy. Our rationale for examining the secondary school age range is that it is a particularly vulnerable time for many pupils as physical and emotional changes occur causing greater self-consciousness and higher drop-out rates in physical activity. Equally, it is at this stage of compulsory schooling that physical education becomes a specialist subject in its own right taught by highly-trained subject experts who are extremely influential on the activity patterns of pupils both within and outside of formal secondary school settings.

For the purpose of this book we have agreed, with our contributing authors that the use of the term 'equity' relates to fairness and respect for all pupils where forms of oppression and discrimination are removed from the classroom setting. Penney (2000) has summarised the term 'equity' and its association with physical education:

> In short, equity is concerned with giving value to, and celebrating social and cultural differences of individuals and in society.
>
> Penney (2000: 60)

Inclusive education has been defined as a journey with a purpose (Mittler 2005) as well as involving the politics of recognition and being concerned with the serious issue of who is included and who is excluded within education and society in general (Hodkinson and Vickerman 2010). Our own use of the term 'inclusion' specifically refers to ways in which schools and teachers value the achievements, attitudes and wellbeing of every young person equally whilst providing a curriculum that is relevant to each individual regardless of ability. It is based on the notion that every child can achieve success irrespective of their personal circumstances and that the term '*gifted and talented*' is a mis-used and inappropriate way to describe a child's educational and physical potential. In this respect, it is often assumed that the terms 'gifted and talented' are synonymous whereas, in fact, the term '*gifted*' refers to up to ten per cent of a school's population measured by actual or potential achievement in the main curriculum subjects whilst '*talented*' refers to subjects such as Art, Music and Physical Education (Cambridgeshire County Council (2011). Tomlinson (2008: 59) has observed that, 'despite twentieth-century moves towards egalitarianism in education, the selection and segregation of those regarded as being gifted, talented, or of higher ability in better resourced schools and programmes is now increasingly acceptable'.

Our use of the term 'inclusion', therefore, follows former UK table tennis Commonwealth Games medallist Matthew Syed and his optimistic, albeit old-fashioned, message in his book *Bounce* that success can be achieved by all young people, but it comes at a price and depends upon hard work, practice and self-belief rather than innate ability or individual social category. In this respect, the book outlines a range of issues within contemporary physical education that involve processes that are not exclusively reserved for individual schools and draws attention to a range of complexities that exist at a time when lifestyle choices, activity preferences and exercise habits amongst young people continue to change. The rhetoric of public policy and the reality of practice in physical education in secondary schools are considered, highlighting the ways and means through which physical education is provided to pupils and how teachers are central players in both perpetuating or challenging discrimination and inequality within physical education classes. Moreover, the physical education experiences of young people are assessed and offer a voice to both those who excel in a physical environment and those who have become disaffected, disinterested and disillusioned with school physical education.

In the previous edition of this book and in keeping with the theme of inclusion we drew upon anecdotal accounts regarding school physical education experiences in order to highlight the extent to which these impressions can have an impact upon future participation. We are keen to provide other personal accounts of school physical education but are aware that these stories could be interpreted superficially and we have no empirical evidence to support the claims that many of these writers have brought to the attention of the profession. These personal accounts, however, may serve to inform those within the physical education profession of how physical education can potentially exclude some pupils and we have decided to include other accounts in this edition, whenever possible, preceding each chapter. From our experiences as teachers of physical education we also recognise that many of these accounts are likely to be the exception rather the rule and that for every one of these types of experiences there are many more pupils with positive memories.

Since the first edition of this book there have been several other characterisations of the stereotypical male Physical Education teacher such as Mr Sugden (played by the actor Brian Glover) from the movie 'Kes' and 'Dynamo Doug Digby' (played by the actor Brian Conley) from the television series 'The Grimleys'. Most recently 'Jasper Woodcock' played by the actor Billie Bob Thornton in the movie 'Mr Woodcock' has arguably exacerbated many of the images that adults and young people may associate with Physical Education. Other stereotypical representations of female physical education teachers and sports coaches have been portrayed by the actress Jane Lynch who plays the fictional character Sue Sylvester, the coach of the William McKinley High School cheerleading squad – a ruthless fascist bully to pupils and staff in the American comedy-drama 'Glee'.

Miller and Armstrong's comedy sketch illustrating the stereotypical male physical education teacher has also reaffirmed the view that some may have of traditional teaching approaches as the following dialogue exemplifies:

> I was on the books of Rangers for a couple of years, but they decided that they did not want to use me professionally anymore, so I did personal training for bit, but apparently I was too aggressive and I had very poor people skills and that's when I thought, why not be a PE teacher … Filled with pent up rage and want to lash out? Then be a PE teacher. (www.take_it_out_on_the_kids. gov.uk)
>
> (www.youtube.com/watch?v=KwDknTtkVdc – Be a PE teacher)

Likewise, the song and accompanying video titled 'Love Lost' by The Temper Trap may be scarily reminiscent of school physical education lessons and the dreaded cross-country run of some individuals who have now reached their twenties and beyond … (www.youtube.com/watch?v=VLTPKKt-pMs)

The intention of this book is, therefore, to make physical education teachers consider a more empathetic approach to learning and teaching physical education for all pupils if the types of experiences cited above are to be counteracted. So where do physical education teachers fit into all this? As former practitioners ourselves, we acknowledge that teachers in schools have the opportunity not only to teach syllabus content but also to influence wider societal issues as indeed they have done in the past. We also accept that physical education teachers, and other professionals in the field, require information, help, support, advice and encouragement as they plan and implement inclusive programmes in physical education. We recognise the extent of the challenges that face the profession in an ever more demanding educational climate with respect to these issues, and suggest that a greater understanding of the inter-relationship between all forms of social categorization may prove a crucial and distinctive aspect of the work of physical educators. To consider the issues of gender, race, culture and social class in isolation is as unhelpful as it is naïve. The central theme of this book, therefore, revolves around inclusive practice in its numerous forms.

In this first chapter we have attempted to provide our rationale for writing a second edition of this book and the impetus for undertaking this task. We refer to the ways in which physical education can be an alienating experience for some pupils and why issues of equity and inclusion are important factors for teachers to consider. We have outlined some of the pertinent issues associated with equity and inclusion in physical education and the rationale for each chapter selection. We briefly highlight the introduction of key UK government landmark policies in relation to education, bringing to the fore changes in education since 1988, and have concluded with an exploration of the rhetoric and reality of inclusion within physical education during the last decade.

In Chapter 2 Gary Stidder discusses the importance and value of reflexivity drawing upon his autobiographical experiences and observations of physical education as a pupil and a teacher to highlight ways of understanding the teaching and learning of physical education, and how this can help to inform inclusive practice. In Chapter 3 Andy Theodoulides continues the theme of social inclusion and draws upon the development of strategies for inclusion within physical education curriculum planning under the heading of 'personalised learning'. This chapter draws upon Andy Theodoulides' previous chapter in 'Equity and Inclusion' and existing literature to draw upon practical experience in order to highlight future strategies for physical education teachers.

In Chapters 4 to 12 a range of contributors have addressed various contemporary issues specific to physical education and social inclusion that have emerged as a key themes since the publication of our previous version of this book, such as teaching physical education within a 14–19 curriculum framework, the development of sport and physical education policy, the introduction of health-related exercise within the formal physical education curriculum and the teaching of citizenship through physical education.

Sid Hayes and Philip Vickerman consider the challenges teachers of physical education face in providing relevant experiences for pupils with special educational needs in Chapter 4 reflecting on their previous chapter in the first edition of this book and bringing attention to changes to contemporary policy and practice. Gary Stidder, Gill Lines and Saul Keyworth investigate some of the pertinent issues with regards to the gender regime in physical education and dance in Chapter 5 and analyse the influence that the hidden physical education curriculum has on the teaching and learning of physical education to boys and girls. Following on from Keyworth and Smith's (2003) previous theme of policing the perpetration of gender crimes this chapter provides a parody of a courtroom drama and offers some rehabilitation strategies for those who have repeatedly offended. Gill Clarke continues this theme by considering the issues surrounding heterosexism, homophobia and transphobia in physical education in Chapter 6. This comes at a time when a Premier League football manager openly used homophobic language in a post-match interview live on national television without being challenged, another internationally acclaimed football manager who was criticised for using a gay slur, the fining of a professional footballer for tweeting homophobic abuse, and Brighton and Hove Albion football supporters belief that the city's large gay community makes them a prime target for offensive chanting. The scale of the problem and importance of these issues are reflected in Chapter 6 particularly in light of the fact that every premier league football team in England has signed the Lesbian, Gay, Bisexual and Transgender (LGBT) Sports charter and the launch of the English Football Association's four-year plan to eliminate homophobia and transphobia and make the sport an open and welcoming place.

John Sugden and Nico Schulenkorf provide, in Chapter 7, examples of how a values-based approach to teaching can enable the development of citizenship as a key theme and outcome of effective planning and management. They reflect upon the need to understand how different, ethnic and religious affiliations impact upon the design and delivery of sport-related programmes within a multi-cultural society highlighting the importance of teacher attitudes. Much of this chapter refers to the ground-breaking and pioneering project 'Football 4 Peace International' which addresses issues of co-existence within divided societies such as Israel and Northern Ireland and how the same principles can be applied in a school setting through the physical education curriculum.

In Chapter 8, Sid Hayes and Daniel Burdsey discuss the importance of inclusion through physical education from the perspective of racism and ethnic stereotyping in Chapter 8 highlighting the need for teachers of physical education to be aware of cultural sensitivities and the way in which physical education is presented to pupils from multi-cultural backgrounds. This comes at a time when the president of the world governing body of football publically declared and subsequently renounced that there was no racism in professional football and in the aftermath of two high-profile public cases of racism involving two millionaire professional footballers playing in the English Premier League leading Downing Street to use Lesbian, Gay, Bisexual and Transgender (LGBT) History Month to host a summit on racism and homophobia in football on 23 February 2012.

In Chapter 9 John Evans and Alan Bairner address the issue of social class and its impact on pupils within the physical education environment. They discuss the inter-relationship between socio-economic class and other social categorizations such as gender, race and sexuality. In their analysis they bring to the fore the question of why the issue of social class cannot be considered on its own with regards to physical education, sport and in particular health, if the quality of young people's lives are to be improved through targeted and 'situated' solutions to issues such as ability, exercise levels, obesity as well as agency and structure. In Chapter 10 Gary Stidder and James Wallis consider some of the issues facing teachers of physical education within a 14–19 framework and offer some suggestion for inclusive practice. This chapter discusses the opportunities teachers have in guiding all pupils towards nationally accredited courses in physical education, such as examination courses and leadership awards, and considers the implications of this type of approach for teachers and for pupils aged 14–19 within the new vocational diplomas.

Marc Keech's contribution in Chapter 11 highlights the UK government's pledge to offer five hours of physical education and school sport to all 5–16 year olds. Former Prime Minister Gordon Brown called for, a 'united team effort' in the run up to the 2012 London Olympic Games to make sport a part of every child's day, building a greater sporting nation and a fitter nation. This should involve schools, parents, volunteers, coaches and the sports world in offering the equivalent of an hour of sport to every child, every day of the school week. This chapter seeks to examine the feasibility of such an approach to physical education in schools and whether it is either realistic or achievable within the framework of the revised National Curriculum for Physical Education (2008). School–community links are identified as the central mechanism for extending opportunities for participation for young people across the social spectrum and addressing the recent shifts in physical education and sport policies. Finally, in Chapter 12, Gary Stidder and Gerald Griggs examine the teaching of health-related exercise within the revised National Curriculum for Physical Education, which now commands a standalone place within the range and content of activities under the heading 'Exercising safely and effectively'. They invite readers to rip up the proverbial rule book and consider the teaching of alternative physical activities in order to appeal to greater numbers of pupils.

Educational researchers and sociologists are usually much better at identifying social problems than they are at finding solutions. Several changes in policy have happened during the course of editing a second edition of this book and the issues highlighted have presented some very hard questions to which we, and our contributors, have no easy answers. This does not mean that these questions should be ignored. Rather, they become part of a reflective and critical framework within which pupils' experiences of physical education will continue to evolve. Pupil disaffection and disengagement from physical education, however, has been and remains a long-term problem and despite policy interventions to combat the levels of sedentary young people, low participation rates persist. This has therefore, provided the over-arching rationale for this book, which aims to assess the barriers and constraints that discourage pupils from developing positive attitudes towards participation in physical education. The amalgamation of each of the areas covered, drawing on the analyses and insights of all the contributors, summarises how teachers might best address the issue of teaching physical education to all pupils regardless of social categorisation. Just as our counterpart John Evans suggested 25 years ago, we have emphasised a need to question the existing status quo, and to challenge, through reflective practice, resistance to change otherwise any attempt to improve the experiences of young people in school physical education lessons might '*tamper with only the surface features of teaching, in how it publicly appears, leaving the deep structure of intention, assumption, process and consequently the outcomes of actions largely untouched*' (Evans 1986: 9). Our readers will, undoubtedly, judge the extent to which we, and our contributing authors, have succeeded.

Notes

1 The Education (School Day and School Year) (England) Regulations 1999 require all children aged 5–16 to attend school for 190 days (38 weeks) a year. Schools must open for 380 half-day sessions (190 days) in each school year, beginning with the first term to start after July. This is consistent with the up to 195 days a year required by a teacher's statutory conditions of service: the additional five days are non-teaching work days. The UK government's expectation is that all children receive a minimum of two hour high quality physical education a week.
2 www.bbc.co.uk/news/10423816
3 www.bbc.co.uk/news/education-11331574
4 The World Summit on Physical Education (1999) defined quality physical education as the most effective and inclusive means of providing all children with the skills, attitudes, knowledge and understanding for lifelong participation in physical education and sport (World Summit on Physical Education: The Berlin Agenda for Action for Government Ministers. Berlin: ICSSPE.)

References

Brown, L. (1997) Boys' training: The inner sanctum, in C. Hickey, L. Fitzclarence, and R. Mathews (eds), *Where the boys are: Masculinity, sport and education.* Deakin: Deakin University Press, 13–27.

Brown, D. and Evans, J. (2004) 'Reproducing Gender? Intergenerational Links and the Male PE Teacher as a Cultural Conduit in Teaching Physical Education', *Journal of Teaching in Physical Education*, 23, 48–70.

Cambridgeshire County Council (2011) www.cambridgeshire.gov.uk/education/parents/learning/giftedandtalentedchildren.htm

Department for Children, Family and Schools (DCFS) (2008) *Physical Education and Sport Strategy for Young People* (PESSYP)' (Ref. 00131-2008LEF/EN), DCSF, 2008.

Department for Education (2010) *The Importance of Teaching: The schools white paper 2010*, The Stationary Office, London.

Department for Education (2011) *Review of the National Curriculum in England: Remit* www.education.gov.uk/nationalcurriculum (accessed 27 January 2011).

Department for Health (2011) *Start Active, Stay Active: A report on physical activity for health from the four home countries; Factsheet 3 Physical activity guidelines for children and young people (5–18 years)*, July 2011, www.dh.gov.uk/en/Publicationsandstatistics/Publications/PublicationsPolicyAndGuidance/DH_127931

Evans, J. (ed.) (1986) *Physical Education, Sport and Schooling-Studies in the Sociology of Physical Education*, Lewes, Falmer Press.

Evans, J. (ed.) (1988) *Teachers, Teaching and Control in Physical Education*, London, Falmer Press.

Evans, J. (ed.) (1993) *Equality, Education and Physical Education*, London: Falmer Press.

Evans, J. and Davies, B. (1988) Introduction: Teachers, Teaching and Control, in Evans, J. (ed.) (1988) *Teachers, Teaching and Control in Physical Education*, London, Falmer Press, 1–20.

Evans, J. and Davies, B. (1993) Equality, Equity and Physical Education, in Evans, J., (ed.) (1993) *Equality, Education and Physical Education*, London: Falmer Press, 11–27.

Evans, J. and Penney, D. (1996) All Things Bright and Beautiful – PE in Primary Schools post the 1988 Education Reform Act', *Educational Review*, 48: 29–40.

Green, K. (2008) *Understanding Physical Education*, London: Sage.

Green, K. (2010) *Key Themes in Youth Sport*, London: Routledge.

Hargreaves, J. (2000) 'Gender, morality and the national physical education curriculum', in Hansen, J. and Nielsen, N. (eds) '*Sports, Body and Health*', Odense, Denmark, Odense University Press, 133–48.

Hayes, S. (1994) 'Winning through Naturally', Unpublished Masters Degree Thesis, University of Leicester.

Hayes, S. and Stidder, G. (2003) 'Social Inclusion in Physical Education and Sport: Themes and Perspectives for Practitioners' in Hayes, S. and Stidder, G. (eds) (2003) *Equity and Inclusion in Physical Education: Contemporary Issues for Teachers, Trainees and Practitioners*, London, Routledge, 1–13.

Hodkinson, A. and Vickerman, P. (2010) *Key issues in special educational needs and inclusion*, London, Sage.

Keyworth, S. and Smith, F. (2003) 'C'mon PE(TE) it's Time to get Changed for Dance' in Hayes, S. and Stidder, G. (eds) '*Equity and Inclusion in Physical Education and Sport: Contemporary Issues for Teachers, Trainees and Practitioners*', London: Routledge, 105–32.

Mills, E. (2011) 'Jump to it, schools – revive kids' sport', *The Sunday Times*, 17 July 2011, 4.

Mittler, P. (2005) *Working towards inclusive education*, London, Fulton.

Morgan, R. E. (1974) *Concerns and Values in Physical Education*, London, Bell.

Ofsted (2006) *School sport partnerships: A survey of good practice*, October 2006, HMI Reference No. 2518.

Ofsted (2009) *Physical education in schools 2005/08: Working towards 2012 and beyond*, April, Reference number: 080249, www.ofsted.gov.uk

Ofsted (2011) *School Sport Partnerships: A Survey of good practice*, June 2011, Reference No. 100237.

Penney, D. (2000) Physical education … In what and whose interests? in Jones, R. and Armour, K. (2000) *Sociology of sports: Theory and Practice*, Harlow, Pearson Education, 58–67.

Penney, D. and Evans, J. (1999) *Politics, Policy and Practice in Physical Education*, London: E & FN Spon Routledge.

Penney, D. and Evans, J. (2002) 'Talking gender', in Penney, D. (ed.) *Gender and Physical Education: Contemporary issues and future directions*. London: Routledge, 13–23.

Peters, R. S. (ed.) (1973) *The Philosophy of Education*, London, Oxford University Press.

Qualifications and Curriculum Authority (QCA) (2007) *Physical Education Programme of Study Key Stage 3*, www.qca.org.uk/curriculum

Quick, S., Dalziel, D., Thornton, A. and Simon, A. (2009) *PE and School Sport Survey 2008-2009*, London, TNS-BMRB.

Stidder, G. (1998) 'Gender Grouping in Physical Education: An Investigation into Mixed and Single Sex Provision and the effects on Secondary School Aged Children', Unpublished Masters Thesis, University of Brighton, 1998.

Stidder, G. and Hayes, S. (eds) (2011) '*The Really Useful Physical Education Book: Learning and Teaching across the 7–14 Age Range*', London: Routledge.

Syed, M. (2011) *Bounce: How champions are made*, London, Harper Collins.

Tomlinson, S. (2008) 'Gifted and Talented and High Ability: selection for education in a one-dimensional world', *Oxford Review of Education*, (34), 1, 59–74.

Walsh D. (2010) 'Kids deserve a sporting chance', *Sunday Times Sport*, 28 November 2010: 20.

2   The value of reflexivity for inclusive practice in physical education

Gary Stidder

From about the age of 15, I used to sit out the double period of physical education behind the local pub. I had come to regard certain curriculum subjects as embodying disciplining regimes of gender and (hetero) sexuality (Clarke 2004), and crouched between the empty crates of Newcastle Brown Ale, I successfully managed to avoid those lessons and especially the male PE teacher whose encouraging comment that 'You are playing like a bunch of girls' had the desired effect of increasing testosterone levels and displays of aggression. My shivering, bespectacled and disinterested frame did not endear me to my team members or the PE teacher as I repeatedly failed to rehearse narratives of hegemonic masculinity within these public performances and rituals of the body.

Vicars, M. (2006)

'Who are You Calling Queer? Sticks and Stones can Break My Bones but Names will Always Hurt Me',

British Educational Research Journal, 32(3), 352

Introduction

This chapter is a modest attempt at taking a reflexive stance towards the subject I trained to teach and the practices I have observed in the past. As with other chapters in this book this is informed by critical self-reflection, drawing upon anecdotal accounts and assessing ways in which my philosophies and practices have evolved with regard to inclusive physical education. This chapter is the culmination of secondary school experiences gained as a pupil, trainee teacher, qualified teacher and teacher educator within the field of physical education. My intention is to highlight ways in which critical self-reflection can aid professional and personal growth. In doing so, insights might be gained from the conformities of practice as practice is being formed and thus allow 'physical educators in schools and teaching institutions to effectively reflect on practice, to move through the superficial inadequacies of an equitable programme, to examining social construction in all its forms' (Laker *et al.* 2003: 76).

What is reflexivity?

The promotion of reflexivity is actively encouraged for those aspiring to become teachers and considered to be central to research as well as pedagogical processes and practices (Zwozdiak-Myers 2010). It is a form of critical self-reflection that requires the articulation of researchers' values, beliefs, investments and life experiences and the potential influence of these on the collection and interpretation of data and in communicating research findings (Hastie and Hay 2012: 82). Reflexivity involves analysis, assessment and improvement of professional practice and requires self-appraisal through the questioning of aims and actions, monitoring practice and outcomes whilst considering alternatives through critical self-reflection both 'in action' and 'on action' (Pollard and Tan 1987; Hayes *et al.* 2001). In this context, reflexivity can be a valuable pedagogical tool which can play an important part in the professional behaviours of teachers and considered to be essential for professional development (Luttenburg and Bergen 2008). Willig (2008) defines reflexivity as either personal or epistemological.

> Personal reflexivity involves reflecting upon the ways in which our own values, experiences, interests, beliefs, political commitments, wider aims in life and social identities have shaped the research as well as thinking about how the research may have affected and possibly changed us, as people and as researchers. Epistemological reflexivity encourages us to reflect upon the assumptions (about the world, about knowledge) that we have made in the course of the research, and it helps us to think about the implications of such assumptions for the research and its findings.
>
> Willig (2008: 10)

My professional journey has involved both types of reflexivity as I have sought to discover ways in which my observations and experiences of teaching physical education may have isolated certain groups of pupils and how my own research can contribute to a better understanding of pedagogical practices in the classroom setting. As Green (2008: 223) points out there is, rhetorically speaking, a common assumption that:

> A good teacher is one who, rather than being a good technician, regularly reflects upon his or her own philosophy and practice.
>
> Green (2008: 223)

Reflexivity has been the subject upon which some qualitative researchers have based their understanding of physical education. For example, Armour and Jones (1998: 10) have stated that physical education teachers have many identities and roles and whilst we understand and learn a great deal about teachers and professionally related issues through listening to their life stories it is important to analyse our own backgrounds and position in relation to the research process. Fernandez-Balboa and Brubaker (2012: 30) invite researchers to join them on a journey of self-discovery and engage in their own (self) inquiry using memory, knowledge and intuition to establish their own position as a researcher so that research can be approached in purposeful and satisfying ways.

In order to understand my professional journey over the past 30 years, I have drawn upon an autoethnographic narrative of myself and taken on a dual role as both researcher and researched. This method of inquiry, if done well, is where the art of storytelling meets the science of research (Armour and Chen 2012: 247). Through phenomenological self-reflexivity, therefore, I have attempted to evaluate various factors that have influenced my professional thinking and how these factors have been responsible for my own perceptions and actions as a teacher of physical education.

During my research career reflexivity has provided the foundations for building a critical view of the provision of physical education. Such an approach has helped me to construct the 'scaffolding' for my research and allowed raw materials to be pieced together through a critical interrogation of my researching self. Through the process of reflexivity I have attempted to understand more about the ways in which my own experiences as a physical education teacher can inform future practice. My own experiences of being trained to teach physical education in schools has shown what Green (2008: 214) describes as 'a marked disjuncture' between what is taught at initial teacher training institutions and what is actually practiced in the gymnasium or on the sports field. I have, therefore, attempted to assess my professional development and provide an account of the experiences which has given me the impetus to write this particular chapter. In this respect, I have assessed the process of my own *'occupational socialisation'* which Laker (2000) refers to as the training, work-related experience and teaching within a particular curriculum model that reinforce and constitute a particular view of what to teach, how to teach, and who to teach. Consequently, I now have a greater awareness of what Brown and Rich (2002: 80) refer to as 'the gendered physical education teacher identity' and how my prior experiences of sport and physical education in schools have led to me accepting standardized (gendered) beliefs and values associated with the teaching of physical education in schools. In other words, my 'rite of passage' in becoming a male teacher of (boys) physical education.

Critical self-reflection and pedagogy through the use of reflexivity in physical education can contextualise and illustrate various topics of educational debate as well as inform research and provide the impetus for innovation and change. This can enable the researcher to view the art or science of teaching through a different pedagogical lens so that instruction, learning and curriculum design can be re-assessed in terms of the selective tradition of practices that are ideological and political in nature (Macdonald 2002). In this respect, Gabbei (2004) refers to the 'author's lens' and how this can inform critical thinking and help to re-appraise established views in the field of physical education. Personal and professional recollections of physical education have provided the 'lens' which has informed much of my thinking and enabled me to assess ways in which physical education can include as well as exclude pupils. Likewise, reflexivity can be an integral part of an individual's professional development that can help to engage in critical reflections of their own learning and teaching with respect to equity, inclusion and physical education.

Macdonald (2002: 171) cites the work of Wink (2000) from the perspective of critical theory encouraging intellectual risk taking, generating a questioning frame of mind and a reflective approach to our actions and the actions of others which critiques different points of view. This chapter is, therefore, underpinned by my own interpretation of critical theory that values the learner's voice and aims to create social change towards more just and inclusive practices (Macdonald 2002: 171). The purpose of this chapter is to raise professional awareness of the value of reflexivity and how it can help to develop inclusive practice. My own experiences in Europe, North America, Israel, the Middle East and elsewhere around the world have reaffirmed the importance of inclusive practice in physical education with regards to participation and the need to engage with young people in order to identify and define their experiences of physical education. This has remained at the forefront of many contemporary debates within the physical education profession and has stimulated a number of cross-national critical discussions (Penney 2002).

Green (2008) indicates that reflexivity has been one of the major developments in teacher education in the past 20 years and cites the work of Williams (1993; 1998) suggesting that reflective practice comes in three forms ranging from a weak to strong sense of the term.

1   A utilitarian mechanism for improving the execution of teaching skills which is purely instrumental. It is intended to help trainees and teachers replicate practices that both experience and empirical research have suggested are effective. It involves the identification of a number of specific strategies which are seen to be central to good teaching.
2   A form of deliberation among competing views of teaching. Teachers who are able to use a variety of teaching styles are more likely to select the most effective one for a specific learning activity.
3   Reflexivity as the reconstruction of oneself as a teacher, with an expectation that a teacher will be more aware of the cultural milieu in which they operate. Teachers reviewing and reconstructing their taken for granted assumptions about teaching physical education and education itself.

Green (2008: 224)

Green (2008) warns, however, that whilst it may be an avowed goal to populate the physical education profession with reflective practitioners, it may seem an '*unlikely prospect and a naïve aspiration*' (ibid.) as most trainee teachers are encouraged to reflect primarily on daily practice and are rarely asked to consider broader, philosophical issues.

The value of reflexivity

At the age of 11 my parents had been informed that I had failed the '11 Plus examination'[1] and therefore was not entitled to a higher standard of state-funded education. On the basis of this one-off examination successful individuals would attend single-sex grammar schools reserved exclusively for those who had passed the examination at the end of their primary education and were therefore considered to be the brightest 11 year-olds. Others, like me, were effectively 'written off' and attended mixed-sex comprehensive schools that were less resourced and had significantly fewer facilities in comparison. The futures of children were essentially decided at the age of 11 when they took the 11 Plus exam. Those who succeeded received an academic education at a grammar school and usually went on to university. Those who failed, which was the result for the great majority, often received an inferior standard of education at a secondary modern school, from which they usually went straight into full-time employment at the age of 16. This was, in effect, a form of social engineering which confined and restricted the career aspirations of many young people subjected to this form of selective education until it was eventually phased out in most UK local education authorities during the late 1970s.

During my five years of secondary schooling in a mixed-sex comprehensive school in the mid-1970s, I was taught in large groups, predominantly through didactic styles of teaching ('chalk and talk') which was very teacher-centred and promoted rote types of learning. I can recall the way in which we were taught using mechanical repetition which might have helped us to remember, but often without real understanding of its meaning or significance. Many of my recollections as a schoolboy were reminiscent of the depictions from the 1970s and 1980s television programmes of the time such as 'Please Sir' and 'Grange Hill' which were supposed to resonate with the values and moral imperative of teachers. I had also experienced forms of discrimination with regards to my own career aspirations. My intention of becoming a journalist was dismissed by the school's careers adviser as being over-ambitious. Likewise, my intended career pursuit of entering the field of journalism was not taken seriously as I was denied the opportunity of taking an elective typewriting course in my fourth year of secondary school as this was reserved for female pupils who wished to become a secretary. If it wasn't for my physical education teacher, I'd never have got to do my work experience at the sports desk of the local newspaper.

Instead, I was given a choice between technical drawing and handicraft. Between the ages of 14 and 16 I was required to take different qualifications compared to my counterparts at the neighbouring grammar school. For children like me the Certificate of Secondary Education (CSE) qualification in a range of different subjects was considered to be appropriate for those pupils attending state comprehensive schools. This particular qualification was intended for pupils in mainstream secondary education, though not taken by the most academic pupils at grammar schools who took O-level (Ordinary level) qualifications designed for more able pupils and were necessary for progression into further education

(Advanced or 'A' level). I can still recall my teachers reinforcing the message that a grade one in CSE was only ever going to be equivalent to a grade C at 'O' level and that it was practically impossible to ever achieve better grades than our grammar school counterparts.

My own physical education lessons at secondary school were less than satisfactory, as facilities were poor and overtly different compared to the manicured playing fields at the respective boy's and girl's grammar schools. My physical education lessons often took place outside on concrete or tarmac surfaces, or in cramped indoor facilities. On the rare occasion that physical education lessons were organised on grass, these were at off-site local council facilities that reduced the time for lessons by half due to the transportation arrangements. On many occasions my physical education lessons were taught by (male) non-specialist physical education teachers who had a keen interest in football or cricket. They would literally choose two captains to select teams and then referee an adult version of their chosen game, often turning a blind eye to any form of dubious physical contact. Needless to say I learnt very little from such experiences but then again I didn't know any different. Now I can look back and have a real sense of empathy with others who had to endure these same experiences during their own formative years at school.

> Yup, great training, particularly the excruciating choosing of teams. I'd stand there as the number of girls around me dwindled, transmitting a message telepathically to the swaggering captains: "Choose me next. Me. I'm one of you, not one of them. Can't you see that?"
>
> Anna Davis 'Down with Sport', *The Guardian*, 13 November 2000

As a trainee physical education teacher during the 1980s, I witnessed physical education in secondary schools undergo significant changes, reflected by important pedagogical debates of the time associated with policies that addressed equality and inclusion. One of the outcomes of research at the time were the potential benefits of mixed-sex and mixed-ability physical education classes within secondary schools (Sherlock 1977, Graydon 1980, Leaman 1984). As a result, some of my training experiences in schools were with co-educational and mixed-ability classes, albeit a limited number and often restricted to the new intake of 11 year-old pupils. These experiences coupled with teaching activities that I had not previously learnt predictably and inevitably challenged my professional competencies and view about the nature and purpose of physical education. However, the vast majority of my training experiences were with single-sex boys' classes that were segregated according to ability and consisted primarily of male-appropriate team games. In one particular school, pupils were divided into higher, intermediate and lower ability single-sex groups for their physical education lessons (a practice known as 'setting' or 'streaming') on the basis of the time they achieved after completing a three-mile cross-country run.

These types of experiences were not exclusively reserved for the teaching of physical education and reflected the way in which inter-school sporting competitions were organised. In most cases boys and girls participated in separate teams and different sports. Even in situations where they were part of the same team boys and girls took part in separate events and competitions despite alternative ways of organising certain activities. For example, a mixed-sex 4-×-100 metre relay involving two male and two female pupils running at specific stages of the race (girls running stages one and three; boys running stages two and four for example) had the potential to bring public (parental) attention to some of the ways in which sex differences could be celebrated. Likewise, a mixed-sex medley relay[2] involving boys and girls swimming at different stages and different strokes could also have had the same desired effect. Needless to say, I never actually witnessed these types of activities taking place so whilst there appeared to be an acceptance of the principles of equity in theory there appeared to be less commitment to the application in practice.

As such I began to acknowledge that despite common policies for all pupils many of their experiences were often based upon the professional discretion of teachers without involving them in the process. In this context, physical education teachers rarely consulted pupils or offered them a voice in curriculum decisions and tended to hold very conventional attitudes and ideas regarding the types of activities they considered to be appropriate. In one training school during the mid-eighties I had witnessed a group of 14 year-old boys participating in a game known as *'British Bull Dog'*[3] where the object of the game was to get from one end of the gymnasium to the other without being tagged (tackled rugby-style). A fellow trainee teacher at the time reported that he had watched in amazement as a teacher replicated the latest computer game of the time called *'Space Invaders'* whereby lines of pupils would walk sideways in unison across the gymnasium hoping to avoid being struck by a football kicked by pupils unable to participate. If successful each pupil would then take one advancing step forward and descend closer until eventually there was one remaining pupil. Other observations of physical education classes during my initial teacher training in schools included groups of boys carrying wooden benches over, under, around and through a maze of obstacles in a gymnasium in an attempt to simulate the 'field gun competition' held at the annual Royal Tournament.[4] Whilst this may have appealed to the very athletic members of the class it had very little appeal to others who were usually the boys who would be forced to shin up a vertical bench to signify completion of the task and be spared the indignity of having to complete ten press-ups as a punishment for failing to win the task. I can also remember certain teachers in the gymnasium asking groups of boys to remove their t-shirts and play basketball bare-chested against other boys wearing their t-shirts (a practice known within boys' physical education and amongst male physical education teachers as 'skins versus shirts'). Although it appeared that the boys didn't seem to mind I was aware that some boys were self-conscious either about their weight, particular dermatological conditions, or physical scarring.

Much of the divide between academic theory and daily pragmatism was often based on the assumption that more experienced and senior physical education teachers knew what was best for the pupils and was regularly reinforced by the old adage *'if it ain't broke don't fix it'*. Consequently, I learnt to teach pre-adolescent and post-pubescent boys a staple diet of competitive, physically vigorous and aggressive invasion games that remained within the confines of acceptable male heterosexuality without questioning the concept of what it meant to be 'physically educated'. A young man, now in his late thirties, recalled to me a physical education lesson that had all the hallmarks of such an approach to teaching during his time as a pupil in the early 1980s:

> I was at the (Professional Football) Academy at the time playing a high standard of football. My PE lessons could not have been any different. He got us playing football in complete silence. If you made any noise the opposition would always know where you were he'd say.

It is perhaps unsurprising that much of my training in secondary schools as a teacher of physical education was often determined by very prescriptive programmes of activity based upon biological sex, physical ability and performance-related outcomes. On reflection, this had limited both my professional development and understanding of issues related to inclusive practice and physical education in schools. What is now clear is that many of my daily practices in physical education during the initial years of my teaching career were influenced by established patterns of provision. For me it was reminiscent of Rich's (2001: 131) reference to Bullough (1987):

> When a beginning teacher enters a school for the first time, they enter more than a building; they enter a culture of teaching that has evolved in response to a school's structure and wider cultural values that establishes what is the appropriate teacher role. To function successfully within the school, the beginning teacher must come to terms with this role and the values that sustain it.
>
> (Bullough 1987: 83 cited in Rich 2001: 131)

As a result, my early experiences of teaching physical education in secondary schools involved me teaching groups of boys how to become fitter, stronger, and competitive young men predominantly through playing territorial war-like games where performance-orientated outcomes were highly valued. I was often reminded that this was what kids (boys) enjoyed, this was what they wanted, this was what was good for them, this would keep them out of trouble and this was what would eventually help them get a (manual or military) job. Male pupils were often reminded of the value of particular team games for developing character-building and asserting male heterosexuality. *'Rugby would sort the men out from the boys'* were the words of wisdom given to me during the formative years of my career which would provide boys with an outlet to channel their pent-up aggression in a controlled way. Male pupils who were less motivated in physical education lessons were told that *'If you're fit and can work with your hands, you'll always be able to earn a crust'* in an attempt to address apathy and motivate the less enthusiastic members of the class. Many of these perceptions were based upon the limited expectations of boys from particular lower socio-economic backgrounds. As you will read in other chapters of this book (John Evans and Alan Bairner; and Gill Clarke for example) that across the home nations of the UK, physical education and sport have historically laid down the rules of belonging to our gender and social class, as well as our masculine and feminine heterosexuality.

At the time I had begun my teaching career antiquated practices such as forcing misbehaved pupils to write repetitive sentences multiple times (otherwise known as writing lines) had been recognised as counter-productive in developing literacy skills. Why would you use writing as a punishment when the whole point was to encourage pupils to write in the first place? And yet, I had observed physical education teachers doing exactly the same – using exercise as a form of punishment whether it was press-ups or running around the outside of the football pitch three times! To challenge established practices in physical education, however, presented me with a compromising dilemma in advocating innovation and change. As a trainee teacher there was the risk of failing my qualification unless I accepted already established views, whilst as a newly qualified teacher I risked my professional integrity and credibility unless I taught what I was obliged to teach and did the things I was told to do. I later discovered that I was not alone and my experiences were commonplace amongst newly-qualified teachers as highlighted by researchers ten years later (Green 2003; 2008; Brown 2005; Rich 2001). For example, the process of becoming a male physical education teacher and the gender identity work that I had to practice and perfect in order to qualify as a teacher has been explored by Brown (2005) and his interpretation of Pierre Bourdieu's embodied sociology. For Brown, learning to teach physical education involves an economy of gendered practices that happen over a period of engagement within the overlapping field of physical education, sport and education through which a gendered habitus is generated and becomes recognised as accepted practice (Brown 2005: 5). As such, I acquired the subject knowledge and craft skills necessary for me to teach and assess physical education to boys and became a technician rather than a critical professional.

A turning point came when I gained an opportunity to teach physical education in the US at the beginning of the 1990s as part of a UK government teacher-exchange programme. This involved me teaching activities I was less familiar with but also working exclusively with mixed-sex classes in a range of different settings. Many of my own perceptions regarding pupil ability were ultimately challenged as a result of such experiences and changed the way in which I viewed the teaching of my specialist subject, making me more aware of the alternatives. Mixed-sex and mixed ability teaching provided me with an opportunity to reflect upon my own practice and consider innovative ways of engaging boys and girls with a range of abilities into purposeful physical activities. On one particular occasion teaching the principles of invasion games through (American) flag football[5] convinced me that 'contact sports' could be adapted, modified and taught in mixed-sex groups involving all pupils irrespective of physical ability or biological sex providing that the lesson had been planned to take into account both the physical ability and physical size of the pupils.

As a result of this 'Mid-Atlantic' experience I was far more prepared to question my own educational philosophy through critical reflection and consider alternative approaches to teaching physical education. At the beginning of the nineties a National Curriculum for Physical Education (NCPE) was due for implementation into UK state-funded schools and promised to provide equal access and opportunity to the physical education curriculum for all pupils. This was an opportunity for physical education teachers to move beyond conventional approaches and re-define the way in which boys and girls experienced their physical education lessons in schools.

On the surface, the physical education profession seemed to embrace the prospect of a National Curriculum for Physical Education and appeared to be very receptive and committed in addressing equality of access and opportunity. For example, I had observed pockets of innovative, imaginative and inclusive practice within physical education lessons which had integrated male pupils with particular physical disabilities into mainstream classes. One boy for example, who was permanently confined to a wheelchair due to brittle bone disease,[6] participated in a basketball lesson with able-bodied pupils (who were also restricted to use wheelchairs). This had given the pupils empathy towards this individual pupil who was more adept in moving on the court compared to his able-bodied peers. A female pupil, also restricted to a wheelchair, was integrated into mainstream physical education lessons and subsequently developed advanced hand and eye co-ordination skills particularly in the divided court games of tennis and badminton. On another occasion a male pupil who had acute scoliosis[7] succeeded in swimming ten meters across the pool with other able-bodied pupils despite being restricted by a corset that had to be worn underneath his clothing except when he was swimming. In this respect, actions were actually speaking louder than words.

Many of my own experiences of teaching physical education provided the impetus for a post-graduate study that assessed the merits of single-sex and mixed-sex physical education in England (Stidder 1998). The study revealed that physical education held particular importance for adolescent pupils, but despite the fact that pupils were ambivalent with respect to the sex of the teacher, physical education teachers often preferred to teach in same-sex schools or teach same-sex classes in mixed-sex schools. There also appeared to be a sub-culture operating between male and female physical education teachers in the mixed-sex school that diametrically pulled them in opposite directions. This had resulted in very different views on how to manage the physical education curriculum for boys and girls respectively. One male physical education teacher in the mixed-sex school, for example, had spoken 'off the record' and confessed that he would *always know when it's half-time in my lesson, because the girls are heading back to the changing rooms'* (a reference to the fact that his female colleagues believed that girls required more time to change after physical education lessons compared to boys).

My post-graduate study of physical education confirmed that class organisation, management, curriculum design and staffing were significantly influenced by gender. As such, I began to question that even if single-sex physical education teaching was inherently beneficial for boys and girls in schools (and there were educational reasons to suggest so) why was opposite-sex teaching the exception rather than the rule? As an undergraduate student my university tutor would constantly remind us that, '*a good physical education teacher can teach anybody anything*'. Teaching opposite-sex groups was an opportunity for physical education departments to play to their strengths by utilising staff expertise and provide activities to boys and girls outside of traditional boundaries. Opposite-sex teaching allowed for professional development and a chance for male and female teachers alike to expand their repertoires and get to know pupils whom they otherwise may not have taught. During my postgraduate study some physical education teachers I spoke with seemed particularly reluctant to teaching pupils of their opposite sex. Some female physical education teachers I spoke with would attribute this to issues associated with classroom management and control as well as concerns that boys would not take them seriously. In contrast, some male teachers expressed reservations about teaching girls for reasons associated with physical contact and lower levels of enthusiasm. I began to question, therefore, why girls and boys were often taught separately and exclusively by same-sex teachers unlike the experiences I had undergone in North America. Equally, it raised questions about equality of opportunity and why boys and girls were often provided with different types of activities within the formal physical education curriculum.

When I left the teaching profession towards the end of the nineties research suggested that some male teachers within the physical education fraternity appeared to be reticent towards adapting existing practices and generally resisted ways of organising 'girl-friendly' teaching and learning (Youth Sport Trust 2000). My own oberservations also confirmed that mixed-sex and/or mixed-ability physical education was largely a tokenistic gesture towards equal opportunities policy and a 'trendy' strategy that paid little more than lip service to mixed-sex and/or mixed-ability teaching during formal school inspections. Any attempts to move towards mixed-sex and mixed-ability physical education were undermined by some male physical education teachers who often threatened disruptive boys with the prospect of taking part with the girls. Consequently, mixed-sex and mixed-ability physical education was adversely affected by an inappropriate curriculum and limited pedagogical developments that resulted in little or no attitudinal change amongst teachers. It was also clear that senior teachers in some schools had very distinctive views especially when it came to same-sex staffing policy in physical education as highlighted by a conversation with a former male physical education teacher who resigned from his school after being denied an interview for the post of '*Head of Girls' physical education*' – a position that he had successfully covered for eight months due to the maternity leave of a female colleague and subsequent resignation of the female member of staff. Anecdotal accounts related to staffing policies in schools such as these may have been, therefore, an (un)intended consequence of maintaining single-sex physical education classes and separate male and female departments.

As I moved into higher education at the end of the nineties, after 13 years of professional practice in secondary schools, I began to visit trainee physical education teachers during compulsory periods of school-based training and realised that many of my own previous teaching experiences and observations were not unique. Whilst I had visited many schools where pupils were offered different pathways and options in physical education where there was high recognition and status for physical education I also saw the types of practices that I had witnessed throughout my own teaching career 15 years previously. As such, I recognised that the school-based training experiences of some trainee teachers of physical education had the potential to re-affirm a self-perpetuating cycle as some male trainees gained limited experience of teaching dance whilst on school-based placements whilst some female trainees remained inside very traditional and rigid gendered boundaries (Stidder and Hayes 2006). In this respect, their school-based training of physical education at school was a key determinant in reinforcing established forms of professional practice that acted to restrain their views towards innovation and change. It became clear to me that some recruits to the physical education profession had been socialised in reproducing and accepting standardised beliefs and values associated with the teaching of physical education in schools. In essence, I was complicit in the production of 'male' teachers of boys' games and 'female' teachers of girls' games. Further evidence of this was the tendency for physical education teachers and mentors in schools to differentiate the training experiences of trainee teachers by sex, thus perpetuating a gendered cycle of events within the training of future recruits to the profession. For example, my observations were that some female trainees taught 'appropriate' activities to classes of girls and were trained exclusively by female mentors whilst some male trainees underwent identical training with single-sex classes of boys under the mentorship of male teachers – a practice that I was equally guilty of in my role as a mentor when I was teaching in secondary schools.

Conclusion

The physical education profession in England may refute and challenge my observations over the past 30 years and claim that much has been done to address issues of equity and inclusion in physical education. My own experiences as a secondary school teacher, teacher educator and researcher would not support such optimism. As with other researchers (Keay 2005) I would concur that critical self-reflection can help to develop fresh approaches to the induction and training of newly-qualified physical education teachers rather leaving them to rely on experienced physical education teachers as their 'standard setters'. In order to move beyond conventional forms of physical education it would seem highly appropriate to consider the views of Keay (2005) if these forms of practice are to be challenged.

Traditions of the past may not be appropriate for the needs of the future and therefore professional development for new teachers must be based upon critically reflective practice in innovative subject communities that are composed of teachers who willingly take responsibility for the development, and not just the maintenance, of the PE profession.

Keay (2005: 154)

Likewise, the value of reflexivity for inclusive practice in physical education is dependent on challenging established forms of practice that can alienate young people from physical activity and should empower teachers to make informed decisions and choices about what they want to teach and what they wish their pupils to learn. Laker *et al.* (2003: 76) maintain that an increased understanding of ways in which teachers perceive their professional identity and their subject specialism can contribute to the facilitation of the development of the reflective practitioner and potentially enhance the professional and personal growth of both the pre-service teacher and his/her future students. Brown (2005: 19) concludes that habitual reflexivity can empower individuals with both a modified form of habitus through which they teach thus re-construct knowledge that challenges stereotypical understandings of gender (for example) and practices in physical education. However, in Brown's analogy of a computer system, this takes time to 'wipe', 'input' and 'store' new information so that a multi-layered, multi-dimensional habitus can be contextualised rather like a hologram as opposed to a hard drive on a computer. As Brown (2005: 20) points out this may involve:

... strategically forcing the boundaries of what people perceive as gender inconceivable, improbable and acceptable in PE and school sport until the inconceivable becomes the acceptable ...

Brown (2005: 20)

Moreover, Rich (2001) suggests that whilst teaching is not monolithic its influence is extremely powerful and difficult to fracture.

To suggest otherwise would be naïve and the possibilities of critical reflection interrupting the reproductive process of teaching culture needs to be seen in this light

Rich (2001: 149)

In essence, (and as shown in the final chapter of this book), reflexivity helps us to consider the alternatives rather like changing the ingredients of a traditional recipe. Over time, new ingredients are added alongside the staple ones and blended together in different ways. The desired outcome is a product that reflects the tastes, trends and fashions of the day and has greater appeal to a much broader population of people. That is not to deny that changes to existing practices might be idealistic rather than realistic. For inexperienced physical education teachers, many have to become conformists and accept the fact that if you can't beat them, you join them.

At the beginning of this chapter I cited the work of Green (2008) and his contention that reflexivity in its strongest sense is almost unachievable as trainee teachers, in particular, are seldom encouraged to reflect on anything other than routine practice which militates against any inclination to reflect (Green: 224). For Green (2008: 214) newly qualified teachers are likely to work in conditions where established patterns of provision are going to be hard to break and the maintenance of a status quo is consequently sustained. Just like me, as a newcomer to the physical education profession, I was obliged to adapt my behaviour and views so that things could carry on as before. As Green neatly puts it:

> The workplace, especially early-on in teachers' careers, is important in supporting or restricting their practices as they find themselves constrained not only by the dominant values and beliefs of their colleagues, departments and schools, but also by practical matters to do with facilities and equipment. This helps to explain why the impact of teacher education tends to be 'washed out' relatively soon after teachers begin teaching properly.
>
> Green (2008: 214)

In Green's opinion reflexivity does not affect the way in which physical education is taught as it misunderstands the nature of physical education as it is practiced (ibid). Instead, the practices of physical education teachers have far more to do with their predispositions and the contexts in which they teach where constraints on practice matter more than theory in determining what teachers do and how they do it. As Green rightly points out physical education is a process which develops inevitably but the longer physical education teachers remain in the profession and the longer individual teachers remain at the same school, the more conservative their practices are likely to become (Green 2008: 225). Whilst I agree with Green's line of reasoning, I hope that this chapter has shown that a strong sense of reflexivity can be achieved and ultimately affect the way physical education is taught but it takes place incrementally over a period of time and cannot been regarded as an overnight cure to improving the experiences of pupils or indeed the pedagogical skills of trainees and teachers.

Notes

1   In the 1944 Education Act, schooling in the UK was arranged so that children would be entitled to free education between the ages of 5 and 15. Children aged 5–11 would attend a primary school, and children aged 11–15 would attend a Secondary school. At this time there were three types of Secondary Schools – Grammar Schools, Secondary Modern Schools and Technical Schools or Colleges. Each school was designed to fit in with the child's capabilities, so a grammar school would suit those who were academic and wanted to go onto university, whilst a Technical School suited those who wished to pursue a trade, with a Secondary Modern fitting somewhere in between. All children took the 11 Plus exam in their final year of primary school and based on their performance in this exam, they would then go onto one of these three types of secondary school. There are now no grammar schools in Wales or Scotland. In Northern Ireland, this is the last academic year to have an 11 Plus style exam. While in England, 164 grammar schools remain, and pupils wishing to attend must still pass an exam. Competition in these areas is fierce, and a BBC Radio 4 programme has found parents spend as much

as £1,800 on private tuition to help their children (http://news.bbc.co.uk/1/hi/magazine/7773974.stm) .

2 A medley relay involves four different swimmers who compete as a team over a variety of distances ranging from 25m to 100m, each swimming one of four strokes beginning with backstroke, butterfly, breaststroke and finishing with front crawl. During formal competitions these are exclusively male- and female-only events but there is nothing to prevent teachers in schools from introducing it as a mixed-sex event during inter-school competitions.

3 The game of 'British Bulldog' was characterised by its physicality often being regarded as violent leading it to be prohibited by many schools and local education authorities.

4 The Royal Navy's 'field gun competition' is a contest between teams from various Royal Navy commands, in which teams of sailors compete to transport a canon (or field gun) and its equipment over and through a series of obstacles in the shortest time. The Royal Tournament was the world's largest military tattoo and pageant, held by the British Armed Forces annually between 1880 and 1999.

5 Flag Football is an adapted non-contact version of American grid iron football played in teams of eight where the object of the game is to manoevre an oval ball through a defended territory to an end zone. Each team has four attempts to score a 'touchdown'. A tackle is represented by removing a Velcro flag attached to a belt from a ball-carrying player. Flag football was designed in an effort to minimize injuries that playing tackle football could bring and has been increasingly introduced to co-educational physical education classes.

6 Osteogenesis imperfecta (OI and sometimes known as brittle bone disease, or 'Lobstein syndrome' is a genetic bone disorder).

7 Scoliosis is a medical condition in which a person's spine is curved from side to side. The spine of an individual with scoliosis may look more like an 'S' or a 'C' than a straight line.

References

Armour, K. and Chen, H. (2012) 'Narrative Research Methods: Where the art of storytelling meets the science of research', in Armour, K. and Macdonald, D. (eds) (2012) *Research Methods in Physical Education and Youth Sport*, London, Routledge: 237–49.

Armour, K. and Jones, R. (1998) *Physical Education Teachers' Lives and Careers*, London, Falmer Press.

Brown, D. (2005) 'An economy of gendered practices? Learning to teach physical education from the perspective of Pierre Bourdieu's embodied sociology', *Sport, Education and Society*, 10(1), 3–23.

Brown, D. and Rich, E. (2002) 'Gender Positioning as a Pedagogical Practice in Teaching Physical Education', in Penney, D. (ed.) *Gender and Physical Education: Contemporary Issues and Future Directions*, London, Routledge.

Evans J. (1989) 'Swinging from the Crossbar: Equality and opportunity in the Physical Education Curriculum', *British Journal of Physical Education*, 20(2), 84–7.

Fernandez-Balboa, J-M. and Brubaker, N. (2012) 'Positioning yourself as a researcher: Four dimensions for self-reflection', in Armour, K. and Macdonald, D. (eds) (2012) 'Research Methods in Physical Education and Youth Sport', London, Routledge: 29–39.

Gabbei, R. (2004) 'Achieving Balance: Secondary Physical Education Gender-Grouping Options: Can teachers legally use occasional single-sex groupings within co-ed physical education, to the benefit of all students?', *Journal of Physical Education, Recreation and Dance* (JOPERD), (75), 3, March 2004: 33–9.

Graydon J. (1980) 'Dispelling the Myth of Female Fragility', *British Journal of Physical Education*, 11(4), 105–6.

Green K. (2003) *Physical Education Teachers on Physical Education*, Chester, Chester Academic Press.

Green K. (2008) *Understanding Physical Education*, London, Sage.

Hastie, P. and Hay, P. (2012) 'Qualitative Approaches' in Armour K. and Macdonald D. (eds) (2012) *Research Methods in Physical Education and Youth Sport*, London, Routledge: 79–84.

Hayes, L., Nikolic, V. and Cabaj, J. H. (2001) *'Am I teaching well? Self-evaluation Strategies for Effective Teachers'*, Exeter, Learning Matters.

Keay, J. (2005) 'Developing the Physical Education Profession: New Teachers Learning Within a Subject-Based Community', *Physical Education and Sport Pedagogy*, (10), 2: 139–57.

Laker, A. (2000) *Beyond the Boundaries of Physical Education: Educating young people for citizenship and social responsibility*, London, Falmer.

Laker, A., Laker, J. and Lea, S. (2003) 'School Experience and the Issue of Gender', *Sport, Education and Society*, (8), 1: 73–89.

Leaman, O. (1984) *Sit on the sidelines and watch the boys play: Sex Differentiation in Physical Education*, York, Longman, Schools Council Publications.

Luttenburg, J. and Bergen, T. (2008) 'Teacher Reflection: The development of a Typology', *Teachers Teaching: Theory and Practice*, 14, 5–6, October–December: 543–66.

Macdonald, D. (2002) 'Critical Pedagogy: What might it look like and why does it matter?' in Laker, A. (ed.) *The Sociology of Sport and Physical Education: An introductory reader*, London, Routledge Falmer: 167–89.

Penney, D. (2002) 'Gendered Policies', in Penney, D. (2002) (ed.) *Gender and Physical Education: Contemporary issues and future directions*, London, Routledge: 103–22.

Pollard, A. and Tan, S. (1987) *Reflective Teaching in the Primary School: A handbook for the classroom*, Abingdon, David Fulton Publishers.

Rich, E. (2001) 'Gender positioning in teacher education in England: New rhetoric, old realities', *International Studies in Sociology of Education*, 11, 2: 131–56.

Scraton, S. (1992) *Shaping up to Womanhood – Gender and Girls' Physical Education*, Buckingham: Open University Press.

Sherlock, J. (1977) 'A feminist view of Coeducational Physical Education', *Scottish Journal of Physical Education*, 5(2), 21–2.

Stidder, G. (1998) 'Gender Grouping in Physical Education: An investigation into mixed and single sex provision and the effects on secondary school aged children', Unpublished Master's Thesis, University of Brighton.

Stidder, G. (2002) 'The Recruitment of Secondary School Physical Education Teachers in England: A Gendered Perspective?', *European Physical Education Review*, 8(3), 253–73.

Stidder, G. and Hayes, S. (2006) 'A Longitudinal Survey of Physical Education Trainees' Experiences on School Placements in the South – East of England (2000–2004)', *European Physical Education Review*, Autumn, 12(3), 317–38.

Turvey, J. and Laws, C. (1988) 'Are Girls Losing Out? The effects of mixed-sex grouping on girls' performance in physical education', *British Journal of Physical Education*, 19(6), 253–5.

Williams, A. (1993) 'The reflective physical education teacher: Implications for initial teacher education', *Physical Education Review*, 16, 2, 137–44.

Williams, A. (1998) 'The reflective physical education teacher; Implications for initial teacher education', in Green, K. and Hardman, K. (eds) (1998) *Physical Education: A Reader*, Aachen, Meyer and Meyer Verlag: 204–16.

Willig, C. (2008) *Introducing Qualitative Research in Psychology*, 2nd edition, Open University Press, McGraw-Hill.

Wink, J. (2000) *Critical pedagogy: Notes from the real world*, New York, Addison Wesley Longman.

Youth Sport Trust (2000) *Girls in Sport: Towards girl-friendly physical education, Final Report*, Institute of Youth Sport, Loughborough University.

Zwozdiak-Myers, P. (2010) 'Teacher as a researcher/reflective practitioner', in Capel, S. and Whitehead, M. (eds) (2010) *Learning to Teach Physical Education in the Secondary School: A companion to school experience*, London, RoutledgeFalmer, 265–85.

3 Personalised learning in physical education

Andrew Theodoulides

I was in the first year of secondary school. At the end of the lesson I was showing off in front of my mates and threw one of my training shoes into the basketball ring. I scored but it got stuck in the netting underneath and just hung there. Then he came into the gym. Everyone stopped what they were doing. 'You are going to get that down and then I'm going to hit you with it'. And he did – right in front of my mates!!!

Adam (aged 39)
Secondary school 1985–1989

Biographical reflections

One would be hard-pushed to find a physical education teacher who did not claim to have the best interests of the pupils they taught at heart. Meeting the needs of *all* pupils is complex, challenging and, one might argue, virtually impossible. During my time teaching physical education in state secondary schools in England I remember vividly being frustrated by the competing demands of trying to engage all pupils in a class, year group, school – all of whom are said to have 'individual' needs. The hustle and bustle of day-to-day physical education teaching meant no time to 'sit back and smell the roses' – or more accurately the time to reflect was very limited. I've come to realise now that regular opportunities to stop, reflect and ask: 'What can I do to enhance the learning of more pupils?' are vital if teachers of physical education are to ensure that their subject is to appeal to a greater number of pupils. In the previous chapter Gary Stidder discussed the value of reflexivity for inclusive practice in physical education. One aim of this chapter is to encourage reflection on that very question.

Introduction

Since my previous chapter in the first edition of this book (Theodoulides 2003) there have been a number of distinct changes to UK government policy and the ways in which it has attempted to strategically address the issue of social inclusion in schools for all pupils notwithstanding a change in political terminology from 'inclusive practice' to 'personalised learning'. My intention in this chapter is to explore factors that underpin curriculum planning decisions, particularly in the light of the revised National Curriculum for Physical Education requirements (QCA 2007).[1] The discussion will examine issues relating to the content and structure of the physical education curriculum, that is, what is taught (the range and content) and how it is organised. As part of a wider policy initiative for placing people at the centre of public services, personalised learning has become an important consideration of the practices of schools and teachers in England and Wales. Whilst elements of the personalised learning agenda have undergone transformation from five components[2] (Miliband 2004; DfES 2004a) to nine key features[3] (DCSF 2008) the general philosophy underpinning personalised learning has remained. This chapter will explore personalised learning and some of the tensions and constraints that exist between aspects of the personalised learning agenda, other government agendas and the way in which physical education is planned and taught in schools. Elements of the personalised learning agenda will be identified and explored with reference to how matters of personalised learning might be pursued further within physical education.

What is personalised learning?

From the outset, personalised learning was part of New Labour government's plan to drive up standards in education by improving the quality of learning and teaching in all schools through a pupil-centred approach to education provision. The DCSF (2007: 64) commented '(t)he distinctive feature of the pedagogy of personalisation is the way it expects all pupils to reach or exceed expectations, fulfil early promise and develop latent potential. Personalised lessons are stretching for everyone'. A central feature of the personalised learning agenda was therefore ensuring schools were focused on ensuring higher attainment for *all* pupils. Furthermore, seen in the context of other education initiatives such as Every Child Matters (DfES 2004b) and later The Children's Plan (DCSF 2007), the personalised learning agenda was also an attempt by policymakers to raise awareness of the educational attainment of pupils from different backgrounds. It was those pupils who fared less well in education who were targeted as most in need within the personalised learning agenda (DCSF 2008). In this context, as the DCSF (2008: 6) pointed out, the personalised learning agenda had a 'moral purpose' to create a more equitable and fair education system.

When outlining personalised learning in a speech at the North of England Education Conference, David Miliband, then the Secretary of State for School Standards, said:

Decisive progress in educational standards occurs where every child matters; careful attention is paid to their individual learning styles, motivations, and needs; there is rigorous use of pupil target setting linked to high quality assessment; lessons are well-paced and enjoyable; and pupils are supported by partnership with others well beyond the classroom.

This is what I mean by 'Personalised Learning'. High expectations of every child, given practical form by high quality teaching based on a sound knowledge and understanding of each child's needs.

(Miliband 2004).

A concern for greater equality and fairness gave the personalised learning agenda an inclusive focus. Central to this focus on greater personalisation was the role of teachers and schools in catering simultaneously for the different needs of all pupils in the class (DCSF 2008) in order to motivate and engage pupils in their learning. One might ask about personalisation, 'what is new about any of this?' Many of the claims made by Miliband (2004) and in subsequent government publications, that personalised learning is characterised by attention to individual learning styles, motivating pupils, target setting and assessment, and well-paced lessons are essentially all features of good teaching that have been central to the work of teachers for a long time. In fact the DfES (2004a) acknowledges this point in an early publication about personalised learning. Whether new or not, what became clear in the years after personalised learning was placed on the education agenda was that it became a key focus of government's education policy and was reinforced within the practices schools and teaching in a short period of time.

One aim of the personalisation agenda has been to affect change within learning and teaching practices. The DCSF (2007: 6) commented that '(p)ersonalised learning is central to a school improvement agenda which has teaching and learning at its heart'. The personalised learning agenda then, places emphasis on teachers and schools to examine their practices and develop more effective ways of making greater provision for all pupils. This focus on high quality teaching and learning through school and classroom practices locates much of the moral obligation in meeting personalised learning outcomes in the hands of schools and teachers. The personalised learning agenda requires teachers and curriculum planners to think more critically about the relationship between the pedagogy, curriculum and assessment (Hipkins *et al.* 2010). In doing so, the personalised learning agenda ignores, or at best marginalises, the impact wider structural constraints such as a prescribed and regulated curriculum, standardised modes of assessment, class organisation based on chronological age and lessons controlled by bells, have on promoting personalisation. As the following discussion will highlight there are tensions, contradictions and constraints in the practices and policies of schools which inhibit the extent to which teachers can fully address the aspirations of the personalised learning agenda. However, before persuing these further the discussion turns to an exploration of learning and teaching methods which address matters of inclusion and personalised learning in physical education.

Personalisation of learning and teaching within physical education

Meeting pupils' individual learning needs within physical education has generally been seen as the responsibility of the teacher. Typically, this has focused on teachers employing appropriate learning and teaching strategies to develop a pupil-centred approach. Published before the personalised learning agenda came into being, three principles of inclusion were identified in the National Curriculum for Physical Education in England (NCPE; DfEE/QCA 1999) which provided useful guidance for inclusive practice and how to meet pupils' individual learning needs. These were: 1) 'setting suitable learning challenges'; 2) 'responding to pupils' diverse needs'; and, 3) 'overcoming potential barriers to learning and assessment for individuals and groups of pupils' (DfEE/QCA 1999; 28–31). The section below will explore three common strategies that are thought to be valuable in personalised learning by virtue of their ability to meet pupils' individual learning needs; these are differentiation, using a variety of teaching styles and employing different learning styles.

As pointed out by Vickerman and Hayes in the following chapter to this book differentiation is thought of as central to personalised learning (DCSF 2008) as well as to inclusive teaching (Vickerman 2004). In general, teachers will set a learning task for the majority of the pupils in their class and then differentiate the task to make it easier for those who are struggling and set a more challenging task for those who find the task easy. So for example, within a unit of work that focuses on outwitting an opponent through the principles of invasion games and in particular goal shooting games, whilst the majority of the group might be working to beat a semi-active defender in a 1v1 situation in basketball before taking a shot, those who find this task difficult could be asked to beat a passive defender whilst those that find the task easy would be required to beat a fully active defender. Through such differentiated tasks a greater number of pupils are likely to be working on tasks that are more closely matched to their ability than if all pupils were doing the same practice. Thus, 'a recognition and commitment to modify and adapt … teaching and learning strategies in order to enable access and entitlement to the physical education curriculum' is at the heart of inclusive teaching (Vickerman 2004: 162) and greater personalisation for pupils' learning. Differentiation is one way of engaging pupils of different abilities in learning activities that enable them to participate fully in physical education lessons.

The use of different teaching styles also allows teachers to meet pupils' individual learning needs. Mosston and Ashworth's (1986) spectrum of teaching styles identifies ten different teaching styles. Movement along the spectrum of teaching styles from command style, where all decisions are made by the teacher, to self-teaching, where the learner is working independently of the teacher, sees decision-making responsibility transferred from the teacher to the pupil in increasing amounts. This movement along the spectrum from command to self-teaching places increasingly greater responsibility for, and involvement in, learning in the hands of the learner. However the extent to which teachers are willing to employ different teaching styles within their lessons is subject to tension. For example, in their study into teachers' and pupils' perceptions of personalised learning Underwood and Banyard (2008) found that to boost pupils performance in examinations teachers tended to over-rely on a command teaching style which is at odds with a pupil-centred approach to learning. Whilst their study was not focused on physical education, what is clear is that the pressure on teachers to meet targets for pupils to pass examinations and meet end of Key Stage attainment levels clearly impacts upon and constrains the teaching styles teachers chose to employ to promote pupils' learning.

The requirements of the NCPE provide opportunities for teachers to employ different teaching styles to promoting pupil's learning in physical education. For example, in addition to developing skills, the NCPE requires pupils to evaluate and improve, make and apply decisions and make informed choices about healthy active lifestyle. The use of different teaching styles is effective in promoting pupils' learning in these areas (Mosston and Ashworth 1986). For example to evaluate, pupils could be asked to teach another pupil a forward roll (reciprocal style) or video their own forward roll and then evaluate it (self-check style) within a unit of work that focuses on accurate replication of actions, phrases or sequences. In a unit of work that aims to promote performing at maximum levels such as in an athletics lesson to accommodate individual differences, each pupil could be asked to decide whether they wanted to practice the javelin throw, for example, from a standing, a 3-step approach or a 5-step approach (inclusion style) thereby learning at their appropriate level. From these examples it is clear that different teaching styles require different levels of decision-making from pupils which require them to take a more active part in their learning than when a command style is used. The use of a wider variety of teaching styles allows teachers to personalise learning to a greater extent by adopting different styles to meet individual pupils' different learning needs.

Along with teaching styles, different learning styles are also effective in meeting children's individual needs. Popular within education are the learning styles proposed by Honey and Mumford (1992); activitist, reflector, theorist and pragmatist.[4] These learning styles address individual needs through the different ways in which Honey and Mumford (1992) claim children prefer to learn new information. Thus, a learning activity which requires problem-solving (for example most effective way in which to throw a discuss like object) would be more suited to theorist learners; one which involves group work (such as working together to sling an object over the world record discus distance) to activist learners; a video analysis task (to determine the arm position at the release of a discus) to reflectivist learners; and a practice task (to implement the release of a discus) to pragmatist learners. Such a variety of learning activities are more likely to both challenge and motivate children by engaging a greater number of them in preferred ways of learning rather than by presenting tasks in a similar manner. The use of different learning styles also makes it incumbent upon teachers of PE to think differently about assessment. Different learning styles require children to draw upon knowledge, skills and understanding in diverse ways and this ought to be reflected in the way in which children are assessed. It is to assessment that the discussion now turns.

Personalised learning and assessment

Rigorous and frequent testing has been viewed by policymakers as important for driving up standards in education (DCSF 2008). Miliband (2004) highlighted how accountability of schools had been effective in raising pupils' levels of attainment and he restated the government's commitment to standardised national tests and examinations as a means of measuring schools' success. In order for pupils to improve and be successful in attainment tests and examinations, it is generally thought to be important that pupils know their current level of attainment and what they need to do to improve. Assessment for Learning (AfL) then is seen as valuable in meeting the personalised learning agenda in that it is said to be an effective way of meeting pupils' individual needs (DCSF 2008) as they move towards summative examinations. However, the extent to which assessment and AfL can make a significant contribution to personalised learning has come in for criticism. Pollard and James (2004) argue AfL only has a superficial impact upon personalised learning. For example, in their study into teachers' perceptions of personalised learning Underwood and Banyard (2008) found that teachers viewed the inter-relationship between personalised learning and assessment as mainly to do with improved record-keeping and providing better feedback to pupils. Pollard and James (2004) argue that what is needed are deeper changes in assessment practices which are likely to lead to a greater impact upon personalised learning. For example, in physical education pupils frequently work in groups but are rarely, if at all, assessed formally on their ability to demonstrate the skills needed for effective group work, or to solve problems. Stidder and Hayes (2010) have shown that there are many opportunities within physical education to assess and develop personal learning and thinking skills as well as address the five outcomes of 'Every Child Matters'. Within the key concepts, processes, range and content and curriculum opportunities of the revised National Curriculum for Physical Education teachers can provide pupils with problem-solving and decision-making tasks whilst enabling them to be healthy, stay safe, enjoy and achieve, make a positive contribution and achieve economic well-being. Pupils could for example, act as coaches and provide other pupils with strategic or tactical advice. In other circumstances, pupils might make independent decisions related to the risks involved in a particular activity whilst evaluating their individual and team performance. All of these tasks can help to develop the key skills of reading, writing, communicating and listening. Teachers can also provide pupils with opportunities to become self-managers, creative thinkers, reflective learners, problem-solvers, team workers, independent learners, and effective communicators according to the style of teaching they adopt in physical education lessons. Ofsted (www.ofsted.gov.uk./resources/physical-education-schools-200508), however, has highlighted how pupils are not often assessed in leadership or coaching roles as teachers tend to focus assessment upon skill performance. Assessing pupils in a wider range of learning outcomes may well result in some pupils being identified as successful learners in physical education which might not have been the case had the focus of assessment been upon technique and skills. A narrow focus on assessment outcomes is perhaps understandable given that the NCPE levels of attainment against which pupils are judged at the end of each Key Stage make very little reference to group work, leadership and coaching. This highlights how the constraints of the curriculum and the pressure to assess pupils against narrow and limited attainment criteria, work to restrict opportunities for physical education teachers to adopt assessment practices that meet the needs of a greater number of pupils.

In the timing of assessment, practice tends to be rather limited too. Typically in physical education summative assessment (AoL) tends to take place at the end of a unit of work. All pupils are usually assessed on the same knowledge, skills and understanding and at the same time. However, to promote personalised learning, where possible why not allow pupils the choice of assessment mode? So for example, in assessing a pupils' knowledge and understanding when evaluating a partner's ability to accurately replicate an action, sequence or phrase of movement such as in gymnastics pupils might be given the opportunity to decide whether they want to be assessed in written form or audio form. Similarly pupils might be offered the choice of the activities on which they are assessed. For example, given that teachers of physical education cannot assess everything pupils do, pupils might decide the physical education activities and/or the learning objectives on which they would prefer to be assessed rather than having teachers decide. Furthermore, pupils might be given the choice of when they want to be assessed within the unit of work. Some might chose to be assessed in week six whilst others might wait to be assessed in week nine thereby giving them more time to learn. What all this highlights is that assessment practices are not set in stone and there is flexibility for teachers to be more creative in how they decide upon what is to be assessed, when and how they plan and implement assessment practices. By adopting such practices as those outlined here this might go some way to addressing Pollard and James' (2004) concern that AfL has had only a marginal impact upon personalising learning. For greater personalised learning it is generally agreed that pupils ought to be involved in decisions about their education and assessment is one aspect in which they can be consulted. The extent to which pupils are consulted on other aspects of their learning is discussed further below and this begins by looking at how pupils learn to learn.

Personalised learning and learning to learn

Whilst one focus of the personalised learning agenda has been the practices of schools and teachers in order to better motivate, challenge and meet pupils' individual learning needs, Pollard and James (2004: 5) stress that personalised learning should be viewed as more than 'an over-simplified consideration of teaching provision'. They argue for looking at personalised learning as a 'dynamic concept', one built upon 'social practices' that require changes in education provision. For example, one of the attractive features of the personalised learning agenda is a focus on 'learning how to learn' (Pollard and James 2004; Crick 2009). In this respect the Association for Physical Education (AfPE 2008) define physical education in the following way:

Physical education is the planned, progressive learning that takes place in school curriculum timetabled time and which is delivered to all pupils. This involves both 'learning to move' (i.e. becoming more physically competent) and 'moving to learn' (e.g. learning through movement, a range of skills and understandings beyond physical activity, such as co-operating with others). The context for the learning is physical activity, with children experiencing a broad range of activities, including sport and dance.[5]

Association for Physical Education (AfPE 2008: 3)

In order to promote greater pupil engagement and involvement in learning there have been calls for changes in the way in which knowledge is transmitted within subjects on the school curriculum (Kirk and Macdonald 1998; Glasby and Macdonald 2004; Crick 2009; Hipkins *et al.* 2010). What is needed it is argued, is the teaching of knowledge that is 'unearthed, encountered and exchanged from the "person up" rather than the "system down"' (Crick 2009: 186). Learning how to learn focuses on developing higher order skills such as problem-solving, critical reflection and skills of enquiry and places a strong emphasis in getting pupils to be creators of knowledge rather than passive recipients. Such a focus requires teachers to think differently about how to educate pupils.

Since its introduction, the NCPE has been conceptualised in narrow terms, that is skills and techniques in the context of élite sport performance (Penney and Evans 1999: Penney 2000). Despite some attempt in the revised NCPE to move towards a thematic curriculum (DfE 2011), the physical education curriculum is still dominated by traditional team games (Quick *et al.* 2010) through which the teaching of sport specific techniques is an enduring factor (Kirk 2010). One upshot of these 'performance discourses' (Tinning 1997) is that they presented knowledge in such a way that it seen as both agreed and static, with the teacher as the mediator of knowledge and the student as the passive recipient. A 'person up' approach would, arguably, have the effect of involving children much more in creating knowledge through which they identify and pursue their own learning goals (Underwood and Banyard 2008). This 'facilitates the individual in acquiring dispositions, skills and attitudes for learning how to learn. And learning how to negotiate the values issues and dilemmas of the real world' (Crick 2009: 187). Within physical education Kirk and Macdonald (1998) have argued that a situated learning approach to pupils' education. Based upon a constructivist approach to learning which views learning as an 'active process', Kirk and Macdonald develop Lave and Wenger's idea of 'communities of practice' to argue that situated learning through a sport education model has potential to offer 'greater opportunities for meaningful, authentic, and differentiated participation' in physical education than traditional forms of the subject (Kirk and Macdonald 1998: 384). Put another way, Kirk and Macdonald argue that situated learning through a sport education model engages pupils in a form of physical education that is relevant to their lives, their social context and their capabilities (Kirk and Macdonald 1998). The idea is that pupils then develop autonomy for their learning and become less reliant upon teacher input. This point was made also above in the discussion on teaching styles and learning styles in physical education. Personalised learning is enhanced through pupils' ownership of their learning. It is clear from this discussion that how pupils learn is intimately related to the nature of the physical education curriculum and it is to this that the discussion now turns.

Personalised learning and curriculum organisation

A key feature of the personalised learning agenda is 'curriculum organisation' and in particular flexibility to design a curriculum that is more relevant to pupils' needs (DCSF 2008). Such flexibility would appear to be an attractive proposition for teachers and pupils alike. Flexibility, the argument goes, allows teachers to plan a curriculum that is pertinent to the needs of the pupils in a particular school. For pupils, a curriculum which is specific to their needs is likely to be one which they find more interesting, stimulating and through which they achieve success. However, Campbell *et al.* (2007) point out government regulation of the curriculum means that 90 per cent of what is taught in schools, and when it is taught, is determined by education policy. Given the current level of government prescription with regard to curriculum content any flexibility to personalise a school curriculum is likely to be constrained by the very structured demands and requirements of the National Curriculum and subject areas. But despite curriculum constraints schools do have some degree of flexibility for teachers to be creative in how they utilise such opportunities. In Chapter 10 Stidder and Wallis provide what they believe to be a compelling case for wholesale accredited awards in physical education for all pupils aged 14 and over. For example, there is at least one school in the South-East of England in which all pupils start their GCSE[6] subjects in year nine rather than year ten thereby in effect, reducing Key Stage three to two years. It is also quite common practice now for schools to 'fast-track' high achieving pupils to start GCSE in physical education in year nine. Indeed, at the time of writing the implementation of the new National Curriculum for England is to be delayed by one year and will take effect from 2014 with the possibility that Key Stage three could be reduced to just two years with Key Stage four changing to three years. This would mean that the lead up to GCSE would be a more substantial and meaningful three-year programme of work but perhaps less personalised as all pupils would follow an accredited award in physical education. One might wonder whether such changes to physical education curriculum in these schools are intended to meet pupil's individual needs or to enhance the school's standing in league tables. These two aims are not necessarily mutually exclusive in leading greater personalisation, but it does not necessarily follow that it is advantageous for pupils to be 'fast-tracked' to start GCSE's in year nine. Whatever the motivation of schools, what this highlights is that some possibilities exist for thinking about different ways of structuring the school's physical education curriculum to meet a wider range of pupils' needs. The challenge for those that plan the curriculum is to seize upon these opportunities and use them to promote greater personalised learning.

Over the last 20 years there have been a number of developments within physical education which have indicated possibilities for changes in physical education pedagogy whilst still meeting NCPE requirements. For example, there have been moves towards a more pupil-centred approach to the way in which athletics is taught within schools with more emphasis on developing the fundamentals of running, throwing and jumping (Morgan 2011 UK Athletics 2005) rather than Olympic-style events. Kirk and Macdonald (1998) have reminded us how games for understanding and sport education have the potential to promote learning in a wider range of outcomes than lessons which focus predominately on teaching techniques. More recently Quick *et al.* (2010) identified that schools are offering a much greater range of physical activities and sports within the physical education curriculum in an attempt to motivate and engage more pupils. As part of a much broader study Stidder and Binney (2011) explored the suitability of 'alternative' physical activities within the formal physical education curriculum through the findings of a pilot survey completed by physical education teachers and pupils after completing a series of 'alternative' activity taster days hosted by a university in South-East England. The results suggested that 'alternative' activities have a great deal of appeal to pupils and there is a willingness amongst teachers to promote 'alternative' types of physical activities within the formal physical education curriculum. On that basis they proposed an 'alternative' physical education curriculum for pupils in secondary schools.

The increase in popularity of what have been termed 'lifestyle' activities (Wheaton 2004; Green 2008) has been said to have the potential to challenge stereotypes and dominant discourses in physical education around notions of gender and ability (see Chapter 5 for a further discussion of these issues). However the reality is that whilst lifestyle sports might have the potential to transgress social identities and challenge notions of masculinity with sport thus far they have failed to do so (Wheaton 2004). As Wheaton (2004: 19) notes, within adult lifestyle sports 'femininities continue to be framed by discourses and practices that perpetuate stereotypes of white heterosexual attractiveness, and masculinities based on normative heterosexuality and whiteness, skill and risk.' What all these initiatives have in common is that they have been seen as alternatives to the dominant pedagogy of 'performance discourses' (Tinning 1997) within physical education which reinforces élitism and defines excellence in terms of a limited range of sports skills and competence (Penney 2000, Green 2002). As such, they have potential to enhance personalised learning through the way in which they promote learning in a different range of outcomes than 'performance discourses' and are therefore able to meet the needs and interests of a wider range of pupils than those who are currently attracted to physical education and school sport.

Personalised learning and the extended physical education curriculum

Alongside curriculum organisation is the extended curriculum through which personalised learning is said to be enhanced (DCSF 2008). Physical education extra-curricular activities have potential in '(h)elping pupils to discover or develop new interests and talents (which) is an important aspect of personalised learning' (DCSF 2008: 44). Between 2003 and 2010 the Physical Education and School Sport Clubs Links strategy (PESSCL; DfES/DCSF 2003) and Physical Education and School Sport and Young People Strategy (PESSYP; Youth Sport Trust 2009) were focused upon increasing the amount of physical activity and sport in which pupils participated outside of curriculum time. Both PESSCL and PESSYP attempted to build links between schools physical education and sport and national governing body sport clubs in order to encourage more pupils to participate in sport outside of school. Whilst much of the focus of PESSCL and PESSYP was aimed at encouraging pupils to take part in more *sport*, by the time PESSYP had replaced PESSCL in 2009 there was greater recognition of pupil's diverse interests in ways of being active which acknowledged preferences for less structured and more informal physical activity as opposed to structured and organised sport (see Chapter 11 for further discussion of these issues). PESSCL and PESSYP are no longer part of the physical education agenda, but encouraging pupils to engage in physical activity or sport outside of physical education lessons and outside of school is one aim that resonates highly with teachers of physical education (Green 2003). Given the strength of this 'ideology' which Green (2003) found in the physical education teachers in his study it seems reasonable to concede that this remains an important aim for physical education teachers today and one way in which this aim might be addressed is through extra-curricular activities.

In essence and as highlighted by Stidder and Hayes in Chapter 1, for teachers of physical education, extra-curricular activities serve two main purposes; to encourage 'sport for all' and to provide opportunities for competitive sport (Green 2003). Whilst some of the teachers in the studies by Green (2003) and Haycock and Smith (2011) claimed to provide extra-curricular activities which were 'open to all' pupils, that is those who wanted to participate for recreational purposes, for fun and enjoyment, and those who wanted to play competitively, Green (2003) noted the tension and confusion that existed between rhetoric and reality. The reality is that in most schools extra-curricular physical education is heavily focused on competitive team sport in which the more able pupils participate (Penney and Harris 1997; Green 2003; Haycock and Smith 2011). The result of this is 'limited opportunities and experiences to only a minority of pupils' (Penney and Harris 1997: 43). If the potential of extra-curricular activities to promote greater personalised learning is to be utilised then extra-curricular provision is one aspect of physical education to which teachers ought to pay attention. As Haycock and Smith (2011) so aptly put it when writing about the experience of pupils with special educational needs such as physical disabilities in extra-curricular physical education:

> ... until those involved (in organising extra-curricular physical education activities) are willing and/or able to bring about desired change in the content, organisation and delivery of ECPE (extra-curricular physical education), it may be that rather than developing more inclusive and non-segregated forms

of provision, teachers in many schools will be constrained and/or inclined to continue providing programmes that, in effect, continue to provide what Penney and Harris call 'more of the same for the more able' pupils in ECPE.

Haycock and Smith (2011: 522)

Pertinent questions to consider would seem to be; how can extra-curricular physical education be planned and delivered so that they appeal to, engage and motivate a wider range of pupils to participate? What activities should be offered to bring about greater participation for all pupils? What are the implicit and explicit messages pupils pick up about the aims and purpose of extra-curricular activities? One way of meeting pupils' extra-curricular needs, as the discussion below highlights, might be to engage with pupils in discussion on some of those questions identified above.

Personalised learning and curriculum organisation in PE: pupil choice and pupil 'voice'

Whilst pupil choice was a key component of the early personalised learning agenda (DfES 2004a) it was less explicit in later publications (DCSF 2008). Nevertheless, pupil choice opens up possibilities for a more personalised learning by providing pupils with opportunities to make decisions about their physical education and thereby better meet their individual needs. Within the curriculum student choice is possible where there is flexibility to deviate away from NCPE requirements. Typically this tends to occur at Key Stage 4 where pupils choose which examination subjects to take and in core physical education where pupils often chose which activities to do as part of their physical education programme. Glasby and Macdonald (2004) alert us to the possibility of greater 'negotiation' between teachers and pupils in physical education in all key stages in order to involve pupils in decision-making about their education. They identify two areas where teachers can negotiate with pupils; the content of the curriculum and assessment and approaches to teaching and learning. They argue this would lead to pupils making decisions about their learning such as what tactics and strategies *they* would want to learn; whether *they* want to be assessed individually or as part of a group and how they prefer to learn. The important thing to note here is that such decisions are being made by the pupils and not by the teacher.

Through greater personalisation which involves pupils in decision-making about what is taught, when it is taught and how learning is assessed '(t)he learner becomes a leader in his or her own journey: the boundaries between the individual learner and the organisation are troubled by subtle shifts in energy as the notion of "a learning eco-system" redistributes and changes conceptions of power' (Crick 2009: 187). One might think that in schools funded by public money that any other approach is simply unacceptable. Such challenges to the power relationships between teachers and pupils' means granting greater power to pupils. Many teachers, head teachers and governors might feel uncomfortable with this. However, in some areas of the physical education curriculum there appears to have been some evidence of a shift in power between teachers and pupils. For example, Smith *et al.* (2009: 218) point out that activity choice is evidence of a 'democratisation of PE'. They continue however, that 'despite the prevalence of "activity choice" the power differentials between young people and teachers remains tilted in favour of the latter' (Smith *et al.* 2009: 217). Where teachers have listened to pupils 'voices' pupils have felt a greater sense of ownership of their education (Ruddock *et al.* 2006). As Glasby and Macdonald (2004: 143) argue 'if schools are for and about pupils, then the way forward in how educators (teachers, parents, curriculum, writers, coaches etc) work with students is clear. Physical education practices need to adopt a pupil-centred negotiated approach to teaching and learning'. One way of adopting a more pupil-centred approach might be to listen to pupils' 'voices', and those of their parents with regard to their preferences for physical education.

The notion of pupils and parents having a 'voice' in the way in which education services are employed is problematic.[7] Campbell *et al.* (2007) distinguish between 'deep' and 'shallow' personalisation. 'Deep' personalisation they argue, occurs when users (in education this would be parents and pupils) 'become "designers and paymasters" of services' (Campbell *et al.* 2007: 136). Shallow personalisation, on the other hand, provides users with a limited 'voice'. Currently, one constraining element within education and physical education in striving for 'deep' personalisation is the level of government regulation of the curriculum which then manifests itself through the decisions made by head teachers and school governors at a school level. Currently, the extent to which pupils and their parents have significant 'voice' room appears limited but the personalised learning agenda opens up possibilities for developments in this area. The extent to which pupils and parents might have meaningful input into curriculum matters is also dependent upon the 'social and linguistic competence' (Pollard and James 2004: 11) of those who are aiming to get heard. Users that 'speak' the language of the school are more likely to be successful in this and typically this is likely to be the middle class (Pollard and James 2004; Campbell *et al.* 2007). Glasby and Macdonald (2004) highlight the time, energy and commitment that is required by teachers and pupils when negotiating upon curriculum matters. Those from middle-class families are much more likely than those from working-class families to possess the social, cultural and economic capital to engage in such negotiation. So while the notion of listening to pupils' and parents' 'voices' is central to the personalised learning agenda a note of caution is required. An education system that ignores, or fails to listen to the 'voices' of the working class is likely to increase inequality rather than reduce it.

Thus the relationship between the personalised learning agenda and matters of equity are deeply related to the nature of the curriculum (Hipkins *et al.* 2010). As other contributors to this book have shown the physical education curriculum has long been complicit in the reproduction of class, gender and race related ideologies. As Hipkins *et al.* (2010) point out:

If it [the curriculum] becomes a programme or pedagogy solely for those who have not been the winners in the curriculum, then it will be seen as a second-class curriculum option which is marginalised from the mainstream. On the other hand, if it is subsumed within the dominant curriculum it will favour those who possess the largest helpings of officially sanctioned cultural capital. We fear that lack of attention to issues such as these will simply enlist the new pedagogies into the project of reproducing the status quo.

Hipkins *et al.* (2010: 115)

If curriculum planners fail to ensure that the curriculum is inclusive and the 'voices' of parents and pupils from all social classes are heard and given equal consideration, then it is not too difficult to imagine how '(p)ersonalisation, therefore, might increase the already large inequalities in educational provision and achievement, deriving mainly from social and economic status' (Campbell *et al.* 2007: 39). The educational attainment of working class pupils still lags behind that of pupils from middle class (Green 2008). The challenge for physical education then, is to develop practices which address issues of inclusion for pupils from all social-classes and marginalised groups.

Conclusion

Despite the tensions and constraints that exist between competing government education agendas and the difficulties these pose for schools and teachers in addressing matters of personalised learning it seems right to claim that physical education has greater potential to enhance personalised learning. A more pupil-centred, pupil-led curriculum; flexibility (where it exists) provides for alternative approaches to a competitive, skills-based, games dominated curriculum; choice and 'voice' through which pupils and their parents have a say in shaping their school experience; learning and teaching methods that place greater emphasis on students to create knowledge, make decisions about their learning and engage more fully in the learning process, are all strategies that open up new possibilities to shape the physical education curriculum into one that will meet the needs of a greater number of pupils. Given the recent UK coalition government's proposal to introduce more competition within school physical education (Conservative Party 2010) it might appear that future policy decisions are more likely to reinforce the focus on sport-specific skills, élitism and competition in years to come particularly in the wake of the London 2012 Olympic and Paralympic Games. But all is not lost. There is often 'slippage' (Penney and Evans 1999) between policy and practices as teachers adapt government policy in order to meet their own priorities (Swaby and Penney 2011). Smith *et al.* (2009) remind us that despite NCPE orders which lead to a narrowing of requirements at Key Stage 4 (particularly with regard to breadth of study) teachers of physical education have continued work against the grain in this area by offering a broad range of recreational-type activities to enhance pupil's motivation for leisure style activities. Therefore, with a commitment to 'desired change' (Haycock and Smith 2011) physical education has to promote greater personalised learning and has potential to do more to meet the needs of *all* pupils. What is required is for teachers to open their minds to new possibilities.

Notes

1   A fourth national curriculum for physical education in England was published by the QCA in 2007 and implemented in September 2008 for all pupils beginning their compulsory secondary schooling at the age of 11.
2   The five components were: assessment for learning; teaching and learning strategies; curriculum choice; school organisation; and school links to the wider community.
3   These nine key features were high quality teaching and learning; target-setting and tracking; focused assessment; intervention; pupil grouping; the learning environment; curriculum organisation; the extended curriculum; supporting children's wider needs.
4   According to Honey and Mumford (1992) a reflectivist learner prefers to learn by watching and thinking through a novel experience; a pragmatist by practicing, that is, applying new learning to practice; a theorist by thinking through the problem; an activist by working with others to meet a challenge.
5   AfPE's view of physical education is as follows:

> The aim of Physical Education is to develop physical competence so that all children are able to move efficiently, effectively and safely and understand what they are doing. The outcome – physical literacy – is as important to children's overall development as literacy and numeracy.

6   The General Certificate of Secondary Education (GCSE) is an academic qualification awarded in a specified subject, generally taken in a number of subjects by students aged 14–16 in secondary education in England, Wales and Northern Ireland.
7   For a more detailed discussion of some of the challenges for children and teachers in allowing children more input into the their learning and the curriculum, see Glasby and Macdonald (2004).

References

Association for Physical Education (2008) *Health Position Paper*, September 2008 http://www.afpe.org.uk/public/downloads/Health_Paper08.doc

Campbell, R. J., Robinson, W., Neelands, J., Hewston R., and Mazzoli L. (2007) 'Personalised Learning: Ambiguities in Theory and Practice', *British Journal of Education Studies*, 55 (2), 135–54.

Conservative Party (2010) *Extended opportunities: A Conservation policy paper on sport*, London: no publisher given.

Crick, R. D. (2009) 'Pedagogical challenges for personalisation: integrating the personal with the public through context driven enquiry', *The Curriculum Journal*, 20(3), 185–9.

DCSF (2007) *The Children's Plan: Building brighter futures*, London: The Stationery Office.

DCSF (2008) *Personalised Learning – A practical guide*, Annesley: DCSF Publications.

DfEE/QCA (1999) *Physical Education: The National Curriculum for England*, London: DfEE/QCA.

DfES (2004a) *A National Conversation about Personalisation*, Annesley: DfES Publications.

DfES (2004b) *Every Child Matters: Change for Children*, Annesley, DfES Publications.

DfES/DCSF (n/d) *Learning through PE and Sport*, Annesley: DfES publications.

Glasby, T. and Macdonald, D. (2004) 'Negotiating the curriculum: challenging the relationships in teaching', in Wright, J., Macdonald, D., and Burrows, L. (eds.) *Critical Inquiry and Problem-solving in Physical Education*, London, Routledge, 133–44.

Green, K. (2002) 'Physical Education Teachers in their Figurations: A sociological analysis of everyday "philosophies"', *Sport, Education and Society*, 7(1), 65–83.

Green, K. (2003) *Physical Education Teachers on Physical Education: A sociological study of philosophies and ideologies*, Chester: Chester Academic Press.

Green, K. (2008) *Understanding Physical Education*, London: Sage.

Haycock, D. and Smith, A. (2011) 'Still "more of the same for the more able?" Including young disabled people and pupils with special educational needs in extra-curricular physical education', *Sport, Education and Society*, 16(4), 507–26.

Hipkins, R., Reid, A., and Bull, A. (2010) 'Some reflections on the philosophical and pedagogical challenges of transforming education', *The Curriculum Journal*, 21(1), 109–18.

Honey, P. and Mumford, A. (1992) *The Manual of Learning Styles* (3rd edn), Maidenhead: Peter Honey.

Kirk, D. (2010) *Physical Education Futures*, Abingdon: Routledge.

Kirk, D. and Macdonald, D. (1998) 'Situated Learning in Physical Education', *Journal of Teaching in Physical Education*, 17, 376–87.

Miliband, D. (2004) *Personalised Learning: Building a new relationship with schools, speech by David Miliband*, Minister of State for School Standards, at the North of England Conference, Belfast, 8 January 2004.

Morgan, K (2011) *Athletics Challenges: A resource pack for teaching athletics* (2nd edn), London: Routledge.

Mosston, M. and Ashworth, S. (1986) *Teaching Physical Education*, London: Columbus.

Penney, D. (2000) 'Physical education, sporting excellent and educational excellence', *European Physical Education Review*, 6(2) 135–50.

Penney, D. and Evans, J. (1999) *Politics, Policy and Practice in Physical Education*, London: E & F Spon.

Penney, D. and Harris, J. (1997) 'Extra-curricular Physical Education: More of the same for the more able?' *Sport, Education and Society*, 2(1) 41–54.

Physical Education in Schools 2005/08: Working towards 2012 and beyond http://www. ofsted.gov.uk./resources/physical-education-schools-200508-working-toward-2012-and-beyond (accessed 14.5.12).

Pollard, A. and James, M. (eds) (2004) *Personalised Learning: A commentary by the teaching and learning research programme*, (no place of publication): Economic and Social Research Council.

QCA (2007) Physical Education: Programme of study for Key Stage 3 and attainment target. http://media.education.gov.uk/assets/files/pdf/p/pe%202007%20programme%20of%20study%20for%20key%20stage%203.pdf (accessed 25 November 2011).

Quick, S., Simon, A. and Thornton, A. (2010) *PE and School Sport Survey 2009/10*, London: DfE.

Ruddock, J., Brown, N. and Hendy, L. (2006) *Personalised Learning and Pupil Voice: The East Sussex Project*, Annesley: DfES Publications.

Smith, A., Green, K. and Thurston, M. (2009) '"Activity choice" and physical education in England and Wales', *Sport, Education and Society*, 14(2) 203–22.

Stidder G. and Binney J. (2011) 'Alternative Approaches to Teaching and Learning Physical Education in Secondary Schools', *Physical Education Matters* (formerly The British Journal of Teaching Physical Education), summer (6)2, 27–32.

Stidder, G. and Hayes, S (2010) 'Thematic learning and teaching through Physical Education', in Stidder, G. and Hayes S. (eds) *The Really Useful Physical Education Book. Learning and Teaching Across the 7–14 Age Range*, London, Routledge, 159–75.

Swaby, K. and Penney, D. (2011) 'Using discursive strategies, playing policy game and shaping the future of physical education', *Sport, Education and Society*, 16(1), 67–87.

Theodoulides A. (2003) 'Curriculum planning for inclusion in physical education', in Hayes S. and Stidder G. (eds) (2003) *Equity and Inclusion in Physical Education and School Sport: Contemporary Issues for Teachers, Trainees and Practitioners*, London, Routledge, 15–32.

Tinning, R. (1997) 'Performance and participation discourses in Human Movement: Towards a Socially Critical Physical Education', in Fernandez-Balboa, J. M. (ed.) *Critical Postmodernism in Human Movement, Physical Education and Sport*, New York: SUNY, 99–119.

UK Athletics (2005) *Elevating athletics: a framework for teaching athletics in schools for pupils aged 11–16*, (no place of publication): UK Athletics.

Underwood, J. and Banyard, P. (2008) 'Managers', teachers' and learners' perceptions of personalised learning: evidence from Impact 2007', *Technology, Pedagogy and Education*, 17(3), 233–46.

Vickerman, P. (2004) 'Planning for an Inclusive Approach to your Teaching and Learning', in Capel, S. (ed.) *Learning to teach physical education in the secondary school: a companion to school experience (2nd edn online)*, London: RoutledgeFalmer.

Wheaton, B. (ed.) (2004) *Understanding Lifestyle Sports: Consumption, identity and difference*, London: Routledge.

Youth Sport Trust (2009) *The PE and Sport Strategy for Young People: A guide to delivering the 5 hour offer*, www.youthsporttrust.org/downloads/cms/PESSYP/PESSYP_small.pdf (accessed 12 December 2010).

4 Special educational needs and disability in physical education

Philip Vickerman and Sid Hayes

I hated PE at school! Now don't get me wrong, I am not adverse to exercise, but in my school for the girls it was netball outside in winter (with regulation netball skirt and polo shirt – no tracksuits) and boys rotated rugby and football (in rugby/footie shirts and shorts) unless it was the middle of a storm in which case the teachers huffed and puffed and 'allowed' us inside to the sports halls where we would either play netball/football on the indoor courts, do bleep tests or be treated to the odd 'fun lesson' where we got to play benchball or dodgeball and then there were the mandatory cross-country sessions on the coldest, rainiest days of the year. Then in the summer, it was athletics for the first half of the summer term ready for sports day ... and then it was back to netball for most of the term with the odd session of tennis and rounders for girls and football with the odd session of cricket for the boys ...

http://www.digitalspy.co.uk/forums/showthread.php?t=798976&page=6

Accessed 25 August 2009

Critical self-reflection (Philip Vickerman)

All children are on a continuum of learning. I have witnessed many developments throughout my working life on the subject of including children with special educational needs and disabilities (SEND) in physical education and school sport. These include the early days of segregated education and a lack of recognition of children's individual entitlements to access PE, through to modern day approaches of empowerment and rights, and responsibilities placed on teachers and schools to facilitate inclusive education.

My educational philosophy is based on a fundamental recognition of empowering children with SEND to speak out about their experiences of PE and for teachers and schools to listen and respond to their experiences and needs. I wholeheartedly believe in inclusive PE, which embraces disabled and non-disabled children learning and progressing in the same environment. For me, this offers opportunities for young people (and teachers) to develop mutual understanding, respect and empathy for diversity. In saying this, I recognise though that on occasions it may be appropriate for segregated teaching and learning to take place where it is educationally appropriate to do so. Critical to successful inclusive PE is an open mind, positive attitude and a readiness to modify and adapt your practices to meet the individual needs of all children.

Critical self-reflection (Sid Hayes)

As we know all pupils offer different challenges when we consider learning and teaching generally and specifically in physical education and school sport. Whilst it has been and still is to an extent, useful to group pupils together based on generalised criteria associated with that group it can also be problematic and divisive. These comments ring true for me when we consider pupils categorised as a group known as SEND. Clearly the needs of this group require some particular interventions and teaching approaches to facilitate their learning but pupils linked together by such a label will cover a diverse range of abilities and needs. Due to the existence of such paradigms it is essential that practitioners develop their own philosophy towards inclusive practice based on a professional commonsense approach, and whichever learning and teaching approach is adopted the important starting point for all practitioners should be the following question – How can I include this/these pupil(s) in the learning experiences of the lesson? If this is the starting point then I think education for pupils classified as having a SEND will have moved forward significantly from the days of segregation and exclusion. Of course this will not always be easy and in some rare cases not always fully achievable but nevertheless this should be the starting point. For me this is morally the right stance to take as society and education progresses into the unknowns of the twenty-first century. The legislation, documentation and political ideology of any specific time will always evolve and change over time and practitioners will of course have to alter some of their practices to suit, but they should not lose sight of the moral obligations placed upon them to try to do the right thing for all pupils irrespective of any label attached to them.

Background and context

The World Education Forum (2000) acknowledged inclusive approaches to teaching and learning as a high priority for schools and these are further supported through the United Nations' (2008) promotion of 'Education for All'. In the context of children with special educational needs (SEND), UK policies have been implemented through the Special Educational Needs and Disability Act 2001 (DfES 2001a); National Curriculum (NC) Statutory Inclusion Statement (QCA/DfES 2007); SEN Code of Practice (DfES 2001b) and the 'Every Child Matters' Agenda (DfES 2005). Furthermore, within the backdrop of PE for children with SEND these policies set out to increase engagement of learning, while recognising the social, psychological and physiological benefits of participation (Vickerman and Coates 2009).

As a consequence, the commitment to inclusive PE for pupils with SEND within the UK is well evidenced in policies and PE teachers need to embrace these in practice (Morley *et al.* 2005) through the delivery of effective learning, teaching and assessment strategies. As a result, this chapter considers how teachers can address the inclusion of pupils with SEND in PE as defined by the Code of Practice (DfES 2001b). It will also address philosophical and practical aspects of PE for pupils with SEND, whilst offering practical strategies to enhance the delivery of barrier-free and inclusive activity. The chapter concludes with a summary of key features for teachers to address when planning and delivering inclusive PE for pupils with SEND.

Developing equality of opportunity for pupils with SEND

In order for teachers to plan for inclusion within mainstream PE lessons it is important to first clarify that pupils with SEND have a fundamental right to an inclusive education, which is supported through legislation. In interpreting this legislation practically, PE teachers must recognise that in facilitating inclusion the critical success factors are an open mind, positive attitude and a readiness to listen, review and modify existing learning, teaching and assessment strategies as necessary (Fitzgerald 2009).

Indeed, it is important to recognise equality for pupils with SEND in PE is socially and morally right (Avramadis and Norwich 2002) in any modern society and that schools offer pupils an ideal platform for learning mutual understanding and respect for difference and diversity. In considering the principles of equality it is therefore important to recognise that equality for pupils with SEND is not about treating all pupils in the same fashion. Thus, for PE teachers to enable full access to the curriculum, they need to recognise individual pupils' needs, then plan accordingly for them. According to Bailey (2005) equality of opportunity in PE should therefore focus upon celebration of difference and diversity amongst children, which is matched by a commitment to treat people differently but fairly according to their individual needs.

Coates and Vickerman (2008) reviewed a range of strategies for differentiating PE for children with SEND and suggested there are three common themes that are evident in most models of inclusive delivery. These are: Curriculum adaptation (changing what is taught); instructional modifications (changing how we teach); and human or people resources (looking at changing who teaches or supports adapted aspects of PE). Furthermore, the social model of disability (Burchardt 2004) recognises that often the greatest disabling factor is not the child with SEND, but the lack of flexibility and or commitment to modify and adapt existing practices by schools and teachers (Block and Obruniskova 2007). Consequently, inclusion for pupils with SEND should be recognised as a process that is responsive and flexible to pupil needs, and moves beyond traditional concepts of integration and mainstreaming in which additional or separate practices are often bolted onto existing provision (Armstrong 2005). Inclusive PE for pupils with SEND is more concerned with recognition of both the philosophical basis of inclusion which is matched by a commitment and desire to support its action through both policy implementation and a readiness to modify and adapt practice.

Indeed, the NC (QCA/DfES 2007) suggests that inclusive PE for children with SEND can be addressed via three principles of:

- **Setting suitable learning challenges**: Here PE teachers should recognise that in order to reflect children's diversity they should develop different objectives for children based upon their individual needs and differences.
- **Responding to the diverse needs of pupils**: This places a requirement on teachers to acknowledge difference and diversity of children with SEN in PE and respond accordingly.
- **Differentiating assessment and learning to meet individual needs of pupils**: This recognises that if PE teachers set appropriate objectives and recognise children are all on a continuum of learning they should also consider alternative methods of assessment which maximise opportunities for children to demonstrate their knowledge and understanding.

Equalities Act 2010

This Act brings together nine separate pieces of legislation into one Act covering disability, age, gender re-assignment, marriage and civil partnership, race, pregnancy and maternity, religion and belief, sex (gender) and sexual orientation. With regards to disability, it sets out to end discrimination experienced by disabled people by giving rights in employment, in education, and to access goods, facilities and services.

With the new Equalities Act essentially nothing really changes from a disability perspective, the rights covered by the DDA have simply been transferred under the new Act. The Equality Act (October 2010) definition of '*disability*' is a 'physical or mental impairment that has a substantial and long-term adverse effect on a person's ability to carry out normal day-to-day activities' (2010: 4).

This definition is more flexible than under the older DDA and makes it more likely that it will apply in a broader range of cases, particularly in relation to mental health.

The Green Paper (2011)

The present government's plan for SEND is outlined in this document and suggests the following proposals:

Figure 4.1 UK government SEND proposals

The UK government wishes to fairly radically alter the system of support and it states that there will be:

> ... a new single assessment process and 'Education, Health and Care Plan' by 2014 to replace the statutory SEN assessment and statement, bringing together the support on which children and their families rely across education, health and social care. Services will work together with the family to agree a straightforward plan that reflects the family's ambitions for their child from the early years to adulthood, which is reviewed regularly to reflect their changing needs, and is clear about who is responsible for provision. The new 'Education, Health and Care Plan' will provide the same statutory protection to parents as the statement of SEN and will include a commitment from all parties to provide their services, with local assessment and plan pathfinders testing the best way to achieve this.
>
> (Green Paper 2011:5)

As identified in the previous diagram and the government statement it is evident that the legislation and potential structure of SEND is likely to change sooner rather than later.

Key guiding principles for pupils with SEN in PE

Vickerman (2007) suggests there are four guiding principles for including children with SEN in PE. These embrace both the philosophy and practice of inclusive education and should be considered as central to any successful PE lesson. These are entitlement, accessibility, inclusion and integrity. In relation to *entitlement*, the premise is to acknowledge the fundamental right of all children to access PE and this is of particular relevance with the emergence of inclusive legislation as noted earlier in this chapter.

The second principle of *accessibility* refers to the responsibility of PE teachers to devise strategies to ensure all pupils with SEND gain their full entitlement to the curriculum. This involves adopting flexible approaches to learning, teaching and assessment with teachers recognising their, rather than pupils', responsibility to modify and adapt activities. This view embraces the social model of disability through which society (i.e. teachers and schools) should adapt provision to accommodate individual pupils' needs. This contrasts with more traditional medical-based models of disability (Murchardt 2004) which centre the location and causation of disability with the disabled individual and focus on the need for the individual to adapt to fit with society's pre-existing structures.

With reference to the third principle of *inclusion* teachers of PE should start with a recognition that in any class there will be a continuum of learning needs. As such, teachers should work upon the premise of planning for full inclusion (Vickerman 2007) then work backwards to alternative and/or separate activities. It is also important to recognise though that for some children separate activities may be the best way of achieving inclusion in PE. For example, it may be more appropriate for a child in a wheelchair to take part in an alternative activity if the rest of the class is on a grass pitch. What is important here though is that the child has been consulted and is happy with any alternative offered. This links to the final principle of *integrity* which suggests that whatever the nature of learning, teaching and/or assessment strategy utilised it must be of equal worth and in no way tokenistic or patronising.

Extending and developing the key guiding principles

As part of their wider teaching philosophy and practice PE teachers should embrace a series of guiding principles if they are to make a genuine commitment to inclusive PE for pupils with SEND. These principles incorporate notions of entitlement, accessibility, inclusion and integrity which have already been discussed. Furthermore, the principles of the NCPE (QCA/DfES 2007) statutory inclusion statement incorporating setting suitable learning challenges; responding to pupils' diverse needs, and overcoming potential barriers to learning and assessment for individuals and groups of pupils should also be considered by teachers.

The NCPE (QCA/DfES 2007) also promotes the importance of personalising the curriculum as a matter of moral purpose and social justice. Indeed, teachers are expected to ensure children with SEND see the relevance of the curriculum to their own experiences and aspirations and have sufficient opportunities to succeed in their learning to the highest standard. The National Strategies 'Waves of Intervention Model' (DfE 2006) is one such way in which PE teachers can adopt inclusive approaches to learning, teaching and assessment for children with SEND. The model is premised on three 'waves of intervention' as indicated below:

Wave 1

This first wave focuses on the notion that effective inclusion for children with SEND in PE has to be based on personalising the curriculum for individual pupils' needs. This includes setting clear, challenging but achievable learning objectives; high quality learning, teaching and assessment that addresses the full continuum of all children's needs; and differentiation of objectives to accommodate a variety of pupils' learning styles. Thus, in adopting these guiding principles inclusive teaching will benefit all pupils and not just children with SEND.

Wave 2

The second wave of intervention builds upon the good inclusive practice identified in Wave 1 but extends this to targeted provision for individuals and small groups of pupils. Here strategies may include the use of specialised intervention strategies such as the 'inclusion spectrum in PE'. This spectrum recognises that teachers should adopt a range of strategies such as open, modified, parallel, disability sport and separate activities to include children with SEND. In relation to open activities this is where all children perform the task in the same way with no or minimal need for differentiation. It is good practice to start from the premise of full inclusion then work back towards separate activities if required. Modified activities may include changing the size of a court, ball or racquet to aid inclusion. Parallel activities incorporate streaming groups of pupils in terms of abilities so they all may be involved in the same activity but compete at different degrees of complexity in relation to rules or conditions you place on a game. Disability sport activities are where PE teachers introduce an activity such as Boccia or seated volleyball for all pupils to gain an appreciation of disability-oriented activities. Finally, in relation to separate activities this recognises that for some pupils it may be appropriate to have separate activities at particular points within a lesson. This may include for example where a child works on wheelchair slalom rather than athletic relays as part of a lesson.

Wave 3

Wave 3 is concerned with intervention for children where 'quality first teaching' in Wave 1 and 'specific intervention strategies' in Wave 2 are not enough to facilitate inclusion in PE for children with SEND. Thus, there is a need for more specialised intervention and individual support for pupils. In PE for children with SEND this may involve the support of a teaching assistant, physiotherapist for movement advice and/or links to a disability sport association for links to lifelong physical activity outside of the curriculum. Consequently, by adopting the waves approach to learning, teaching and assessment, schools and teachers will be able to target their resources in a more focused way at those children with SEND that need it most. Furthermore, the wave approach has the potential to benefit all children and enhance their learning experiences and not just those with SEND.

Leaning to move – moving to learn

Sugden and Wright (1998) suggest PE has a distinctive role to play for all children regardless of their individual needs as it does not just focus on the education of the physical, but also has social, emotional, cognitive, moral and language dimensions. Consequently, for children with SEND a first step in the teaching and learning process is to consider the learning outcomes of the PE lesson. If these are not set within a context of appropriate learning challenge and potential for success it will potentially lead to barriers to learning which limit opportunities for children to gain their full entitlement and maximise opportunities to succeed in PE. Therefore, in order to address this issue learning outcomes should be developed around a focus of learning to move and/or moving to learn.

Learning to move can be considered an intrinsic benefit of PE and is a traditional outcome of any physical activity lesson. Here, PE teachers identify the specific skills to be taught and learned by the pupils and for those with SEND this may have a particular focus if a child has movement difficulties in which outcomes may need to be modified to accommodate these. For example a child with cerebral palsy may struggle to hop, skip and jump in athletics. Thus, the task of learning to move may have to be modified to include travelling via crawling or the use of a frame to move around a space. In contrast, *moving to learn* involves developing outcomes that are based upon the results of broader experiences in PE rather than a focus on quality of movement. Mouratadis *et al.* (2008) suggest that by teachers focusing upon extrinsic benefits such as developing pupil's co-operation, empathy, team work, leadership skills and the like this can enable more pupils to access PE by simply changing the focus of the learning outcome for some children. For example, if a child needs to learn how to take turns or listen to the views of others this can be identified as a specific outcome for the child to work on. Another example may be where teachers introduce pupils to a disability sport activity for non-disabled pupils to gain mutual understanding and respect for difference and diversity.

Inclusion and Emotional and Behavioural Difficulty (EBD) pupils

As already noted, schools and the PE profession are well placed to take on board the processes required for developing an effective inclusion strategy for pupils with a variety of SEND. Developing inclusive practices for pupils who regularly demonstrate behavioural difficulties, however, poses a somewhat different set of issues for the teacher. As the Office for Standards in Education (Ofsted) states in its report Managing Challenging Behaviour (2005):

> The challenging behaviour of many younger pupils arises mainly as a result of poor language and social skills and emotional development fitting to their age. The most common form of poor behaviour is low-level disruption of lessons, perpetrated much more often by boys than by girls.
>
> (Ofsted 2005: 5)

The reasons for such behaviour may be due to a complex number of circumstances, which may have their roots either within or outside the school environment, and these are well-documented (see Smith *et al.* 2004; Travell and Visser 2006). It is not the purpose of this chapter to re-examine these causes but to consider how these pupils can be a part of a school-wide inclusive strategy. As we have pointed out, it is reasonable to assume that challenges posed by pupils with behavioural difficulties are somewhat different from those challenges posed by pupils with other learning needs. We do, however, feel it is correct and necessary to view these pupils as part of any overall inclusive strategy whilst also accepting that they constitute a different set of demands and occupy a distinctive, separate part of the whole inclusive spectrum. Behavioural problems are a key challenge facing a number of schools as highlighted by Ofsted in its annual report on schools for 2009/2010 where it is stated:

> Behaviour was good or outstanding in 89% of primary schools and 70% of secondary schools inspected in 2009/10. Behaviour was almost always good

or outstanding in the schools where teaching was at least good. In the minority of the schools where behaviour was poor, teaching was frequently also weak.

Ofsted (2010 p. 32)

It is prudent and realistic to suggest that the teaching profession should address issues of inclusive practice in stages as part of previously mentioned guiding principles. It may be that, presently, issues of behaviour management within schools need to be tackled at a managerial level before we can expect PE teachers and teachers in general to embrace inclusive processes for pupils with major behavioural difficulties within their daily teaching regimes, as well as other inclusive processes that are already being developed. In some schools this is clearly happening, in others, there is still some way to go (Ofsted 2010). If managerial guidance and structure occurs then it should be possible for all teachers, including PE practitioners, to move forward in achieving long-term inclusive practices for all pupil needs including EBD pupils as part of an overall inclusive school strategy.

Practical examples of inclusive PE for pupils with SEND

When planning inclusive PE for pupils with SEND, it is important to start from the premise of full inclusion within the activity, and, where this may not be possible, to consider adaptation and/or modification of learning and teaching strategies or activities.

The central success factor for teachers is to consult initially, where appropriate with the child with SEND and relevant professionals as part of a multi-disciplinary approach. This enables the pupils and teachers to consider, at the planning stage, any differentiation that may be required. This further supports the principle of equality and the social model approach that acknowledges individual diversity. It also responds accordingly to the needs of pupils with SEND by modifying or adapting activities as appropriate.

An example of this could be in games activities such as hockey, where pupils may initially require lighter, larger or different coloured balls in order to access the activity. Adaptations to rules (modified activities) may need to be considered, such as allowing a player with movement restrictions five seconds to receive and play the ball. In addition, if utilising such a strategy, it is vital that all members of the group understand the need for such an adaptation in order that they can play to this rule during a game.

In dance, activities can be adapted through consultation with the disabled and non-disabled pupil, as part of the requirements of the curriculum to work co-operatively. For example a pupil in a wheelchair can use the chair as an extension of their body to move around a particular area. If group tasks are to be performed, then the group can work together on themes for inclusion in which the movement patterns of the pupils with SEND can be incorporated into the overall group piece being performed.

Another example of inclusive participation in athletic activities with physically disabled pupils may involve one push of their wheelchair, rather than a jump into the sandpit, or reducing distances to run or travel. In addition, if there are pupils with visual impairments teachers can organise activities such as a 100-metre race in which a guide stands at the finish line (separate activity) and shouts out the lane number they are in, or a guide runs alongside them for support.

Opportunities for SEND pupils outside the curriculum

Teachers should be aware of the structure of sport in the UK (see Figure 4.2) and call on the support of the relevant organisation to help facilitate pupils' accessing sports-related opportunities outside normal curriculum hours..

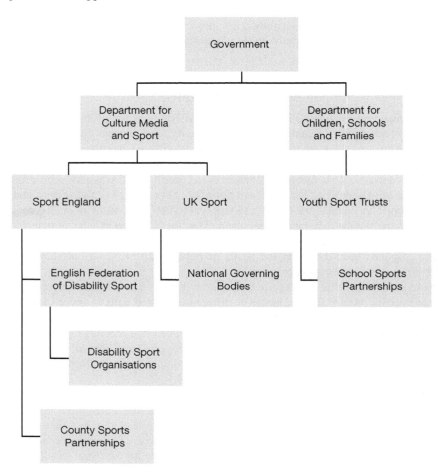

Figure 4.2 UK structure of sport

Structure of disability sport

Although the central focus of this chapter relates to core curriculum matters in PE, it is necessary to briefly highlight how pupils may access activity outside of curriculum time through extra-curricular activities or within the community. There are a number of organisations (see Figure 4.2) and initiatives aimed at providing activity for pupils who have additional learning needs and PE departments may wish to develop partnership links with such organisations to serve the needs of the pupils' post-curriculum time.

Sport England advocates the mainstreaming of disability sport into the work of Governing Bodies of Sport. There is recognition, however, that this will not occur in the short-term and a considerable amount of work is going to have to be undertaken to achieve this objective. The English Federation of Disability Sport (EFDS) was therefore established in order to help achieve this. Its aims are to expand sporting opportunities for people with disabilities; increase the numbers actively involved in sport; and work with mainstream governing bodies of sport. There are nine EFDS regions where teachers can access information about local and national opportunities.

EFDS as the national body responsible for developing sport for disabled people in England work closely with the National Disability Sports Organisations (NDSOs; as recognised by Sport England) to develop sporting opportunities for disabled people. In 2011 there are eight NDSO members of EFDS. Each of these organisations provided sporting opportunities for a specific impairment group namely:

British Amputee & Les Autres Sports Association
British Blind Sport
Cerebral Palsy Sport (CP Sport)
Dwarf Sports Association
Mencap Sport
Special Olympics
UK Deaf Sport
WheelPower – British Wheelchair Sport.

Finding local opportunities

There are two key pathways that can be followed outside school-based provision: disability-specific sports clubs or mainstream sports clubs. Most local authorities will have a sports/leisure development officer who will know where local sports clubs meet and how accessible they are to disabled people. Some local authorities produce directories of sports clubs that provide opportunities for disabled people. Sports Development Officers (SDOs) can also provide an invaluable link between the school PE department and the local sports community.

Development work in disability sport concentrates on providing people with disabilities with a choice. Clearly there is still some way to go before we reach total inclusion and mainstreaming of disability sport. It is easy to be critical but it should be recognised that inclusion is a reality and not just a possibility. For example, there are many examples of athletes with disabilities competing at the same venue as mainstream competitors. Furthermore, initiatives such as those organised by the Youth Sports Trust (YST) have added a new dimension to the area of inclusive PE provision. YST have produced bags of equipment and resource cards aimed specifically at special or mainstream schools. The equipment is aimed at both young people with SEND and non-disabled young people of all abilities. Additionally five separate games were included in an equipment bag issued by the Youth Sports Trust which can be used to help those pupils with severe disabilities. These games: Boccia (a bowls-type game), Table Cricket, Table Hockey, Polybat (an adapted version of table tennis), and Goalball, a game played by visually impaired people. Four of these games have pathways for young people to go on and progress from recreational level through to National, International and Paralympic competition, the exception being Table Hockey.

The tabletop games (although designed primarily to be played on a table tennis table) have the versatility to be played at most tables. Polybat was designed for those young disabled people with control and co-ordination difficulties. The development of a glove bat has ensured that those pupils who find it hard to grip a bat can handle the Polybat and so participate successfully. Another game that can be used for this equipment is table skittles, using plastic cups if skittles are not available. Goalball is a 3-a-side game developed for visually-impaired people; sighted players can join in as everyone wears adapted goggles. This is an example of reverse inclusion where sighted people can be included in a disability-specific game. It is important to consider how these activities can be developed further. One possibility could be an inter-school competition or perhaps establishing a lunchtime or after school club. Although these activities may go some way to addressing activity levels for people with disabilities, research undertaken by Sport England (2011) has highlighted some interesting differences in sports participation between people with disabilities and their non-disabled peers. These include acknowledgement that:

- currently 93% of disabled people in England are not taking part in sport according to the latest Sport England Active People Survey.
- sports participation among disabled adults has decreased by 42,800, from 429,500 to 386,700.

Opportunities are, however, being created for young disabled people to participate either recreationally or competitively in sport. It is knowing, however, where and how to access the network of provision available at both local and/or national level. The situation could be improved through better-informed partnerships between school PE departments and disability organisations, both nationally and regionally, and this could be a developing role within a PE department's structure.

'You can't beat practical experience. Coaches need more of it. In terms of the older generation, they don't understand disability. In their time, disability was shut out of the way, so they've had to learn what disability is and change their view on it. A few weeks after coaching us they change their view.'

(ROSS)

Stop being so negative!

- Don't assume you can't coach disabled people. As well as your previous coaching experiences, a willingness and open mind are important qualities that will help you to coach disabled athletes.

- Not all disabled people want to only participate with other disabled people. Welcome more disabled people into your coaching sessions.

- Don't learn everything you can about every impairment. Talk to the individual and adapt your session – they have the best knowledge of what their body can do.

- If an activity isn't working for everyone, adapt it. Use the great coaching knowledge you have.

- Don't hide in your shell. Talk to, and learn from, other coaches and share your experiences and ideas about coaching disabled athletes.

'I've had experiences in the past where a coach has basically said he can't do anything for me, that he thinks I can't be helped to improve. So I was told not to bother to train. It's not exactly inviting you to a session if you've been told nothing can be done for you.'

(JOHN)

Here's what our interviewees want to see:

From the start

- A warm welcome goes a long way. Confidently approach your participant and talk to them about what experience they have had, and what they want to get out of your sessions. (Scope: #endtheawkward)

- How do disabled people get to hear about your coaching sessions? You could advertise your sessions via the Internet and local social networks supporting disabled people (try your local county sports partnership)

- If you have not coached disabled people before, be open-minded and see it as an opportunity to extend your experiences on your road to becoming a better coach.

- When playing sport or being active, some disabled people may prefer to be with other disabled people. Others may prefer to be coached together with disabled and non-disabled people.
Get to know what other opportunities are available locally, so you can signpost people if necessary.

- Check your coaching venue is accessible (contact EFDS for more details). It's not just about ramps and lifts!

'A good coach has to be able to understand me. You know, know my body, know how it moves. There's no point thinking I'm like someone without a disability. So for me, my coach needs to be in tune with my body. To do this they've got to keep thinking all the time; they need to be reflective.'

(MARK)

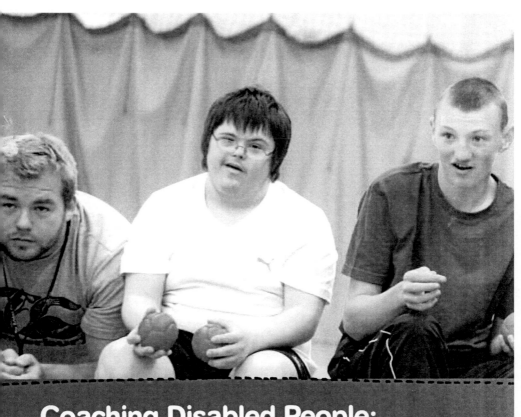

Coaching Disabled People:
What Coaches Need to Know

COACHING DISABLED PEOPLE:
WHAT COACHES NEED TO KNOW

You should not underestimate the impact your coaching can have on disabled people. You can inspire and motivate them to continue to play their sport.

Current sports participation statistics tell us that there is still much work to be done to support disabled people in sport.

Did you know that:

- sports participation among disabled people is significantly lower across all age groups than the overall population
- the proportion of disabled people receiving tuition or coaching is lower than the overall population?[1]

sports coach UK spoke to a number of disabled people involved in sport at all levels. The following responses and guidance have been taken from those conversations.

> 'A good coach is someone who is understanding. I think the most important thing is having a coach that you can get on with and one who communicates well with you. I think you both need to be on the same wavelength. If your coach wants different things to what you want, or if they have different goals to the athlete, I don't think it works. I think the most important thing is that you are both clear on what you are trying to do.'
>
> (STEVE)

Positive lessons to learn:

- Involve disabled people in all of your sessions.
- Recognise a disabled athlete as an individual, not an impairment.
- Have a shared vision with your participants in terms of coaching goals and expectations. Communicate and work together to achieve them.
- Talk to your disabled participants about their impairment to plan effective coaching sessions and adapt practices.
- Know the sport you coach. Have a passion to develop yourself as a coach.

> 'We need people who are really, really good at the sport, who are prepared to work with disabled athletes – not the other way round. We need people who are good at coaching the sport, who can adapt it. That is how we are going to move forward. What you find with some people is that it's limited because they will pick up the coach who will work with a disabled person, and they are not necessarily the best coach.'
>
> (JOY)

EFDS (2010) 'Overall Participation of Disabled People in Sport'. *Active People Survey 5*. Loughborough: EFDS.

During your session:

- Don't get hung up on labels (for example, someone has CP; someone else has attention deficit hyperactivity disorder [ADHD]). See through the label and talk to the person.

- Remember, we are all individuals. One disabled person will not be the same as another, so coach the individual not the impairment.

- Remember to develop your sport-specific technical knowledge as well as your understanding of disability. This will help you to work more effectively with disabled people.

- Communicate continually with everyone in your session and get their views on how it went at the end.

'Coaches have a lack of understanding. There isn't enough on offer to help them understand about cerebral palsy (CP) or dwarfism etc. It isn't until they coach someone or talk to someone that they think, "hang on a minute, it's not as scary as it first seemed" and then they carry on.'

(ROSS)

Developing as an inclusive coach

- Network with other coaches and share your experiences or ideas for coaching disabled participants. Join the Coaching Disabled People group through LinkedIn, or check with your CSP when the next coaching forum or conference is being held.

- Develop a better understanding of how your sport (eg rules and equipment) can be adapted for people with different impairments. Try a sports coach UK workshop to learn more about adapting sport appropriately for disabled people, coaching disabled people, or communicating effectively with deaf people in sport. The workshops also provide a great opportunity to talk to other coaches.

- Know where you can go locally (eg contact your CSP or governing body of sport disability/equity development officer, or visit a local disability sports club) for further support.

- National organisations can also help. Check out the sports coach UK website for the disability contacts information.

4

Oscar Pistorius

We think it would be remiss of us not to mention before the end of this chapter the inclusion of Oscar Pistorius the 400 metres athlete, who competed in the 2011 Daegu world athletics championship recently. This was a landmark decision by the International Association of Athletic Federations (IAAF) allowing a disabled athlete to compete with non-disabled athletes in the same event. His inclusion in the event certainly atrracted considerable media attention. Although he was eliminated in the semi-final it will be interesting to note how things develop in forthcoming years with regards to the inclusion of disabled athletes into mainstream sport: will the momentum build or will this prove to have been a unique, one-off situation. Watch this space!

Summary: facilitating inclusive physical education for pupils with SEND

Inclusive PE is a key issue for government, schools and teachers to address in the coming years. The philosophical basis of inclusive PE for pupils with SEND is both socially and morally sound, and is supported through legislation and the development of new practices in teacher education.

The role of schools and teachers is central to the success or otherwise of the government's agenda for inclusion. Teachers need to adopt a clear and consistent framework in relation to PE for pupils with SEND. A necessary framework for inclusion should encompass a combination of philosophy, process and practice, drawing together a number of key points for consideration when planning and delivering PE to pupils with SEND.

PE teachers should recognise and spend time analysing, planning and implementing their delivery through the consideration of a series of interrelated factors. The first being to recognise and embrace the philosophy behind inclusion discussed within this chapter as a basic and fundamental human right, which is supported by professionals in society through statutory and non-statutory guidance such as the Special Educational Needs and Disability Rights Act 2001 (DfES 2001a), the revised Code of Practice (DfES 2001b), the NCPE (QCA/DfES 2007) and the Equalities Act (2010).

In order to facilitate this process schools and teachers must embrace a purposeful approach to fulfilling the requirements of inclusive PE. Thus, time should be spent examining philosophical standpoints to achieve clear recognition of the rationale and arguments behind inclusive education. Teachers must be proactive in the development and implementation of inclusive PE and consult actively as a whole school, with fellow teachers and with pupils with SEND, in order to produce a collaborative approach to their delivery within the school.

Inclusive PE for pupils with SEND requires a recognition and commitment to modify and adapt existing learning and teaching styles in order to facilitate full access and entitlement to the curriculum, and an obligation to undertake this through a social model of disability. The development of inclusive PE for pupils with SEND must, therefore, be recognised as a process that evolves, emerges and changes over time, and, as such, will need to be regularly reviewed by all the key stakeholders.

In summary, PE teachers and schools must ensure that inclusion is reflected within policy documentation, as a means of monitoring, reviewing and evaluating delivery. The critical factor, however, is the need to move policy through into the pedagogical practices of PE teachers. Whilst philosophies and processes are vital for schools and teachers, they must ultimately measure their success in terms of effective inclusive practice, which is embedded within a 'person-centred' approach to the education of pupils with SEND.

References

Armstrong, D. (2005) *Reinventing 'Inclusion: New Labour and the Cultural Politics of Special Education*, Oxford Review of Education, 31(1), 135–51.

Avramadis, E. and Norwich, B. (2002) 'Teachers' Attitudes towards integration/inclusion: A review of the Literature', *European Journal of Special Needs Education* 22(4), 367–89.

Bailey, R. (2005) 'Evaluating the Relationship between Physical Education, Sport and Social Inclusion', *Educational Review*, vol. 57(1), 71–90.

Block, M. and Obruniskova, I. (2007) 'Inclusion in Physical Education: A review of the literature from 1995–2005', *Adapted Physical Activity Quarterly*, 24, 103–24.

Burchardt, T. (2004) 'Capabilities and Disability: The capabilities framework and the social model of disability', *Disability and Society*, vol. 19(7), 735–51.

Coates, J. and Vickerman, P. (2008) 'Let the Children have their Say: A review of children with special educational needs' experiences of physical education', *Support for Learning* 23(4), 168–75.

Department for Education (2006) *The Primary National Strategy Waves of Intervention*, London, HMSO.

Department for Education (2011) *Support and Aspiration: A new approach to special educational needs and disability. A consultation*, London HMSO.

Department for Education and Skills (2001a) *Special Educational Needs and Disability Rights Act 2001*, London, HMSO.

Department for Education and Skills (2001b) *Special Educational Needs Code of Practice*, London, HMSO.

Department for Education and Skills, (2005) *Every Child Matters: Change for Children in Schools*, London, HMSO.

Equalities Act (2010), London: HMSO.

Fitzgerald, H. (2009) 'Still feeling like a spare piece of luggage? Embodied experiences of (dis)ability in physical education and school sport', in Bailey, R. and Kirk, D. (eds), *The Routledge Physical Education Reader*, London, Routledge.

Green Paper (2011) 'Support and Aspiration: A new Approach to special needs and disability – A consultation', London, HMSO.

Morley, D., Bailey, R., Tan, J. and Cooke, B. (2005) 'Inclusive Physical Education: Teachers' views of teaching children with special educational needs and disabilities in physical education', *European Physical Education Review* 11(1), 84–107.

Mouratidis, A., Vansteenkiste, M., Lens, W. and Sideris, G. (2008) 'The Motivating Role of Positive Feedback in Sport and Physical Education: evidence for a motivational model', *Journal of Sport and Exercise Psychology*, vol. 30, 240–68.

Office for Standards in Education (2005) *Managing Challenging Behaviour*, London, Ofsted Publications.

Office for Standards in Education (2010) *The Annual Report of Her Majesty's Chief Inspector of Education, Children's Services and Skills 2009/10: Maintained schools summary*, London, Ofsted Publications.

Qualification Curriculum Authority/Department for Education and Skills (2007) *National Curriculum Physical Education*, Qualification Curriculum Authority, HMSO, London.

Smith, D., Travell, C. and Worton, L. (2004) 'You, Me and Us: How a project set up by an LEA educational psychology service helped a school to support the inclusion of pupils with EBD', *Emotional and Behavioural Difficulties*, 9(3)171–80.

Sport England (2011) *Active People Survey*, Sport England, London.

Sugden, D. and Wright, H. (1998) *Motor Co-ordination Disorders in Children*, London, Sage.

Travell, C. and Visser, J. (2006) '"ADHD Does Bad Stuff to You": young people's and parents' experiences and perceptions of ADHD', *Emotional and Behavioural Difficulties*, 11(3), 205–16.

United Nations (2008) *Education for All: Overcoming Inequality – Why Governance Matters*, Oxford, Oxford University Press.

Vickerman, P. (2007) *Teaching Physical Education to Children with Special Educational Needs*, London, Routledge.

Vickerman, P. and Coates, J. (2009) 'Trainee and Recently Qualified Physical Education Teachers Perspectives on Including Children with Special Educational Needs', *Journal of Physical Education and Sport Pedagogy*, 14(2), 137–53.

World Education Forum (2000) *Inclusion in Education: The Participation of Disabled Learners*, Dakar, Senegal.

5 Investigating the gender regime in physical education and dance

Gary Stidder, Gill Lines and Saul Keyworth

In my early years I have no recollection of ever kicking a ball. As a girl, I just didn't! At school I took part in a range of team games, gymnastics, dance, swimming and athletics. As I grew older my love of dance and gymnastics developed at the expense of other activities. I had plenty of opportunities to take part in virtually any sport I wanted, except perhaps football or rugby, which at that time just weren't played by girls. It was perhaps only when I began working in the field of teacher training that the absurdity of the 'missing men and boys' hit home. The subtlety of access to certain team games, whilst important for equity, is on reflection a minor point when compared to a far greatly tragedy. Namely, the exclusion of so many boys from dance; the only activity within the PE curriculum that offers young people the chance to use their body is an expressive way to communicate ideas, feelings and moods, and the unwillingness, fear and dread felt by so many men forced to teach it. Whilst there are small pockets of progress, no other area of PE stands out so obviously as a beacon of poor inclusive practice.

Fiona Smith,
Principal lecturer in Physical Education and Dance,
University of Brighton, Chelsea School of Sport

Introduction

Members of the Jury.

In the previous edition of this book we saw that due care and attention was given to achieving gender equity for girls and boys in physical education through changes to teaching approaches, group organisation and alternatives to more established (and prescribed) activities in the secondary school physical education curriculum (Lines and Stidder 2003). In order to emphasize the possible ways of achieving greater parity for boys and girls Keyworth and Smith (2003: 189) contributed to the debate surrounding gender equity by sharing male stories of 'gender troubles' (Butler 1990) in dance and encouraged male (and female) physical educators to grapple with gendered beliefs by engaging in critical autobiographical work (Sparkes 1999). Through our continued surveillance as under-cover detectives within the Physical Education Gender Police (PEGP), new evidence has come to light. We now examine the evidence related to 'the gender regime' (Connell 1996) in physical education and dance and how it might be policed. In particular, we reveal that that there have been very few changes made to encourage more gender equitable practice to flourish in physical education and dance. Our purpose is to prove allegations of gender-bias teaching in our capacity as Gender Equity Compliance Officers (GECO) accountable to the Department of Inclusive Policies and Practices for Youth (DIPPY). Through our own judicial review we investigate the influence of the so-called 'hidden curriculum' (Fernandez-Balboa 1993) and will show you how the perpetrators of gender crimes are guilty of 'damage limitation' (a process of limiting the damaging effects of an action or mistake). In this context members of the Legal Office for Gender Order and Compliance (LOGOC) stand accused and will be interrogated. Through our cross-examination we will highlight the contribution of their accomplices in aiding and abetting the perpetration of heinous gender crimes. It is our intention to present you with evidence that proves the defendants are not only habitual criminals but are also guilty beyond reasonable doubt.

To begin our case against the accused we draw your attention to the fact that the editors of this book have stated in their introduction that physical education and dance is 'genderised' possibly more than any other secondary school curriculum subject, influenced by male and female perceptions of heterosexual masculinity and femininity. This is often incompatible with the types of physical activities and sports offered to young people in secondary schools. For example, in its form and content games teaching is openly gendered and has been progressively privileged in respect to its place on the physical education curriculum (Green 2008). Whilst girls prefer individual activities (HMI for Wales 2007), traditional feminine-appropriate team games have guaranteed themselves a secure place on the girls' physical education curriculum in secondary schools. The privileged place of sex-stereotyped team games at the expense of other forms of physical activity within the physical education curriculum is a significant contributory factor in the genderisation of physical education and dance. It is frequently based on sex-stereotyped assumptions about the appropriateness of particular patterns of provision reserved exclusively either for boys or girls, typically staffed by male and female teachers respectively thus reinforcing acceptable forms of heterosexual masculinity and femininity (Flintoff and Scraton 2005). We have expert witnesses who are willing to give evidence and ensure that the perpetrators of these gender crimes are prevented from perverting the course of justice. Our witnesses will testify that it is for these reasons that physical education in schools makes both friends and enemies. That it inspires and it alienates. That it is nice for some (disproportionately middle-class male pupils) and nasty for others (Evans and Davies 2002: 20). Or as one author has commented:

> Physical education as it currently exists in many British schools is a masculinised form of the subject which does not meet the needs of many girls and at least some boys. Consequently, many pupils are prevented and deterred from leading active lifestyles. In schools funded by public money this is simply unacceptable.
>
> (Kirk 2002: 35)

Your Honor, some of the most serious gender crimes that have been committed have resulted in damaging long-term effects on our clients such as an aversion to competitive team games amongst many of our female clients, a reluctance to participate in dance activities amongst our male clients, an inability to perform in mixed-sex environments, negative body image and low self-confidence (Penney 2002a; Flintoff and Scraton 2005). Much of this can be attributed to the actions of the defendants who tend to have very clear ideas of the kinds of activities they view as appropriate for boys and girls regardless of recent developments towards broader and more varied physical education programmes of activity. Our investigations have uncovered sufficient evidence to prove that the types of physical activities provided in schools bears little or no resemblance to those on offer later in adult life. We would like to provide you with the following statement to support our case:

> Boys and girls continue to be confronted by (PE) curricula dominated by competitive, physically vigorous games; that is 'Traditional' PE.
>
> (Green 2008: 143)

The extent to which gender crimes in physical education and dance have encouraged teachers to reflect and change is limited, as pointed out in Chapter 2. For, despite research on gender issues in physical education (Leaman 1984; Scraton 1992; Wright 1999; Penney 2002b; HMI for Wales 2007; Ofsted 2009), and calls for innovation and change to traditional (gendered) forms of physical education the process of rehabilitation has been slow and the issues remain hardly different to those experienced by pupils across the decades (Flintoff and Scraton 2005). Your Honor, we would like to point out that sport and physical education in the UK has become highly politicised with the advent of the London 2012 Olympic Games and that the focus of UK government attention has revolved primarily around talent identification and performance development at the expense of socially inclusive programmes of physical education and dance for boys' and girls' schools. We would like to present evidence of research that has assessed the relative scope and freedom to implement alternative (and gender inclusive) approaches to teaching and learning physical education and dance in secondary schools since revisions to the national curriculum for physical education in England (Stidder and Binney 2011; Griggs 2008). And yet, we bring to your attention that some teachers have remained resistant to anything but conventional gendered types of physical education and dance in schools (Ofsted 2009). It is our contention, therefore, that whilst the physical education research community has been proactive in highlighting gender inequalities in schools it has made little progress in leading the proverbial horse to water and making it drink.

You will hear from the Defence that the value of educational research in the social sciences is considered by some to be too abstract, too far removed from practitioners, unusable by politicians and too much aimed at fellow academics. They will argue that educational research is too arcane and far removed from the real world of teaching and that a damaging dichotomy remains between the need to disseminate and publish research and that of interpretation and application within the school context (Evans and Davies 2002). They will also try to convince you that:

> The PE profession is not unique here – this is a normal characteristic of occupational groups who have a built-in tendency to resist change that threatens to make life highly uncomfortable by disrupting established routines.
>
> (Green 2003: 161)

But, don't be fooled. As prosecutors we will argue that insights from educational research in physical education and dance can be both dangerous and threatening as it can generate change both educationally and socially thus reflecting the conservatism that exists in the physical education profession (Evans and Davies 2002: 15). We will show that this is not surprising as many physical education and dance teachers have themselves been socialised into playing the 'gender game' (Keen 1992) throughout their engagement in physical activity and may inevitably find it difficult to reflect constructively on threats to their own gendered identities and practices. We have obtained evidence that a fuller understanding of gender, gender relations and pupil achievement in physical activity requires deeper insights into teachers and the embodiment of self (Brown and Evans 2004: 66) and it is on this basis that the defendants stand accused.

We reject the suggestion made by the Defence that physical education has been successful in combating gender crimes and maintain that boy's physical education especially has changed even less. Our witnesses will testify that the experiences of marginalisation and alienation are not the sole prerogative of girls and will provide you with compelling evidence that gender differences are not being obliterated in terms of the nature of physical education provision or the lessons to be learnt through physical education regarding gender-appropriate behaviour (Green 2008: 152). Moreover, we suggest that girls' participation in physical education programmes after the age of 14 has also come under greater scrutiny, and as it will be shown in Chapter 10 of this book, boys continue to outnumber girls by at least three to one with respect to following accredited forms of physical education between the ages of 14 and 16.

Likewise, the defendants have been responsible for perpetuating the low ratio of boys in the 14–19 age range, opting to study dance compared to girls which is one-in-ten. The Youth Sports Trust (2008) found significant gender differences with regards to the teaching of dance in schools and concluded that further work is needed to increase the proportion of boys completing dance-related courses, particularly post-16 Performing Arts courses. Key findings within the report revealed the following gender bias in the teaching of dance.

> Single sex boy's schools were the least likely of all school types to provide dance in curriculum time, or out of school hours (OOSH);
>
> Specialist dance teaches make up only seven per cent of the curriculum delivery dance workforce;

Entries for GCSE Dance between 2005 and 2007 increased by 28 per cent overall, and by 55 per cent for boys, and by 27 per cent for girls;

In 2008 girls made up 94 per cent of all GCSE dance entries; (in 2010, 85% of candidates for GCSE dance were girls compared to 15% of boys - Joint Council for Qualifications 2010);

A-Level entries in performing arts between 2004-07 rose by 34% with girls showing the largest increase. However girls are making up a growing proportion of all those entered rising from 67% in 2004 to 72% in 2007.

(Youth Sports Trust 2008: 3)

These statistics alone indicate that there are clear gender differences and distinctions between boys and girls in the area of physical education and dance and if we are to make sense of the underlying causes and effects then a thorough cross-examination of the Defence is required.

In this chapter, Connell's (1996) notion of 'a gender regime' provides a framework for our initial discussion' as we re-open the case file and identify significant factors with regards to the inclusion of boys and girls in physical education and dance. It is evidenced by our own experiences as pupils and teachers in schools. We will, therefore, be making a case for abandoning the 'Gender Game' (Keen 1992), encouraging teachers to acknowledge diversity and to use physical education and dance as a space that can challenge understanding of gender. We wish to offer young people experiences which can be transformative and will help them see alternative identities which step outside and destabilize the traditional gender binary. To this end we are willing to provide formal written statements, give evidence under oath and to tell the truth, the whole truth, and nothing but the truth. Our officers within the Physical Education Gender Police (PEGP) have provided us with an account of their investigative work on gender-based mal(e)-practice and subsequently issued a warrant for the arrest of those who are being held to account. It is for these reasons that they stand before you in the Dock. Your Honor, with your permission, we would now like to proceed with our case.

Personal reflections

Gary

My experiences of teaching physical education in schools have confirmed that the adolescent stage of development is a particularly important time for boys and girls due to changes in physical and emotional growth. I often observed that many pupils felt awkward and self-conscious as they experienced these changes in their personal and physical development. As a teacher of physical education I was sensitive to the fact that friendship groups, body image, developing sexuality and self-esteem were issues that presented teenage girls and boys with certain anxieties. These issues were often exacerbated by the types of physical activities forced upon girls and boys ,which on reflection, actually had very little relevance to their participation in activities outside of school or once they had left school. In other words, the physical education curriculum that was prescribed had very little importance for a significant number of pupils whom I taught.

Gill

As a young girl growing up in the 1960s, I was fortunate to be encouraged by my parents and teachers to be physically active and sporty. As an only child my dad taught me to throw, hit and kick balls so that we could play cricket, football, tennis and other games he knew together in the garden. I really enjoyed watching 'Match of the Day' with him and going along to football matches – already I was stepping outside the 'gender game'. At primary school my (male) classroom teacher too encouraged me to develop my sporting interests too, and although we had mixed physical education classes in some activities when it came to games, the girls played netball whilst the boys played football. I never did get the opportunity to play a full-sided game of football throughout my secondary school or teaching training course. Although I could kick a ball I don't think I questioned why at the time – besides 'I loved netball! So I hung up my boots and began to play the gender game'. Dad made me a netball post and learnt the rules – we had a new garden game – he by now was stepping outside the 'gender game'.

Saul

> Some men are surely, albeit with great difficulty and in slow motion, responding to recent debates about the nature of gendered identity and dancing towards more acceptable ways of being.
>
> (Burt 1995: 198–9)

Entering physical education teacher education as a seasoned games player I had little idea how salient Burt's discussion of dance and its potential to transform limited and limiting notions of gender would become. Although I was a keen b-boy (break-dancer) in the early eighties, I had little conception of how this and my dancing repertoire more generally could be broadened through physical education. At school, physical education was the personification of Keen's 'gender game', whereby boys were differentiated and separated from the girls and taught accordingly. Dance didn't fare well here. It was only upon furthering my teacher education at university that I realised dance could, indeed should have been part of the curriculum mix. Aside from having a long historical association with physical education, dance's inclusion in my own physical education socialisation/ practice has enabled me to 'question' how physically educated I am. Was it right that I stood before pupils espousing the wonders of PE, when I could barely stretch and touch my own toes? My own shortcomings became evident and open to critical reflection whilst attending a week-long beginner's contemporary dance workshop. I felt out of place here and my awkward reflections in the dance mirrors highlighted that I was little more than a narrow mind on broad shoulders. I painfully realised I needed to undergo a fair dose of mental and physical recreation to become the physical educator I aspired to be. Dance has been, and continues to be, an invaluable part of this professional, physical, emotional and gendered re-awakening/alignment (see Warburton 2009).

Identifying the gender regime in physical education and dance

Connell's (1996) notion of a 'gender regime' has been used to develop greater understanding of boys and their developing masculinities whilst the social construction of gender in physical education in schools has been identified in research about the hidden curriculum in schools (Bain 2009 cited in Bailey and Kirk 2009). Berg and Lahelma (2010: 32) suggest that the 'gender regime is described as the state of play in sexual politics within a school.' With regard to physical education spaces and sexual politics it is important to see how practices and discourses construct gender difference and can work to legitimate particular types of gendered behaviour and expectations. Nutt and Clarke (2002) for example, believe that the (not so) hidden curriculum promotes gendered ideologies and stereotyped notions of femininity and masculinity which teachers, pupils and parents accept as natural and legitimate processes that become taken for granted, and therefore, followed and promoted without question. Consequently:

> ... it is possible to appreciate how the hidden curriculum, that is the norms, values and ways of behaving that pupils are exposed to (both consciously and unconsciously) serve to legitimate stereotyped gendered (and racialised) subject positions which impact on teachers' and pupils' identities in damaging ways.
>
> (Nutt and Clarke 2002: 149)

Fernandez-Balboa (1993) has highlighted the impact of the 'hidden curriculum' in physical education and dance, and suggests that there is a need to challenge traditional practices in physical education in order to create a more equal society and disturb the unequal power structures and social inequalities that are part of the maintained status quo in society and schools. Many of the assumptions that teachers hold for example, often result in stereotypical expectations of girls' and boys' behaviour that is reinforced by lesson content and organisation, and thus transmits covert messages to pupils about the status and acceptability of certain activities to boys and girls. Nutt and Clarke (2002: 150) further suggest that physical education departments are saturated with ascendant values and ideologies that do much to reflect and sustain existing practices. Thus, what a typical physical education curriculum consists of and what pupils learn derives from perceived notions of what teachers regard as suitable programmes of activities for boys and girls (Green 2008).

Laker (2000: 73) has suggested that the 'hidden curriculum' in physical education (and dance) acts as a subtle and often unnoticed means of reinforcing particular values and attitudes amongst pupils and 'is so successfully hidden that its implementation is totally subliminal'. Acknowledging the existence of a gender regime and a hidden curriculum in physical education and dance has increased attention on equity and inclusion within physical education. This has raised the issue of meeting the needs and interest of all individuals in schools and has become an established agenda item for UK policymakers and practitioners. Much of this has been attributed to different (and open) interpretations of UK government education policy and, therefore, different implementations of inclusive practice. For example, it has been suggested that a national curriculum for physical education in state (government-funded) schools could not and would not be the same for all pupils and was limited by pragmatic and economic agendas and constraints in very varied school contexts (Penney and Evans 2005). In seeking to uphold the professionalism of teachers it was deemed important to allow an element of flexibility in implementing a revised national curriculum for physical education. Consequently, the specific requirements of the national curriculum for physical education at Key Stages 3 and 4 gave teachers the freedom to choose particular activities from the official text and, therefore, make decisions regarding time allocation, groupings strategies and teaching styles. This has resulted, however, in an over-emphasis on traditional (gender-differentiated) team games (Ofsted 2009) which some have considered to be part of not only a hidden curriculum in physical education but also a hidden UK government agenda with regard to the increased emphasis on providing more competitive sport in schools.

Defining the rules of the gender game

In order to play the 'gender game' it is important to understand a few fundamental rules prescribed by the democratically elected national governing body (the State). These are overseen by qualified appointed referees and umpires (headteachers and school governors) who have overall jurisdiction for ensuring fair play. To achieve clarification of the key terms is essential so that the 'gender game' can be played without misinterpretation or confusion by the participants. To begin with the terms 'sex' and 'gender' have to be dissected so that the intricacies and subtle nuances associated with the terms can be fully understood. In order to understand the complex processes of gender construction in physical education and dance it is important to establish a clear definition of what is meant by the two terms as this is a central focus for understanding the relationship between males and females. Green (2008: 138) refers to the term 'sex' as being an aspect of gender which is genetically inherited, anatomical and physiological whereas 'gender' is learnt normative and appropriate sex-specific behaviours referred to as either masculine or feminine. Consequently, the terms masculinity and femininity can be defined in relation to this. In other words, masculinity and femininity depend upon the social definitions of gender in which a stereotyped set of expected attributes and qualities can be associated. To emphasise this point Connell's (1996) framework for understanding gender issues in the education of boys helps to explain the ways in which different versions of masculinity develop.

Gender is constructed within institutional and cultural contexts that produce multiple forms of masculinity. Normally one form is hegemonic over others. Schools are active players in the formation of masculinities. Schools overall gender regimes typically reinforce gender dichotomy, though some practices reduce gender difference. Masculinising practices are concentrated at certain sites: curriculum divisions, discipline systems, and sports.

(Connell 1996: 206)

We would argue that it is in the physical education department that the terms 'sex' and 'gender' have often been substituted for each other when discussing issues related to boys and girls involved in physical activity. Research has shown that physical activities play an important part in the social process of gender construction (Wright 1996). In this context, the biological sex of an individual (being male or female) determines a person's gender through which appropriate behaviour is learnt. Thus, what is constituted as the appropriate, expected and different behaviours for boys and girls can be categorised as either masculine or feminine. This can differ within a particular society as Humberstone (2002) observes:

Femininity and masculinity are often viewed as immutable and natural arrangements. Although biological sex is usually fixed, masculinity and femininity are constructs of a particular culture or society and may therefore be open to change.

Humberstone (2002: 59)

Nowhere is this more overt than in the way schools and physical education departments label particular activities and games as either 'boys' or 'girls' or in the ways that schools separate male and female physical education departments within the same school (Stidder 2002; Stidder 2005). For example, physical education departments in UK schools frequently have gender-specific managerial roles such as 'head of boys' PE' and 'head of girls' PE'. Teachers remain unaware that they label some activities as gender appropriate in their curriculum, even though this labelling may be unconsciously done without malice aforethought. Other ways that activities could be labelled is by association with the teacher who most commonly teaches it, or by the group to whom it is offered (Laker *et al.* 2003: 83). Gendered labelling of teachers is, therefore, reinforced through gender-appropriate activity programmes, single-sex groupings and same-sex staffing. As Saul Keyworth pointed out in the first edition of this book, secondary schools often restrict employment opportunities for male and female teachers through the vocabulary used in national advertisements, thus perpetuating gender divisions within physical education and dance. For Saul, it was very seldom that he located a physical education job advertisement asking for a male that could, would and wished to teach dance. Needless to say it became quite clear that if he was going to teach physical education in schools he would have to make some major compromises. He wasn't prepared to do that!

These issues are further exacerbated by the tendency of schools to label physical education as either 'boy's physical education' or 'girl's physical education'. This is manifested in the vocabulary schools often use to overtly promote gender divisions through appointing pupils to senior roles within the school such as 'Head Boy' and 'Head Girl' rather than 'student leader' or 'senior prefect' or awarding separate prizes for achievement during whole school celebrations. For example, pupils may be given subject awards for outstanding performance over the course of an academic year such as in English, Mathematics and Science but quite often there are separate awards for boy's physical education and girl's physical education and even separate awards for boy's dance and girl's dance, a situation that does not occur in any other curriculum subject. In other aspects of school life the gendered terminology and language associated with subject areas and, in particular job descriptions, have been successfully addressed. For example, the terms 'headmaster' and 'headmistress' have long become redundant terms and have since been replaced with the more acceptable title of 'Headteacher'. It would seem to be the case that the physical education profession has undoubtedly got a long way to go before they can legitimately and legally claim to be innocent of any involvement in committing gender crimes. Indeed, they could be categorised as repeat offenders and therefore, should be held in custody pending an application for bail.

Physical education and dance can act to sustain different gendered embodiment for boys and girls. In simple terms, physical education and dance are subjects within the secondary school curriculum in which boys and girls 'learn to be what men and women are supposed to be in our society' (Sparkes 1997: 95). For example, where schools only offer access to masculine or feminine appropriate activities girls and boys may have limited opportunities to experience the different physicality required of non-stereotypical activities. Despite more limited attention to boys' experiences in school physical education it can be argued that boys too experience inequalities and are encouraged into particular versions of masculinity that restrict male possibilities for challenging the gender binary particularly through dance. Green (2008) maintains that the way in which the physical education curriculum is presented to pupils often implicitly, if not explicitly, reinforces the physical and psychological attributes of being, or becoming, a man through a dominated ideology of masculinity. The result is a prevalence amongst boys to view dance as not only pointless but 'gay' (homosexual) or unmasculine (Green 2008: 147).

Parker (1996) maintains that boys' physical education within secondary schools is pivotal in the development of masculinity. Parker's study found the existence of various pupil masculinities within his case study school. The boys concerned provided evidence as to the way in which a selection of masculine forms can evolve according to differing internalised value structures, and how the academic ethos of the institution itself might influence the personal identity and hierarchical peer group position of certain individuals. Based on his findings Parker concludes:

> If these findings are to achieve anything, it is hoped that in locating physical education as a significant site in the construction of masculinities within

schools, they may encourage a forthright attack upon the implicit and explicit masculine ideals which continue to permeate this curricular area, and which serve to create unequal educational conditions for many pupils.

(Parker 1996: 153)

Within the gender regime a clear distinction between boys and girls is all too often assumed. Connell (1996) for example, identifies that there is no one pattern of masculinity and likewise despite idealized versions of femininity there are in reality different groups of boys and different groups of girls with varied identities and physicality that do not always fit the socially constructed binary divide or hegemonic ideal. As other contributors to this book have shown, social class (Evans and Bairner), race (Vickerman and Hayes), sexuality (Clarke), culture and religion (Sugden and Schulmann) have been identified as other key determinants with regards to sporting preference and participation and are clearly important intersections with gender. Flintoff and Scraton (2005) maintain that physical education and dance teachers should recognise different plural femininit*ies* and masculinit*ies*, rather than the singular terms femininity and masculinity. Within this there are multiple identities the teaching of physical education and dance contributes to (but can also challenge) including a narrow range of 'accepted' ways of being masculine/feminine. In this respect, heterosexuality is central to gendered physicalities.

In other words, there are multiple masculinities and femininities across different social groupings that do not always match the stereotypical views and values often projected in and through physical education, dance and sport.

The relationship between over-competitive and aggressive sport (often a characteristic of boys' physical education programmes) with developing female sexuality is frequently a factor that impacts on girls participation rates, but is known to impact on the participation rates of boys who have expressed a dislike for these forms of activities (Macdonald 2002). In this context, PE teachers believe that there is a strong rationale for separate programmes of activity, but as a result are responsible for, and therefore guilty of promoting stereotyped outcomes and behaviours. The Youth Sports Trust (2000) suggest that ascendant forms of masculinity and femininity have been developed and reinforced in schools through the teaching of physical education and in particular competitive team sports. Ten years on, Ofsted (2009: 40) also found that schemes of work are insufficiently broad and often reflect stereotypes of male and female activities, particularly in Key Stage three. Traditional forms of gender-differentiated practice, therefore, have characterized the development of physical education and dance in schools and have established dominant notions of what is appropriate for girls and boys.

Playing the gender game

Within the rules of 'the gender game' physical education and dance play an integral part as they have been epitomised by gendered patterns of organisation. Whilst some schools have bent the rules by advocating the use of mixed-sex groups in order to address the 'gender regime' in physical education and dance, the use of single-sex groups and same-sex teachers continues to reflect the collective voice of many teachers in the profession. In this respect, Lines and Stidder (2003) confirmed that mixed-sex grouping policies in physical education adversely affects the attitudes of girls particularly as they get older due to pressures to conform to stereotypical notions of femininity within the physical environment. Consequently, girls with a particular interest in sport can feel uncomfortable when participating with boys particularly in activities that are male-dominated.

Green (2008) has concluded that mixed-sex physical education has resulted in a number of unintended consequences particularly for girls. In this context, lessons are typically orientated towards boys who dominate and monopolise the learning environment which is exacerbated by teachers who are unable to control the class effectively. One of the outcomes of poorly managed mixed-sex physical education lessons is that girls' behaviours are constrained by the competiveness of boys particularly in situations where team games are the focus of the lesson. It is hardly surprising, therefore, that girls are likely to withdraw and retreat from these types of activities within mixed-sex classes. Thus, the taking part in football or rugby during mixed-sex physical education lessons can exacerbate many of the pressures for girls, encouraging them to revert to gendered notions of acceptable femininity. For some girls this can be a very negative and off-putting experience. Likewise boys wishing to take part in perceived feminine appropriate activities may also run the risk of having their masculine heterosexuality called into question.

Dancing to a different tune

At this point one of our chief prosecutors will now proceed with the case against the Defence for the perpetration of gender crimes specifically in dance.

Your Honor, thinking more deeply and critically about social justice issues is a leitmotif[1] of recent debates about how best to educate boys and girls in order to create a socially just and inclusive physical education curriculum (Martino *et al.* 2009). As such best practice is seen as being that which blends theory and practice – *praxis* (McCaughtry 2006; Wellard 2009). With particular reference to dance education, there is a paucity of research that shows how democratic dance curricula can be realised in the studio and gymnasium (Lehikoinen 2006). To add to this small but significant body of work (Risner 2007 2009) the non-use, misuse and positive use of dance in physical education can be explored through legal precedent and the respective cases of Tom Waddell, Edward Villella and Kristopher King. Each case evolves within a tightly guarded and largely unforgiving hetero-normative frame that has meant 'trying on the daunting title of dancer' (Benjamin 2002) has not been without its 'costs' (Butler 1993). A recurring motif of each story, therefore, is that heterosexist and homophobic prejudice serves to minimise both the frequency and style of dancing boys and men partake in. This was nowhere more evident than in the plight of Dr Tom Waddell, founder of the Gay Games. Although an accomplished and aspiring ballet dancer his anxieties about his participation revealing his non-proclaimed homosexuality were sufficient for his dancing to cease. In his autobiography (Schapp and Waddell 1996: 19) he reveals he 'liked feeling male' and was 'bothered that gayness meant femininity'. As a result Waddell replaced dance with sport as this was (and still largely is) an arena where masculinity and heterosexuality are presumed and unquestioned.

Now let us consider the case of Edward Villella. During the 1970s Edward Villella received worldwide acclaim as a principal dancer with the New York City Ballet. Despite such accolades his autobiography (Villella 1998: 151) reveals his 'success was a front, a façade concealing a lack of true accomplishment'. As is the case with many male ballet dancers, he was expected to show athleticism and virtuosity at every turn. In other words, bring a man's touch to proceedings. Here Villella laments 'I got tired of being typecast in the public eye as the macho ballet dancer. This was simplistic to me and insulting to other male ballet dancers' (Villella 1998: 184). Villella wished to loosen the shackles of the 'gender game' (Keen 1992) which tightly governed how, where and with whom he could dance. He was desperate to be considered a 'complete artist and not just a technical spitfire' (ibid. 11) but his longing to re-write the mores of the gender game did not meet public and media approval. Audiences continually flocked to see this macho-athlete dance while television and university campus audiences were offered Villella as a 'boy-friendly' vision of promoting increased male participation in dance.

Failing to play by the rules of the 'gender game' is a costly business as the tragic story of the young ballet dancer Kristopher King reveals. Touted as Derby's Billy Elliot, Kristopher's ballet career was prematurely cut short due to a physical assault that hit the national press. Accosted by several of his 11 year-old peers whilst walking home from school he was pushed to the floor where his legs were repeatedly stamped on and ridden over with a bicycle. The final straw in a long line of bullying, his parents sought to sue both his primary school and local education authority for neglect. What wasn't revealed in the press was that Kristopher attempted to escape this nightmare by taking his own life. Regrettably as Marr and Fields (2001) shocking *Bullycide: death at playtime* reveals, this is an all too common experience, especially among boys and men who have their sexuality brought into question (see Dorais 2004).

Calling in the gender police

It is clear that no matter how many public enquiries and policy reviews are undertaken there are greater influences on girls' and boys' physical activity patterns outside of formal school settings (Green 2008) and that the gender police have limited powers in issuing arrest warrants to those who are habitual criminals. In this respect, there is compelling evidence to suggest that there are other very influential socialising factors that continue to work against an egalitarian approach to the teaching of physical education and dance in schools. For example, family expectations and support, peer group values and the cult of masculinity and femininity all play an important part in the numbers of girls and boys who are willing participants in physical education. Likewise, the maleness of sport and patriarchal control within society alongside pressures to conform to modes of feminine and masculine appropriate behaviour and sporting activities deter many girls and some boys and cause them to withdraw from physical activity prematurely due to a lack of role models, perceptions of sport inequality, and the value and function of sport in lifestyle (Sport Scotland 2005; Flintoff and Scraton 2005; Hills 2007; Green 2010).

At present it seems that the UK coalition government policy is moving very firmly in the direction of school sport (rather than physical education) as its focus in order to motivate more young people to take part in competitive sport. The intention to re-direct and re-structure the place of school sport towards physical education may enable and facilitate the achievement of UK élite sporting success, but will do little to engage more girls and boys into physical education and physical activity. Competitive sport is an intimidating experience for some girls and boys as it often exacerbates feeling of self-consciousness and embarrassment. Consequently, this has the potential to marginalise those pupils who are disaffected and unmotivated by what is on offer within the school physical education curriculum and could be deterred from physical education altogether when they perceive it to be a substitute for competitive sport. The UK coalition government and their accomplices are, therefore, guilty on two counts: Acting with intent to short-change the majority of young people; and denying them the opportunity to engage in relevant and purposeful physical activity in schools.

Whilst there have been advances and developments in research into gender and physical education it is difficult to identify simple policy changes that will make an impact in all contexts, in all schools. Flintoff and Scraton (2005) have suggested, however, that a shift from 'gendered physical education' to 'gender relevant physical education' is critical in engaging more girls (and boys) and must involve changes in the way physical education is presented to pupils in schools. In this respect, policies must account for difference, be centred on physical empowerment for all and involve pupils in critical enquiry and critique of the physical education curriculum. The ideas developed in this final section argue that physical education and dance could be a platform for challenging understandings of gender and have the potential to offer young people experiences which can be transformative and help them to see 'alternative' identities which step outside or cross the traditional gender binary. How then might the gender police help the physical education and dance profession to challenge gendered physicality, expectations and provide empowering opportunities?

Challenging the gender game

Where physical education is seen to function to reinforce the ideals and values of sport in the wider society it is difficult to see how it can readily break down some of the reified and long-standing stereotypical traditions. The UK coalition government's vision for more competitive sport in schools seems to reinforce long-standing male versions of physicality. It is difficult to see how this will challenge dominant hegemonies – indeed it contradicts many of the more recent strategies that have sought to encourage participation in sport and re-engage disaffected young people. The revised versions of the English national curriculum for physical education too have never explicitly offered a critical pedagogical dimension to the subject that might encourage transformation of young peoples' views about the world of sport and their own sporting identity and physicality (see Macdonald 2002). Even where teachers have attempted to introduce strategies to challenge traditional views of gender there have been a number of issues. For example, as mentioned in a previous chapter of the first edition of this book (Lines and Stidder 2003) mixed-sex physical education has merely developed masculine versions of physical education rather than challenged it. In other words giving girls more of what boys have always had in physical education reinforces traditional hegemony and acts to sustain the value of masculine versions of sport. For change to happen the practices and pedagogy of teachers need to provide challenging versions of masculinity.

On observing attempts to promote male dance in physical education many male pupils avoid dance as they believe their sexuality will be placed under critical scrutiny and judgement. For those who remain, many will, like Villella, 'boy up' proceedings by restricting or having their dancing restricted by teachers to movements which 'fit' traditional conceptions of hetero-masculinity (strong, fast, spacious). This process of changing dance to meet (some) boys is a short-term strategy that needs to be used with caution. Rather than challenging and transforming the limited and limiting movements espoused by the gender game it will rehearse and reinforce them. A longer-term strategy should see teachers encouraging boys to meet a breadth and depth of dance experience by:

> ... providing students with the full range of movement experiences including those that are energetic, powerful, skilful and dynamic and those that use the body softly, flexibly and sensitively.
>
> (Nilges 2000: 305).

To do so will require teachers and pupils to develop a critical understanding of gender as a socially constructed set of power relations that serve to sanction and police limited modes of being for many boys and girls – the gender game. As tragic stories like Kristopher King's reveals, many young boys and girls are held hostage to its accurate replication and play. Such tales can be used sensitively as a means to place gender on the agenda, and open to positive re-articulation. As Butler (1990 2004) reminds us, the intelligibility of gender has been made and as such is always open to being undone and re-made in more socially just and equitable ways. In this respect, physical educators' should be at the forefront of this movement. The process of overcoming anxieties in dance, moving beyond the restrictive shackles of the gender game to re-write how, where and with whom the body can move is very much an ongoing process. But for the time being the dance continues.

Critiques of the gender regime have identified how, too often pupils are expected to respond in the same way to the opportunities provided whereas in reality there are diverse ways of engaging in, and enjoyment of physical activity.

As suggested by Theodoulides in Chapter 3, consideration should be given to personalised programmes of activity that provide varied opportunities. This can be achieved by providing male and female – only spaces and opportunities to take on different roles and responsibilities, trying new activities. This has the potential to erase some of the concerns of the body on display for the opposite sex – the male gaze especially. In contrast, mixed-sex spaces offer teachers working with pupils further opportunities to challenge issues of perceived male superiority and the assumption of dominant roles. This can develop pupils' knowledge of gender; raise girl's awareness of cultural tensions; develop understanding of perceptions and individual agency and empowerment to gendered ideals. Moreover, this can encourage girls and boys to move out of their gender 'comfort' zones and attempt new activities which extend their perceptions of their own physicality. For example, girls could explore their power and strength whilst boys are given opportunities for creative, sensitivity in movement activities.

Combating gender crimes in physical education and dance, however, is not necessarily a straightforward task. Consultation with leading witnesses such as pupils, parents and members of staff is required along with the forensic evidence that is available. Other people matter and deserve a voice so that opportunities for reflection by pupils and teachers might help to understand how gender is constructed in and through physical education, dance and sport, and in print and electronic media (Wright 1999: 194). Consequently the social construction of gender and the role of physical activities in the process can be better understood with a greater appreciation that the sex of the individual is not problem but rather the issue is socio-cultural. It is how society constructs femininity and masculinity. To achieve this, efforts need to focus on girls, boys, men and women in challenging stereotypical notions of femininity and masculinity within physical activities. Teachers should reflect on their own practice and establish an anti-sexist pedagogy in physical education and dance that will change deeply-held sexist beliefs and values. Equal opportunity and access, curriculum content, grouping policy, sex-role socialisation, physical education department structure, teachers' expectations and attitudes, recruitment and selection of staff, extra-curricular provision, and pupil's activity choices and preferences are all key components within the established rules of the gender game. For those who are currently standing on trial, in custody, serving sentences, have been released or are on remand, a period of probation may be required so that an understanding of their crimes can be developed.

Changing the rules

Your Honour, to avoid any miscarriages of justice it is important to consider how the gender regime might be challenged. We suggest an overhaul of the existing rules is required and due consideration paid to the following:

- Policies that recognise and address social and cultural perceptions of gender and their relationship to physical education and dance are critical in raising the participation rates of girls and boys in secondary schools.
- Policies that privilege traditional team games activities in the physical education curriculum are not in the best interests of all girls and boys.
- Policies that permit some single-sex physical education classes in co-educational schools would benefit a proportion of 14–16 year-old pupils with regards their participation and enjoyment of physical education and dance lessons.
- Policies that involve pupils in the decision-making process and provide greater levels of choice are critical in capturing girls and boys interests in physical education and dance.
- Policies that are sensitive to the developing sexualities of adolescent girls and boys which confront heterosexism and homophobia are imperative in engaging more girls and boys into physical education and dance lessons at school.
- Policies that acknowledge diversity and individuality are essential to increasing the numbers of girls and boys who enjoy physical education and dance lessons at school and are willing participants.
- Policies that raise the public profile of female achievement in a wide range of sports contribute significantly to raising the numbers of girls who are willing participants in school physical education and challenge the patriarchal view of sport.
- Policies that make clear distinctions between what constitutes 'Physical Education' and 'School Sport' can help girls and boys to overcome the anxieties they experience when participating in physical education lessons.

Conclusion

At this point, Your Honor, we would like to present our closing argument and in summing up highlight some important points. To support our case we have obtained evidence of individuals being caught 'red-handed' committing a series of inexcusable gender crimes. During the course of writing this chapter high profile sports personalities and television presenters were apprehended live on television manifesting sexist views reaffirming the position of bigotry within the world of professional sport. For many the punishment of Andy Gray and Richard Keys fitted their crimes and reflected the level of unacceptability amongst the general public towards the types of language they used whilst still 'on air'. From our perspective neither of these personalities nor others who have committed similar gender crimes deserve time off for good behaviour, parole, suspended or reduced sentences.

As stated in the introduction to this book, sport (and by inference physical education) as it publically appears is perhaps nothing more than a façade behind which old habits hide. We would also add that the perpetrators of these gender crimes have been associated with larger syndicates and gender cartels in the form of the broadcast and print media who themselves have failed to challenge homophobic language used by a high profile English football manager and have been complicit in perpetuating the notion that sport is a man's world. In November 2011, the BBC announced their shortlist of candidates for the BBC Television Sports Personality of the Year for 2011 based on the votes of 27 newspaper and magazine editors – just six months before the London 2012 Olympic Games not one single British female sport star or athlete appeared on that shortlist. We rest our case!

Ladies and gentlemen of the jury. Have you reached a verdict upon which you are all agreed? Do you find the Defendants guilty or not guilty?

Note

1   A leitmotif is a musical theme that recurs in the course of a work to evoke a particular character or situation. Leitmotifs are typical of the operas of Richard Wagner.

References

Bailey, R. and Kirk, D. (eds) (2009) *The Routledge Physical Education Reader*, London, Routledge.

Bain, L. (2009) 'The Hidden Curriculum Re-examined', in Bailey, R. and Kirk, D. (eds) (2009) *The Routledge Physical Education Reader*, London, Routledge: 39 –47.

Benjamin, A. (2002) *Making an Entrance: theory and practice for disabled and non-disabled dancers,* London: Routledge.

Berg, P. and Lahelma, E. (2010) 'Gender processes in the field of physical education', *Gender and Education*, 22, 1: 31–46.

Brown, D. and Evans, J. (2004) 'Reproducing Gender? Intergenerational links and the male PE teacher as a cultural conduit in teaching physical education', *Journal of Teaching in Physical Education*, 23: 48–70.

Burt, R. (1995/2007) *The Male Dancer: Bodies, spectacle, sexualities,* London: Routledge.

Butler, J. (1990) *Gender Trouble: feminism and the subversion of identity*, London: Routledge.

Butler, J. (1993) *Bodies that Matter*, London: Routledge.

Butler, J. (2004) *Undoing Gender*, London: Routledge.

Cockburn, C. and Clarke, G. (2002) '"Everybody's looking at you": Girls negotiating the femininity deficit they incur in physical education', *Women's Studies International Forum*, 25(6): 651–65.

Connell, R. W. (1996) 'Teaching the boys: New research on masculinity, and gender strategies for schools', *Teachers College Record*, 98(2) 206–35.

Dorais, M. (with Lajeunesse, S. L.) (2004) *Dead Boys can't Dance: sexual orientation, masculinity and suicide,* London: McGill-Queens University Press.

Evans, J. and Davies, B. (2002) 'Theoretical background', in Laker, A (ed.) *The Sociology of Sport and Physical Education: An Introductory Reader*, London, Routledge: 15–35.

Fernandez-Balboa, J-M. (1993) 'Socio-cultural characteristics of the hidden curriculum in physical education', *Quest*, (45), 2: 230–54.

Flintoff, A. and Scraton, S. (2005) 'Gender and Physical Education', in Green, K. and Hardman, K. (eds) (2005) *Physical Education: Essential Issues*, London, Sage: 161–79.

Green, K. (2003) *Physical Education Teachers on Physical Education*, Chester, Chester Academic Press.

Green, K. (2008) *Understanding Physical Education*, London, Sage.

Green, K. and Scraton, S. (1998) 'Gender, Coeducation and Secondary Physical Education: A Brief Review', in Green, K. and Hardman, K. (eds) *Physical Education: A Reader*, Aachen: Meyer and Meyer: 272–89.

Griggs, G. (2008) 'A new curriculum for girls' Physical Education', *PE and School Sport Today*, October 2008 available online at: http://www.teachingexpertise.com/articles/new-curriculum-girls-pe-496

Her Majesty's Inspectorate for Education and Training in Wales (2007) *'Girls participation in physical activity in schools'*, July 2007, www.estyn.gov.uk

Hills, L. (2007) 'Friendship, physicality, and physical education: An exploration of the social and embodied dynamics of girls' physical education experiences', *Sport Education and Society*, 12, 3: 317–36.

Humberstone, B. (2002) 'Femininity, Masculinity and difference: what's wrong with a sarong?', in Laker, A. (ed) *The Sociology of Sport and Physical Education: An Introductory Reader*, London: Routledge: 58–78.

Joint Council for Qualifications (2010) *'Results 2010 GCSE, Applied GCSE, Entry Level, Diploma*, www.jcq.org.uk

Keen, S. (1992) *Fire in the Belly: on being a man*, London: Piatkus.

Keyworth, S. and Smith, F. (2003) 'C'mon PE(TE) it's Time to get Changed for Dance', in Hayes, S. and Stidder, G. (eds) (2003) *Equity and Inclusion in Physical Education and Sport: Contemporary Issues for Teachers, Trainees and Practitioners*, London, Routledge: 105–32.

Kirk, D. (2002) 'Physical Education: A gendered history' in Penney, D. (Ed.) (2002) 'Gender and Physical Education – Contemporary Issues for Future Directions', London, Routledge, 24–37.

Laker, A. (2000) *Beyond the Boundaries of Physical Education: Educating young people for citizenship and social responsibility*, London, Falmer.

Laker, A., Laker, J. and Lea, S. (2003) 'School Experience and the Issue of Gender', *Sport, Education and Society*, 8, 1: 73–89.

Leaman, O. (1984) *Sit on the sidelines and watch the boys play: Sex Differentiation in Physical Education*, York, Longman, Schools Council Publications

Lehikoinen, K. (2006) *Stepping queerly? Discourses in dance education for boys in late 20th century Finland*, Oxford: Peter Lang.

Lines, G. and Stidder, G. (2003) 'Reflections on the Mixed and Single Sex PE debate', in Hayes, S. and Stidder, G. (eds) (2003) *Equity and Inclusion in Physical Education: Contemporary Issues for Teachers, Trainees and Practitioners*, London, Routledge: 65–88.

Macdonald, D. (2002) 'Critical Pedagogy: What might it look like and why does it matter?', Laker, A. (ed.) *The Sociology of Sport and Physical Education: An Introductory Reader*, London: Routledge, 167–89.

Marr, N. and Field, T. (2001) *Bullycide: death at playtime*. Success Unlimited.

Martino, W., Kehler, M. and Weaver-Hightower, M. B. (2009) *The Problem with Boys' Education: Beyond the Backlash*, New York: Routledge.

McCaughtry, N. (2006) 'Working politically amongst professional knowledge landscapes to implement gender-sensitive physical education reform', *Physical Education and Sport Pedagogy*, 11(2), 159–79.

Nilges, L. (2000) 'A non-verbal discourse analysis of gender in undergraduate educational gymnastic sequences using Laban effort analysis', *Journal of Teaching in Physical Education*, 19(3), 287–310.

Nutt, G. and Clarke, G. (2002) 'The hidden curriculum and the changing nature of teachers' work', in Laker, A. (ed.) *The Sociology of Sport and Physical Education: An Introductory Reader*, London: Routledge, 148–66.

Ofsted (2009) *Physical education in schools 2005/08: Working towards 2012 and beyond*, April, Reference No. 080249, www.ofsted.gov.uk

Parker, A. (1996) 'The construction of masculinity in boys' physical education', *Gender and Education*, 8, 2: 141–58.

Penney, D. (2002a) 'Gendered Policies', in Penney, D. (2002) (ed.) *Gender and Physical Education: Contemporary issues and future directions*, London, Routledge: 103—22.

Penney, D. (2002b) 'Equality, Equity and Inclusion in Physical Education and Sport' in Laker, A. (ed.) *The Sociology of Sport and Physical Education*, Routledge Falmer: 110–28.

Penney, D. and Evans, J. (2005) 'Policy, Power and Politics in Physical Education', in Green, K. and Hardman, K. (eds) (2005) *Physical Education: Essential Issues*, London, Sage: 21–38.

Pringle, R. (2007) 'Fear and Loathing on the Sports Field: Masculinities, social transformation and creative teaching strategies', *Journal of Artistic and Creative Education*, (1)2: 46–67.

Qualifications and Curriculum Authority (QCA) (2007) Physical *Education Programme of Study Key Stage 3*, www.qca.org.uk/curriculum

Risner, D. (2007) 'Rehearsing masculinity: Challenging the boy code in dance education', *Research in Dance Education*, 8(2), 139–53.

Risner, D. (2009) *Stigma and Perseverance in the Lives of Boys who Dance: an empirical study of male identities in Western theatrical dance training*, Lewiston: The Edwin Mellen Press.

Schapp, D. and Waddell, T. (1996) *The Life and Death of Dr Tom Waddell*, New York: Alfred A. Knopf.

Schilling, C. (2010) 'Physical capital and situated action: a new direction for corporeal sociology', *British Journal of Sociology of Education*, 25, 4: 473–87.

Scraton, S. (1992) *Shaping up to Womanhood – Gender and Girls' Physical Education*, Buckingham: Open University Press.

Sparkes, A. (1997) 'Reflections on the Socially Constructed Physical Self', in Fox, K. (1997) *The Physical Self: From Maturation to Well Being*, Champaign Ill, Human Kinetics.

Sparkes, A. (1999) 'Beyond romantic views of the self: critical autobiography as a challenge to teacher development', P*aper presented at the Physical Education Association (UK) Centenary Conference, University of Bath*, 8–11 April.

Stidder, G. (2002) 'The Recruitment of Secondary School Physical Education Teachers in England: A Gendered Perspective?', *European Physical Education Review*, Autumn, (8), 3: 249–269.

Stidder, G. (2005) 'Trainee Teacher Perceptions of Job Advertisements in England with Regards to Gender and Physical Education', *European Physical Education Review*, Autumn, (11), 3: 309–333.

Stidder, G. and Binney, J. (2011) 'Alternative Approaches to Teaching and Learning Physical Education in Secondary Schools', Physical Education Matters' formerly The British Journal of Teaching Physical Education, Summer, (6), 2, 27–32.

SportScotland (2005) 'Making Women and Girls More Active – A good practice guide', Womens Sport Foundation, SportScotland.

Villella, E. (with Larry Kaplan) (1998). *Prodigal Son: dancing for Balanchine in a world of pain and magic,* Pittsburgh: University of Pittsburgh Press.

Warburton, E. (2009) 'Viewpoint: Of boys and girls', *Research in Dance Education,* 10(2), 145–8.

Wellard, I. (2009) *Sport, Masculinities and the Body,* Oxon: Routledge

Williams, A. and Bedward, J. (2001) 'Gender, Culture and the Generation Gap: Student and Teacher Perceptions of Aspects of National Curriculum Physical Education', *Sport, Education and Society*, 6, 1: 53–66.

Wright, J. (1996) 'The construction of complementarity in physical education' *Gender and Education*, 8, 1: 61–79.

Wright, J. (1999) 'Changing Gendered Practices in Physical Education: Working with Teachers', *European Physical Education Review*, (5), 3: 181–97.

Youth Sports Trust (2000) *Girls in Sport: Towards Girl-Friendly Physical Education, Final Report*, Institute of Youth Sport, Loughborough University.

Youth Sports Trust (2008) *Audit of Dance Provision in English Schools 2006/07 Final Report*, March 2008, Loughborough University.

6 Challenging heterosexism, homophobia and transphobia in physical education

Gill Clarke

When I was at school, the attitude of most teachers to homophobia was somewhere between turning a blind eye and active encouragement. I vividly remember one chemistry teacher making a boy's life hell, in punishment for the heinous crimes of having a slightly camp voice and not liking rugby. This was not an isolated case: off the top of my head I can think of three others who, if confronted with a child being picked on because they 'acted gay', would routinely side with the bullies. Several more would gleefully take any opportunity to set out the religious case for why they disagreed with homosexuality. This is an issue for all young people, not just those who are gay or lesbian. Many children are targeted not because they are gay, but because they don't fit in with a set of assumptions about what makes a 'proper' boy or girl. So boys might be picked on because they don't like football or girls because they do. 'Gay' is also liberally used as a catch-all term of abuse, rather than literally meaning homosexual.

John Connolly

'Too many teachers still turn a blind eye to homophobic bullying – we have to rewire their attitudes'

The Times Educational Supplement, 12 November 2010

Introduction

This chapter explores the social construction and manifestations of heterosexism, homophobia and transphobia within physical education and the impact this has in particular on pupils. By doing so the conservative and heteronormative traditions of the PE profession are revealed insofar as their pedagogical practices and expectations contribute to and reinforce stereotyped ideologies of masculinity and femininity. It is these narrow and privileged definitions which have led many within the subject to fear the display of any emotional or physical characteristics which do not fit these hegemonic images. Connected to this, we see how these prejudiced behaviours operate on multiple levels, that is, the personal; interpersonal; institutional; cultural or societal. This, despite progressive legislation which has introduced unprecedented rights and protection under the law for lesbian, gay, bisexual and transgender (LGBT) people in Britain and the appearance of a more 'socially just society, [yet with], harassment, violence, and discrimination continu[ing] to be experienced by non-heterosexual identities or those perceived to be [so]' (Ferfolja 2008: 108). Some strategies are offered to challenge and eliminate heterosexism, homophobia and transphobia while promoting equity and inclusion so that all pupils may achieve their full potential within PE.

Autobiographical note and rationale

The impetus for the research draws upon reflects upon my own experiences of teaching PE in secondary schools and higher education institutions and the lack of research into the lives of lesbian PE teachers. At the time I commenced my doctoral research into the lives of lesbian PE trainees and teachers as little was known about lesbian PE teachers' lives in the UK (Clarke 1996). The limited research that had been published related only to lesbian PE teachers in North America (Griffin 1991; Woods 1992) and had failed to address the impact of compulsory heterosexuality on lesbian teachers' lives (see Rich 1981). A small number of studies in England were to follow the lead of Pat Griffin and Sherry Woods (see Sparkes 1994; Squires and Sparkes 1996). These were significant in that they brought issues around lesbian PE teachers' lives into the public domain, however, it was apparent that there was still much to find out and understand about lesbian women's (and gay men's[1]) lives and how heterosexism, homophobia and transphobia impact on all pupils and teachers within the 'gymnasium'.

Given my own experiences as a lesbian educator and researcher I was anxious to use my own teaching and sporting experiences to help understand and interpret why lesbian PE teachers largely felt the need to conceal their sexual identities within schools. These experiences and insights were, as I have argued elsewhere, both a strength and a resource rather than a threat to the integrity of the research endeavour (see Clarke 1998a). There is now a growing corpus of research in this field emanating from Australia, the UK and North America. 'Nevertheless, while there may have been a rise in academic study it is questionable what impact this has had on grass roots physical education' (Clarke 2006: 723).

Heterosexism, transphobia and homophobia: defining practice in physical education

Other chapters within this edition of the book as well as the previous edition have pointed to the gendered, racialised, classist and ableist nature of PE in schools. These traditional practices and associated stereotyped beliefs have contributed to the marginalisation and subjugation of those pupils and teachers who might be deemed different to what it is to be a 'normal' girl/boy, female/male. This process of othering needs to be located and understood within the confines of homophobia, transphobia and (compulsory) heterosexuality (Rich 1981; Clarke 1998b). I use the concept of '*Other*' like Kumashiro (2002: 26) to 'refer to those groups that are traditionally marginalised from society, i.e., that are *other than* the norm, such as students of colour, students from under- or unemployed families, students who are female, or male but not stereotypically "masculine"'.

Discussions about heterosexism have until relatively recently been absent from debates within PE (Clarke 1998b, 2002, 2006; Sykes 1998, 2011). Moreover, the task of deconstructing heterosexuality as both an institution and practice has been conducted largely outside of this arena (Butler 1990; Jeffreys 1990; Wilkinson and Kitzinger 1993). Heterosexism 'is the set of assumptions, norms and discriminatory actions that leads to heterosexuality being the presumed, and even compulsory, sexuality for students within physical education' (Sykes 2011: 21). Strongly associated with heterosexuality is *heteronormativity* which is 'expressed, for example, through the fact that many of our social rituals are built around heterosexuality, manifested in pictures, cultural signs, and symbols, and through concrete acts in the social "game": the social game that is formed around the two-sex model – the couple comprised of him and her' (Eng 2006: 51).

Transphobia is the dislike, fear or hatred of transgender people. Transgender is an umbrella term which describes:

> ... a range of gender identities (how you think of yourself in terms of gender internally) and gender expressions (external ways of expressing gender, for example, clothes, gestures). Some people find that their gender identity, gender expression and physical bodies do not match up.
>
> (Scottish Government 2009: 27)

The expression '*trans*' is often used synonymously with *transgender* in its broadest sense (see GIRES 2008). To date there is little research in the UK on trans people's experiences in education. A notable exception was the review undertaken by Mitchell and Howarth in 2009 for the Equality and Human Rights Commission which suggests that discrimination in educational settings is a significant problem for trans people. This is important to understand as Sykes (2011: 2) points out 'being trans is especially difficult in physical education because binary discourses about gender permeate so many aspects of the profession from ideas about the body, the curriculum and even the built environment'.[2]

Turning to defining homophobia Sears's (1997: 16) conceptualisation is helpful, he describes it as 'prejudice, discrimination, harassment, or acts of violence against sexual minorities, including lesbians, gay men, bisexuals, and transgendered persons, evidenced in a deep-seated fear or hatred of those who love or sexually desire those of the same sex.' Within England and Wales these fears and prejudices were shored up by Section 28 of the Local Government Act (specifically subsection (2)) which was passed in 1988 by the Conservative government. It stated:

(1) A local authority shall not —
   (a) intentionally promote homosexuality or publish material with the intention of promoting homosexuality;

(b)   promote the teaching in any maintained school of the acceptability of homosexuality as a pretended family relationship.

(2)   *Nothing in subsection (1) above shall be taken to prohibit the doing of anything for the purpose of treating or preventing the spread of disease.* [emphasis added]

(Smith 1994: 183)

Although repealed in 2003 Section 28 has left a 'lingering shadow of uncertainty about whether it is appropriate or even safe to address sexualities' equality in classrooms' (DePalma and Atkinson 2008: xiv). Indeed, Jones and Clarke (2007: 126) found that 'concerns about possible complaints from governors and parents, and the repercussions that discussing LGB[T] lifestyle issues might have for a teacher's career, still persist'.

How this relates to PE and issues of (in)equity and inclusion in schools is discussed below ('Towards a theory of homophobic, transphobic and heterosexist oppression' and 'Manifestations of heterosexism, transphobia and homophobia'). Suffice for now to say that schools in general, and PE departments in particular, are sites for social and moral regulation wherein gender and gender roles are produced against a dominant heterosexuality and a marginalised, often vilified, homosexuality. These gender roles and relations are constructed along narrow, highly demarcated lines which are exemplified through normative and stereotyped expectations about what it is to become or be male or female.

I turn now to examine how these restrictive conceptions of masculinity and femininity negatively impact on all in PE.

Playing the masculine and feminine game or not ...

In the preceding chapter of this book, Stidder, Lines and Keyworth discuss and re-visit some of the pertinent issues related to 'the gender regime' (Connell 1995) in physical education and dance and how it might be policed. In this chapter I also bring attention to the fact that PE is about schooling bodies (and minds) into socially sanctioned and publicly approved ways of being. For boys, to be 'real' men revolves around the public display of particular forms of hegemonic masculinity. This 'is experienced by many men [and boys] as a straitjacket; a set of conventions of behaviour, style, ritual and practice that limit and confine, and are subject to surveillance, informal policing and regulation' (Whannel 2007: 11). These conventions equate with sporting success: to fail or even dislike PE and sport is to render the sexual identity of the self open to question and ridicule, and results in anti-gay jibes (see Renold 2005).

Playing the physical game successfully becomes for boys a signifier of a 'normal' masculine identity, that is, one that is not queer. It is an identity that is exalted as strong, competitive, skilful, aggressive and heterosexual. Nevertheless, 'the nature of hegemonic masculinity is precarious, and ... need[s] to be continually defended and maintained' (Swain 2000: 104). Accordingly, those who fail to maintain and display this hegemonic masculinity are frequently subject to heterosexist and homophobic abuse (see Aldridge 2011; Rivers 2011). If sporting performances are viewed in such narrow ways it is no wonder that many boys (and male teachers) fail to engage with the more aesthetic and creative aspects of the subject, and in particular dance (Keyworth 2001; Keyworth and Smith 2003; Gard 2006), aspects too, that have been associated with the female tradition (Fletcher 1984).

For girls to be successful in physical education is to be caught in a double bind since being a successful performer (and the associated social power/and 'spotlight' that attracts: Gilroy 1997) also brings the potential for vilification by peers and others. The tensions here relate to the fact that the criteria for a successful physical performance are those deemed to be masculine, and thus incompatible with the holding of a stereotypical feminine heterosexual identity, in other words if a girl is successful, she must be 'playing like a man'. It is unsurprising that girls drop out from physical activities and especially those that require the visible display of strength and aggression. Further, where girls/women are successful they are likely to have the pejorative label, lesbian, attached to them. Consequently, girls/women (and boys/men) are likely to employ strategies to protect and project their feminine/masculine identity, hence, we see respectively hyper-femininity and hyper-masculinity regularly being performed within and through the domain of the physical (Connell 1995; Sartore and Cunningham 2009). Those girls and boys who seek to resist the normative gender regime run the risk of being seen as gender deviants (see Ringrose and Renold 2010) and they may also face alienation from those important to them such as friends, parents, carers and neighbours (Cockburn and Clarke 2002; Jones 2011). The following section seeks to explain and offer a framework for understanding how this cycle of oppression operates so successfully and why resistance is so hard won.

Towards a theory of homophobic, transphobic and heterosexist oppression

While for the purpose of this chapter I am focusing on homophobic, transphobic and heterosexist oppression I want to acknowledge the multiplicity, the intersectionality (see Flintoff *et al.* 2008) and the situatedness of oppression and to question the actual adequacy of oppression as a term. Thus, I am inclined like Ramazanoglu (1989), to use the term 'oppression' as a relatively loose concept that can be qualified in different situations. Further, I recognise the danger of seeing those who are oppressed (in this case, teachers and pupils) as just passive victims, without agency. Phelan's work is useful on this question, since she explains that:

> Oppression is a word with many contexts and shades ... The problems and issues involved in the category of oppression are manifold. When does another impose on me? What sort of power must be involved to make this imposition oppressive? How are we to correct this situation: is it a matter for political action, or a matter for education and social discussion? Are there perhaps many places to deal with aspects of this problem?
>
> (Phelan 1989: 15–16)

These are key questions which have escaped some of the research that has focused on the oppression of lesbians and gay men within the educational system. Notwithstanding the complexities of teaching and learning these are also key questions for physical educationalists to address vis-à-vis pedagogical practices within their subject area. In seeking a more complete understanding of why homophobia, transphobia and heterosexism continue to oppress all in PE, regardless of their sexual identity it is helpful to ask: Who benefits? Who is empowered? Who is shackled by it? (Messner and Sabo 1994).

So we see that male hegemony is reinforced in and through PE, insofar as identities that don't fit this hierarchical model are deemed deviant and stigmatised. Further, traditional gender roles are upheld and reinforced since the price for transgressing is all too often too painful (Clarke 2001 2006). Moreover as Ferfolja (2007a: 570) found 'those who transgress the "acceptable" standards of (hetero) normality may be "punished" through overt and covert harassment, stigmatization, ostracism, exclusion and silence'.

Osterman's model (Figure 6.1) provides a useful framework for making sense of these (in)actions and the failure to challenge homophobia, transphobia and heterosexism in physical education:

Osterman uses this model to explain how people justify their rationale for oppressing others. Looking at each aspect in turn we can see first how 'limited knowledge and/or isolated experience' in the case of schools in general and PE departments specifically would apply. Many teachers may have limited knowledge about LGBT issues and how these pertain to the curriculum and effective teaching and learning. In relating this to PE, teachers may for instance have limited

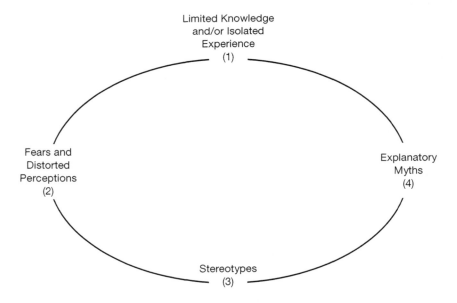

Figure 6.1 Elements of Developing Rationale for Oppression

knowledge about openly lesbian or gay athletes, thereby denying all pupils the knowledge of positive role models. Moreover, Section 28 was used by some teachers as a way of legitimising their not talking about homosexuality, yet, this is precisely what the PE (and teaching) profession needs to do. Teachers need to increase (and disrupt) pupils' knowledge and assumptions (and perhaps their own) about the diverse sexualities of sports participants. Disrupting knowledge is no easy task when conceptions of masculinity, femininity and heterosexuality become so 'naturalised' and 'normalised' that they are unquestioned and taken for granted as *the* way to be. Further, given that schools and PE departments do not exist in a social vacuum and are part of a broader set of social relations, change in schools without wider societal change is inevitably problematic. So what can PE teachers (and pupils) do to make the gym safe for all?

In terms of the curriculum it is crucial to include specific reference to the Other.

> By making visible the 'Other' within classrooms it may be possible to extend the students' critical consciousness to acknowledge and interrogate what it can mean to be different and, in doing so, challenge the ideologies and effects of living in a heterosexist society.
>
> (Vicars 2006: 353)

Such challenges might occur in nationally accredited and recognised physical education courses (but *not* exclusively) through for instance, discussing the international Gay Games which 'developed as an inclusive sport and cultural event engaging the communities of sexual minorities' (Symons and Hemphill 2006: 109; see also Hargreaves 2000; Symons 2007) and by drawing attention to the recent Government Equalities Office Charter on Homophobia and Transphobia in Sport, which aims to make sport a welcoming place for LGBT people. Other opportunities to break the culture of invisibility of LGBT people is through utilising LGBT History Month which runs annually throughout February and the International Day Against Homophobia and Transphobia on May 17 and using examples of openly gay or lesbian athletes such as Gareth Thomas, the former captain of the Welsh rugby union team or Steven Davies, the 24 year-old England cricketer, or John Amaechi who played basketball in the NBA in the USA, or tennis players Martina Navratilova and Amélie Mauresmo or sports commentator Clare Balding. Further, teachers and pupils must cease assuming that heterosexuality is the 'norm' and engage in a more critical pedagogy (Macdonald 2002; Meyer 2008).

Turning to the issue of 'fears and distorted perceptions', these perceptions were embedded within the discourse of Section 28 and specifically in subsection (2), its association of disease, i.e. AIDS, with homosexuality (Clarke 1996). Despite its repeal, much remains to be done if there is to be lasting change in attitudes towards LGBT people and genuine commitment to creating more inclusive practices and deep change in PE. Undoubtedly legislative advances have made some differences so that 'the official policy climate is markedly different after Section 28, both at a UK national government level and in the way school policy interprets and encourages new thinking ... The detailed operation of such policies and the question of responsibility for implementation remain doubtful however' (Nixon and Givens 2007: 466). It is too early to assess the impact of the Equality Act 2010 which replaced previous anti-discrimination laws with a single Act. A key provision of the consolidated legislation is a new public sector *equality duty*, which came into force on 5 April 2011. It covers age, disability, gender reassignment, pregnancy and maternity, race, religion or belief, sex and sexual orientation. The duty has three aims. It requires public bodies to have due regard to the need to:

- eliminate unlawful discrimination, harassment, victimisation and any other conduct prohibited by the Act;
- advance equality of opportunity between people who share a protected characteristic and people who do not share it; and
- foster good relations between people who share a protected characteristic and people who do not share it.

Schools are required to comply with the new equality Duty. Further in 2012, the new Ofsted framework came into force which includes 'behaviour and safety' as one of its key criteria for inspections. Schools should be able to demonstrate the impact of anti-bullying policies.[3]

The issue of stereotypes forms the third part of the model for the rationale for oppression in Figure 6.1. Osterman points out how stereotypes feed myths. The most common and pernicious of these as we have seen pertain to gender roles and appropriate gender behaviour and the participation of girls and women in PE and sport. The damaging nature of these was recognised over two decades ago in the Interim Report of the National Curriculum Physical Education (NCPE) Working Group (1991). In the section on Equal Opportunities in Physical Education it drew attention to:

> ... the physical nature of physical education, and the emergence of sexuality during key stages 2, 3 and 4, providing both problems and opportunities for physical education in challenging body images, sex stereotypes and other limited perspectives which constrain the choices and achievements of disabled children, and of both girls and boys ...
>
> (NCPE Working Group 1991: 17)

It is difficult to see substantial evidence of these 'sex stereotypes and limited perspectives' having been transformed. Stereotypes are pervasive and influence the ways teachers treat their pupils, the expectations they have of them and the amount of attention they give them.

Such a situation is not confined to the UK as Ferfolja (2007b: 148) notes, 'Anti-lesbian/gay discrimination, harassment and marginalization in schools are an international phenomenon ...'.

The transmission of stereotypes is, however, by no means simplistic or uncontested. Nonetheless, stereotypes of female PE teachers being lesbian have been well documented (see for instance, Squires and Sparkes 1996; Clarke 2004). As Sartore and Cunningham (2009: 289) argue 'the lesbian label exists within sport's heterosexist and heteronormative context as a means to subvert women's status, power, influence, and experiences.'

Finally, turning to 'explanatory myths' these are used to explain our (in this case oppressive) actions. Osterman (1987: 21) contends that they are 'usually held over long periods of time ... [and] only when additional information or experience "proves" to us that our myth is distorted or limited will we replace [that myth]'. In applying this to PE and sport we can see that one of the most persistent and damaging myths is that of female frailty and the 'notion that females partaking in sport are masculine, butch, and/or lesbians' (Sartore and Cunningham 2009: 294). Other harmful myths are those that see homosexuality as a sickness/mental illness and a deviation from the (heterosexual) norm. If all are to be valued and receive equal treatment in PE then information must be provided to counter these myths thereby enabling difference, diversity and physical power to be respected and celebrated. As Hemphill and Symons (2009: 404) state 'educational programs are still crucial for attitudinal and behaviour change in workplace, sport, school, university, and community settings.'

Having sought to explain the cycle of homophobic, transphobic and heterosexist oppression it is now pertinent to see in more detail how these oppressive practices operate in schools in general and PE departments in particular.

Manifestations of heterosexism, homophobia and transphobia

Blumenfeld (1992) makes a strong case for recognising that homophobia (and I would add transphobia) operates on four distinct but interrelated levels, namely the: personal; interpersonal; institutional and the cultural or societal. Personal homophobia refers to a personal belief system based on prejudice, stereotyping and misinformation which 'to put it quite simply ... [sees homosexuals as] generally inferior to heterosexuals' (Blumenfeld 1992: 4). Such beliefs 'limit people's choices and chances in life' (Equality and Human Rights Commission 2009: 4).

Interpersonal homophobia 'is manifest when a personal bias or prejudice affects relations among individuals, transforming prejudice into its active component –discrimination' (Blumenfeld 1992: 4). This includes name-calling which is insulting and often disparaging of girls/women. For boys 'the most prevalent and hurtful accusation ... was to be called "gay". Like its counterpart "slag", the accusation was virtually impossible to refute without a dramatic change in social behaviour ...' (Duncan 1999: 106). This accusation is frequently levelled at boys whose sporting prowess is deemed inadequate. These unsporty boys or 'wimps' must therefore be 'gay' and not real men, i.e. they become feminised by heterosexual others (Parker 1996; Aldridge 2011). For sporty girls, that is those who perform well and are not stereotypically passive they must be a lesbian or a 'lezzie', that is, they are exhibiting stereotypical masculine type behaviours which are viewed as being outside the bounds of the cult of femininity and its association with heterosexual romance.

Related to this discussion about name-calling Wallace (2001: 9) has pointed out that 'The word "gay" has suddenly become the ultimate put down in schools ...'. Such a put down refers to 'something that is rubbish, inferior, pathetic-exactly what some people think of others who identify as gay' (LGBT Youth Scotland 2009: 26). This language is powerful and controlling and leaves little room for resistance or other ways of being. As Aldridge (2011: i) found in her research with adolescent males in physical education 'Any deviation, however small, from the "ideal" was subject to ridicule.' Further, the 'prevalence of this discourse in schools allows homophobic attitudes to develop and grow as students learn that this language is tacitly condoned by educators who fail to intervene when it is used' (Meyer 2008: 36).

In connection with this, it is apposite to recall the research of Wright (1996) who concluded that boys-only PE classes become sites where hegemonic forms of (heterosexual) masculinity are valued. Moreover, there are expectations of boys to demonstrate and exhibit dominant forms of masculine behaviour (win at all costs; go into battle; be aggressive, courageous, determined and tough). Boys who do not fit in, are not skilled or have little liking for contact sports can be marginalised or bullied. Forms of solidarity develop between most boys and their male teachers around common experiences in sport, usually cricket or football. Single-sex boys PE classes can therefore, promote homophobic/sexist language (Nancy, pansy, poof, fag, queer, big girls blouse, my sister can throw further) and behaviour which is often used to insult and humiliate other boys.

Returning to Blumenfeld's conception of the third level of operationalisation of homophobia which he sees as institutional homophobia, this refers to the ways educational organisations discriminate on the basis of sexual orientation or identity. This discrimination may be entrenched and as shown 'reinforced through institutional practices, policies and representatives' (Ferfolja 2007b: 149 and see Equality and Human Rights Commission 2009). It impacts on knowledge as it pertains to the official, visible and legitimate discourse of the NCPE insofar as heterosexuality and homophobia remain unchallenged and legitimated, and (hetero)sexual relations retain their power and normalcy.

Cultural or societal homophobia is Blumenfeld's (1992: 6) fourth and final level of homophobia. This he claims takes the form of 'social norms or codes of behaviour that, although not expressively written into law or policy, nonetheless work within a society to legitimize oppression.' The so-called hidden curriculum of PE is a useful way of both unpacking and illustrating this form of homophobia: insofar as the hidden curriculum refers to the ways in which the school, classrooms and playgrounds operate, the underlying rules and rituals, the ways teachers and pupils behave and interact, and the beliefs and values that are transmitted within such practices. The power of the peer group to influence and reinforce hegemonic ways of being male or female is especially significant here (see Aldridge 2011). Indeed, we have already seen how name-calling acts as a way of controlling behaviour that falls outside of hegemonic heterosexual norms. The fear of not being seen to be heterosexually desirable/attractive to their male peers leaves many girls regulating their behaviour and policing their appearance so as to appear 'normal'. These interactions within the peer group involve the communication both implicitly and explicitly of a particular set of values about 'normality'.

Concluding remarks

Physical Education is not a neutral inclusive arena; rather it is an arena that continues to marginalise and exclude those who do not match stereotypical expectations of what it is to be female or male. This situation holds for pupils and teachers alike.[4] Physical education remains a largely male preserve where status and privilege is ascribed to hegemonic forms of masculinity and others are subordinated. To transgress traditional gender norms is to risk censure and harassment (Clarke 2002; Meyer 2008).

For PE to be a truly inclusive, empowering and democratic arena requires open acceptance of the existence of multiple, shifting and contested femininities and masculinities, a rejection of a hierarchy of identities and the destabilisation of the heterosexual status quo. Physical educationalists need to use their privilege and power and work productively to ensure that the sporting turf is a safe place, free from discrimination, prejudice and harassment where all are valued and respected. 'Awareness without action is insufficient' (McCaughtry *et al.* 2005: 437). As such heterosexist, transphobic and homophobic language and jokes should be challenged and clear policies and procedures established for dealing with such incidents. Moreover, these need to be robustly enacted at a whole-school level. Teachers need to acknowledge their role in the construction of masculinities and femininities and vigilantly monitor their own actions and attitudes, and establish within lessons and the co-curriculum opportunities for all pupils to participate in ways (and in activities) that are free from verbal harassment and intimidation to conform to traditional and restrictive notions of what it is to be stereotypically female or male. Further, teachers need to seek out and provide role models and diverse images of masculinity and femininity. Adopting such an approach will require more effective equality training for teachers and trainees to raise awareness about sexualities and possibilities for change and a shift in ideological and pedagogical approaches so as to emphasise co-operation, self expression and social responsibility rather than competition.

If we are to have lasting forms of change in PE departments and the culture of schools, and more sexuality sensitive schooling (see McCaughtry *et al.* 2005) then the dismantling of heterosexism, transphobia and homophobia must continue to be an integral part of working for equity and inclusion in physical education and sport.

Notes

1 I have written elsewhere about the difficulty of identifying gay men in the macho masculine world of physical education (Clarke 1998b: 2002). For an account of one male teacher's experiences, see the ethnographic fiction written by Sparkes in 1997. Sparkes (2002: 166) explains 'I produced it for pedagogical reasons, and I had critical intentions, in an attempt like that of Duncan (1998), to speak for the absent other - in this case, gay, male physical education teachers.'

2 Brill and Pepper (2008) in *The Transgender Child* provide useful guidance on physical education albeit in relation to policies specific to the State of California and the San Francisco Unified School District.

   Hinton (2008: 77) in 'A Transgender Story: From birth to secondary school' relates the story of J, 'a child who seemed to understand from a very early age that the gender assigned to him at birth did not adequately describe his identity.' Attention is directed to the implications for physical education and an Appendix: working with a Transgender Pupil is provided.

3 See the Department for Education (2011) document *Preventing and Tackling Bullying: Advice for School Leaders, Staff and Governing Bodies* which replaces previous advice – *Safe to Learn: Embedding Anti-Bullying Work in Schools*. See also GIRES (2008) *Guidance on Combating Transphobic Bullying in Schools* and in particular the Model transgender policy, pp. 69–70. Ofsted is the UK inspection agency for schools.

4 This is not to deny the innovative work that is happening in some schools. For example at Stoke Newington School, London the boy's football team made a video on how to tackle homophobia and the PE Department used LGBT History Month to challenge gender stereotypes. For further examples of good practice see the report from the Lesbian Gay Bisexual Trans History Month 2011 Pre Launch: Twickenham Rugby Stadium, 2 November 2010. www.lgbthistorymonth.org.uk/resources/sport.htm accessed 1 November 2011.

References

Aldridge, M. (2011) '(In)Visible Bodies: The significance of body image in the lives of adolescent males', Unpublished PhD Thesis, University of Southampton.

Blumenfeld, W. J. (1992) *Homophobia: How we all pay the price*, Boston: Beacon Press.

Brill, S. and Pepper, R. (2008) *The Transgender Child: A handbook for families and professionals*, San Francisco: Cleis Press.

Butler, J. (1990) *Gender Trouble: Feminism and the subversion of identity*, London, Routledge.

Clarke, G. (1996) 'Conforming and Contesting with (a) Difference: How lesbian students and teachers manage their identities', *International Studies in Sociology of Education*, 6(2), 191–209.

Clarke, G. (1998a) 'Voices from the Margins: Lesbian teachers in physical education', Unpublished PhD Thesis, Leeds Metropolitan University.

Clarke, G. (1998b) 'Queering the Pitch and Coming Out to Play: Lesbians in physical education and sport', *Sport, Education and Society*, 3(2), 145–60.

Clarke, G. (2001) 'Outlaws in Sport and Education? Exploring the sporting and education experiences of lesbian physical education teachers', in Scraton, S. and Flintoff, A. (eds), *Gender and Sport: A Reader*, London: Routledge.

Clarke, G. (2002) 'Difference Matters: Sexuality and physical education', in Penney, D. (ed.), *Gender and Physical Education: Contemporary Issues and Future Directions*, London: Routledge.

Clarke, G. (2004) 'Threatening Space: (Physical) education and homophobic body work', in Evans, J. Davies B. and Wright J. (eds) *Body Knowledge and Control. Studies in the Sociology of Physical Education and Health*, London: Routledge.

Clarke, G. (2006) 'Sexuality and Physical Education', in Kirk, D., Mcdonald, D. and O'Sullivan, M. (eds) *The Handbook of Physical Education*, London, Sage.

Cockburn, C. and Clarke, G. (2002) '"Everybody's Looking at You!" Girls negotiating the "femininity deficit" they incur in physical education', *Women's Studies International Forum*, 25(6), 651–65.

Connell, R. W. (1995) *Masculinities*, Cambridge: Polity Press.

DePalma, R. and Atkinson, E. (eds) (2008) *Invisible Boundaries: Addressing Sexualities Equality in Children's Worlds*, Stoke on Trent: Trentham Books.

Duncan, N. (1999) *Sexual Bullying: Gender conflict and pupil culture in secondary schools*, London: Routledge.

Eng, H. (2006) 'Queer Athletes and Queering in Sport', in Caudwell, J. (ed.) *Sport, Sexualities and Queer/Theory*, Abingdon: Routledge.

Equality and Human Rights Commission (2009) *Beyond Tolerance: Making sexual orientation a public matter*, London and Manchester: Equality and Human Rights Commission.

Ferfolja, T. (2007a) 'Teacher Negotiations of Sexual Subjectivities', *Gender and Education*, 19(5), 569–86.

Ferfolja, T. (2007b) 'Schooling Cultures: Institutionalizing heteronormativity and heterosexism', *International Journal of Inclusive Education*, 11(2), 147–62.

Ferfolja, T. (2008) 'Discourses that Silence: Teachers and anti-lesbian harassment', *Discourse: Studies in the Cultural Politics of Education*, 29(1), 107–19.

Fletcher, S. (1984) *Women First: The female tradition in English physical education, 1880 to 1980*, London: Athlone Press.

Flintoff, A., Fitzgerald, H. and Scraton, S. (2008) 'The Challenges of Intersectionality: Researching difference in physical education', *International Studies in Sociology of Education*, 18, 2: 73–85.

Gard, M. (2006) 'More Art than Science? Boys, masculinities and physical education research', in Kirk, D., Mcdonald, D. and O'Sullivan, M. (eds), *The Handbook of Physical Education*, London: Sage.

Gilroy, S. (1997) 'Working on the Body: Links between physical activity and social power' in Clarke, G. and Humberstone, B. (eds) *Researching Women and Sport*, London: Macmillan.

GIRES (Gender Identity Research and Education Society) (2008) *Guidance on Combating Transphobic Bullying in Schools*, London: Home Office.

Griffin, P. (1991) 'Identity Management Strategies among Lesbian and Gay Educators', *Qualitative Studies in Education*, 4(3), 189–202.

Hargreaves, J. (2000) *Heroines of Sport: the Politics of Difference and Identity*, London: Routledge.

Hemphill, D. and Symons, C. 'Sexuality Matters in Physical Education and Sport Studies', *Quest*, 61: 397–417.

Hinton, K. (2008) 'A Transgender Story: From birth to secondary school', in DePalma, R. and Atkinson, E. (eds) (2008) *Invisible Boundaries: Addressing sexualities equality in children's worlds*, Stoke on Trent: Trentham Books.

Jeffreys, S. (1990) *Anticlimax: a Feminist Perspective on the Sexual Revolution*, London: The Women's Press.

Jones, R. (2011) 'Managing the Self: A grounded theory study of the identity development of 14–19 year old same-sex attracted teenagers in British Schools and Colleges', unpublished PhD Thesis, University of Southampton.

Jones, R. and Clarke, G. (2007) 'The School Experiences of Same-Sex Attracted Students in the 14 to 19 Year-Old Secondary Sector in England: Within and beyond the safety and tolerance framework', *Journal of Lesbian and Gay Social Work*, 19(3/4), 119–38.

Keyworth, S.A. (2001) 'Critical Autobiography: "Straightening" out dance education', *Research in Dance Education* 2(2), 117–37.

Keyworth, S. and Smith, F. (2003) 'C'mon PE(TE) it's Time to get Changed for Dance', in Hayes, S. and Stidder, G. (eds), (2003) *Equity and Inclusion in Physical Education and Sport: Contemporary issues for teachers, trainees and practitioners*, London, Routledge: 105–32.

Kumashiro, K. (2002) 'Towards A Theory of Anti-Oppressive Education', *Review of Educational Research*, 70(1), 25–53.

LGBT (2009) *'Toolkit for Teachers. Dealing with Homophobic Bullying in Scottish Schools'*, Glasgow, Learning and Teaching Scotland.

Macdonald, D. (2002) 'Critical Pedagogy: What might it look like and why does it matter?' in Laker, A. (ed.), *The Sociology of Sport and Physical Education: an Introductory Reader*, London: RoutledgeFalmer.

McCaughtry, N., Rocco-Dillon, S., Jones, E. and Smigell, S. (2005) 'Sexuality Sensitive Schooling', *Quest*, 57: 426–443.

Messner, M. and Sabo, D. (1994) *Sex, Violence and Power in Sports: Rethinking masculinity*, Freedom: The Crossing Press.

Meyer, E. J. (2008) 'A Feminist Reframing of Bullying and Harassment: Transforming schools through critical pedagogy', *McGill Journal of Education*, 43, 1: 33–48.

Mitchell, M. and Howarth, C. (2009) *Trans Research Review. Research Report 27*, London and Manchester: Equality and Human Rights Commission.

National Curriculum Physical Education (NCPE) Working Group (1991) *Interim Report*, London: The Department of Education and Science: 8.

Nixon, D. and Givens, N. (2007) 'An Epitaph to Section 28? Telling tales out of school about changes and challenges to discourses of Sexuality', *International Journal of Qualitative Studies in Education*, 20(4), 449–71.

Osterman, M. J. (1987) *Homophobia is a Social Disease*, Evanston, IL: Kinehart Program on Sexuality and Homophobia.

Parker, A. (1996) 'The Construction of Masculinity within Boys' Physical Education', *Gender and Education*, 8, 2: 141–57.

Phelan, S. (1989) *Identity Politics: Lesbian Feminism and the Limits of Community*, Philadelphia: Temple University Press.

Ramazanoglu, C. (1989) *Feminism and the Contradictions of Oppression*, London: Routledge.

Renold, E. (2005) *Girls, Boys and Junior Sexualities: Exploring children's gender and sexual rlations in the primary school*, Abingdon: RoutledgeFalmer.

Rich, A. (1981) *Compulsory Heterosexuality and Lesbian Existence*, London: Onlywomen Press.

Ringrose, J. and Renold, E. (2010) 'Normative Cruelties and Gender Deviants: The performative effects of bully discourses for girls and boys in school', *British Educational Research Journal*, 36(4), 573–96.

Rivers, I. (2011) *Homophobic Bullying: Research and Theoretical Perspectives*, New York: Oxford University Press.

Sartore, M. L. and Cunningham, G. B. (2009) 'The Lesbian Stigma in the Sport Context: Implications for women of every sexual orientation', *Quest*, 61: 289–305.

Scottish Government (2009) *Toolkit for Teachers. Dealing with Homophobia and Homophobic Bullying in Scottish Schools*, Glasgow: Learning and Teaching Scotland.

Sears, J. T. (1997) 'Thinking Critically/Intervening Effectively about Heterosexism and Homophobia: A twenty-fiveyear research retrospective', in Sears, J. T. and Williams, W. L. (eds) *Overcoming Heterosexism and Homophobia: Strategies that Work*, New York: Columbia University Press.

Skelton, A. (1998) 'Eclipsed by Eton fields. Physical education and equal opportunities', in A. Clark and E. Millard (eds), *Gender in the Secondary Curriculum: Balancing the Books*, London: Routledge.

Smith, A. M. (1994) *New Right Discourse on Race and Sexuality: Britain, 1968–1990*, Cambridge: Cambridge University Press.

Sparkes, A. (1994) 'Self, Silence and Invisibility as a Beginning Teacher: A history of lesbian experience', *British Journal of Sociology of Education*, 15(1), 93–118.

Sparkes, A. (1997) 'Ethnographic Fiction and Representing the Absent Other', *Sport, Education and Society*, 2(1), 25–40.

Sparkes, A. (2002) *Telling Tales in Sport and Physical Activity: A qualitative journey*, Leeds: Human Kinetics.

Squires, S. and Sparkes, A. (1996) 'Circles of Silence: Sexual identity in physical education and sport', *Sport, Education and Society*, 1(1), 77–101.

Swain, J. (2000) '"The Money's Good, The Fame's Good, The Girls are Good": The role of playground football in the construction of young boys' masculinity in a junior school', *British Journal of the Sociology of Education*, 21(1), 95–109.

Sykes, H. (1998) 'Turning the Closets Inside/Out: Towards a queer-feminist theory in women's physical education', *Sociology of Sport Journal*, 15(2), 54–73.

Sykes, H. (2011) *Queer Bodies: Sexualities, genders, and fatness in physical education*, Lang: New York.

Symons, C. (2007) 'Challenging Homophobia and Heterosexism in Sport: The promise of the Gay Games', in Aitchison, C. (ed.) *Sport and Gender Identities: Masculinities, Femininities and Sexualities*, Abingdon: Routledge.

Symons, C. and Hemphill, D. (2006) 'Transgendering Sex and Sport in The Gay Games', in Caudwell, J. (ed.) *Sport, Sexualities and Queer/Theory*, Abingdon: Routledge.

Vicars, M. (2006) 'Who are You Calling Queer? Sticks and stones can break my bones but names will always hurt me', *British Educational Research Journal*, 32(3), 347–61.

Wallace, W. (2001) 'Is this Table Gay? Anatomy of a classroom insult', *Times Educational Supplement*, 19 January: 9–10.

Whannel, G. (2007) 'Mediating Masculinities: The production of media representations in sport', in Aitchison, C. (ed.) *Sport and Gender Identities: Masculinities, femininities and sexualities*, Abingdon: Routledge.

Wilkinson, S. and Kitzinger, C. (eds) (1993) *Heterosexuality. A feminism and psychology reader*, London: Sage.

Woods, S. (1992) 'Describing the Experiences of Lesbian Physical Educators: A Phenomenological Study', in Sparkes, A. C. (ed.) *Research in Physical Education and Sport: Exploring alternative visions*, London: FalmerPress.

Wright, J, (1996) 'The Construction of Complimentarity in Physical Education', *Gender and Education*, 8(1), 61–79.

7 Sport for development and peace in divided societies

Developing cross-community sport partnerships in Israel

John Sugden and Nico Schulenkorf

The Football Association continues to play a lead role in tackling discrimination in football. I firmly believe in widening participation and diversity within the game at all levels. The FA is determined to provide an inclusive football experience for anyone who wishes to play, coach, officiate or support English football. An experience that is reflective of our diverse communities, safe for all and free from abuse and discrimination.

David Bernstein
Chairman of the English Football Association

'Downing Street hosts summit on homophobia and racism in football',
Stephen Gray for PinkNews.co.uk 23 February 2012

Introduction

The idea of using sport for social, cultural and community development has been promoted for decades; however, only limited empirical research can be found that analyses the strategic potential of sport projects in contributing to conflict resolution, reconciliation and peace building in deeply divided societies. This chapter overviews the experiences of a number of Football 4 Peace (F4P) projects operating in Israel between 2001 and 2010, and concentrates in more detail on two 'typical' CCSP (Cross Community Sport Partnerships) – one that was established in 2004 and another in 2009. Among other things, the chapter focuses on and assesses the role played by external change agents in facilitating project delivery and development. Following an interpretive mode of enquiry, observations, diary records and focus group discussions with key project facilitators and sport coaches were conducted exploring participant experiences and using this information to develop practical recommendations for social development through sport.

Israel and Palestine: the 'perfect conflict'?

The shape and structure of F4P has not evolved in a vacuum. Those wishing to use sport to assist with the achievement of broader development goals need to carefully study and understand the nature of the cultural setting in which they choose to operate. The State of Israel was controversially created in 1948 in the long shadow of the Holocaust, the apogee of the millennia-long story of Jewish exile and persecution. While on the one hand this is considered by some as a major achievement for the hitherto nation-less and diasporic Jewish people, in equal measure it is viewed by others as a catastrophe for the Palestinians on whose land the fledging state took shape. For neutral observers – and it is so hard to be neutral in the Palestinian/Israeli conflict – both of these positions seem tenable which is why Alan Dowty has described the situation in the former British colony of Palestine and Trans-Jordan as 'the perfect conflict': a conflict at the core of which are a series of counter-balancing claims of land rights, injustice and victimisation: 'this sense of victimhood on both sides, on top of a strong belief that one is in the right, is what has made this into a 'perfect conflict', in the same sense as a 'perfect storm'. It would be difficult to design a conflict with more self-generating power for continued devastation and destruction (Dowty 2008: 222).

In 1948 only 160,000 Arabs stayed in Israel, the rest (some 640,000) fled, mainly to neighbouring Jordan, Syria and Lebanon. Today the Palestinian Diaspora number in the region of 3.5 million). Approximately 2.5 million Palestinians live in the Occupied Territories (West Bank and Gaza), some of the most densely populated places on earth. Perhaps rightly so, the situation of the Palestinians within the Occupied Territories, the plight of the Palestinian Diaspora, and the Israeli State's engagement with these external factors attract continuing global attention. By 2010 Israel's population numbered approximately 7.5 million, made up of 6 million Jews and 1.5 million Arabs. Often forgotten by the international community is the status of relations between the 20 per cent+ Palestinian Arabs who remained within the State of Israel after 1948 and their Jewish neighbours.

It is here that F4P targets most of its programmes, following the philosophy of the late and highly respected Palestinian academic and activist, Edward Said who believed that co-existence, not separation, is the way forward if a lasting peace is to be achieved in Israel. He points out: 'we cannot coexist as two communities of detached and uncommunicatingly separate suffering ... the only way of rising beyond the endless back-and-forth violence and dehumanisation is to admit the universality and integrity of the other's experience and to begin to plan a common life together' (Said 2002: 208).

Sport for development and peace in divided societies

The sport-for-development phenomenon has been advanced as an active, inclusive and exciting vehicle for inter-community wellbeing along a number of dimensions. Different sport programs have been conducted to create social capital and social change within and between communities (Kay 2009; Skinner *et al.* 2008); to positively alter gender roles and increase female participation in sport (Meier and Saavedra 2009); and to support trauma-relief efforts as a post-disaster intervention in disadvantaged communities (Gschwend and Selvaranju 2007; Kunz 2009). In culturally or ethnically divided societies, international aid organisations, NGOs and grassroots initiatives have further engaged in sport and event projects to assist disparate groups in establishing contact, reducing and resolving conflict, and building inter-community bridges (Gasser and Levinsen 2004; Schulenkorf 2010b; Sugden 2006).

This chapter is concerned with one particular dimension of the sport-for-development phenomenon: the use of sport in the service of conflict resolution, peaceful co-existence and reconciliation in deeply divided societies (Gasser and Levinsen 2004; Levermore and Beacom 2009; Sugden and Wallis 2007). For a long time, empirical evidence for positive social outcomes from sport and event projects has been difficult to find (Coalter 2010). Recently however, some empirical studies have presented limited evidence that sport-for-development initiatives can indeed encourage healthy competition, promote friendship and develop intergroup understanding, resulting at times in long-term social, cultural and psychological development (Gasser and Levinsen 2004; Schulenkorf 2010b; Stidder and Haasner 2007; Sugden 2006). From a theoretical perspective, Misener and Mason (2006) expected that people who participate in sportive or cultural expression could be empowered through being creative, developing and using skills, and contributing to inclusive social identities. Confirming this claim empirically, Kay (2009) in her study on young women and adult sport workers in Delhi, India, found that sport can be an agent of personal and social change. Kay argued that sport can provide people from disadvantaged groups with increased self-confidence, which was derived from increased body confidence or the ability to be a team-player and leader during sport activities. Similarly *et al.* (2008) suggested that as a result of team sport activities a broad array of positive social outcomes such as the development of personal and community networks which can result in high levels of inclusive social capital for disadvantaged communities.

Overall, it has been argued that social development contains three main interrelated constructs: social capital; social change; and capacity building (Moscardo 2007). While social capital refers to the development of trust, networks and reciprocity among people, social change refers to the establishment of emotional connections and bonds among communities, such as the creation of a common social identity and a sense of belonging. Capacity building describes the enhancement of material opportunities or particular skills, talent, attitudes and knowledge that contribute to community empowerment. In order to build capacities within and between communities, it is necessary for all participating groups – communities, project organisers and external stakeholders alike – to actively engage and cooperate (Lawson 2005). From a social perspective, inter-community development should therefore be understood as an ongoing process, in which commitment, active participation and cooperation between all groups are the preconditions for creating positive social experiences and achieving lasting social outcomes.

Agents of change

In order to avoid the problems of overwhelming communities with the staging of development projects, several authors highlight the importance of establishing creative and cooperative partnerships with external institutions or 'change agents' which are able to guide and support the process (Lawson 2005; Naparstek *et al.* 1997). In cases where international change agents are involved in the inter-community development process, they are required to respect local traditions and avoid paternalistic behaviour in an attempt to share control and power with local communities (Schulenkorf 2010a; Skinner *et al.* 2008). In fact, change agents should be serving as a supportive enabler and facilitator for projects and networks of partnerships between residents, management, and community organisations (Ife 1995; Kramer and Specht 1975). They are expected to foster grassroots participation and integrate people and communities from different backgrounds, so that they 'rub shoulders' in common tasks and seek common goals. As a supporting contact, change agents must try to foster collective solidarity by respecting and using the individual characteristics of each community in a way that every group is satisfied (Lawson 2005; Midgley 1986; Uruena 2004). Finally, change agents are supposed to merely guide communities to use their capacities effectively, rather than dictating 'the way to go'.

Football 4 Peace

Football 4 Peace (F4P) is a grassroots, sport based, co-existence project that focuses on improving intergroup relations between disparate communities in societies in conflict. In 2001 – operating under the label of WSP (World Sport Peace Project) – six volunteer coaches from the University of Brighton and one staff leader conducted the first F4P project week in Northern Israel (Whitfield 2006). They engaged in a seven-day coaching camp in the Arab town of Ibillin and provided football sessions for approximately 100 Muslim Arab and Christian Arab children (10–14 years old). The intention had been to involve the nearby Jewish community of Misgav. However, the planning phase for this first intervention conincided with the start of the second *intafada* or 'uprising' which saw violent confrontations spread from Palestine's West Bank into Israel, including towns and cities in Galilee. Under these circumstances Misgav withdrew its initial commitment, but did return to the programme a year later along with the neighbouring Jewish community of Tivon. Today the cross community partnership between Ibillin and Misgav is stronger than ever and represents the exemplary bedrock of Football 4 Peace.

Within nine years of operation, F4P grew to encompass 13 project collectives, or Cross Community Sport Partnerships (CCSPs), with 33 participating communities, mainly in the Galilee region. Today F4P is supported not only by the University of Brighton, but also through partnerships with the British Council Israel, the Israeli Sports Administration, the German Sports University in Cologne, Cologne City Council, the (English) FA, the German FA, and hundreds of voluntary co-workers and volunteers. In terms of the latter, as active change agents their overall goal is to contribute to peace and reconciliation through sport, and to support local Jewish, Arab and other minority communities in transcending their social, cultural, ethnic, and religious divides.

While accommodating local nuances and differences, since 2004 F4P projects have followed a common format: targeted pro-rata recruitment of 100 children from an identified cluster of Arab and Jewish communities; two age groups (9–11; 12–14); activities are presented as taking place in neutral, politics-free zones, and all project participants – players, coaches, parents, administrators – are asked to leave their political views and ideological positions outside the project zones; within this relatively safe space participants engage in a variety of sporting and cross-cultural activities divided into 'on-pitch' (football) and 'off-pitch' (cultural and adventurous activities); all activities are underpinned with a values-based educational curriculum centred on the five key principles of inclusiveness, equality, respect, trust, and responsibility which all feed into the ways through which the projects are structured and delivered; this delivery is led by overseas volunteers in collaboration with local volunteers who have all experienced a period of F4P volunteer training either on a European university campus or in 'cascade training' events in Israel; each year, in respect of local tradition and custom, there is at least one project for girls and women only.[1]

Research design and methodology

This study attempts to investigate and identify the inter-community sport management strategies employed in the F4P programme and then use this information to develop practical recommendations for more general social development through sport. To achieve this, the study examined the organisation and implementation phases of two different CCSPs with a five-year time-span between them: the 2004 Kaukab/Nahalal/Shfraram Project and the 2009 Buena Nujeidat/Kfar Kama/Kfar Tavor Project. Both CCSPs were in Northern Israel's Galilee region and were similar to the extent that they worked with the area's sectarian geography to bring together a trio of neighbouring, but segregated ethno-religious communities. There were also however differences that have to be accounted for when trying to draw more general conclusions.

In CCSP, one of the community partners had quite distinctive characteristics in so much as they did not fit the standard make-up of towns and villages in the region. In the case of the Kaukab/Nahalal/Shfraram CCCP, Nahalal is a Moshav: a members' cooperative; a settlement of individual farms and (increasingly) small businesses. It resembles a Kibbutz, with the significant difference being that, in a Moshav individuals own their businesses and personal property. Work is organised collectively, equipment is used cooperatively, and produce is marketed jointly. A Moshav needs to be viewed historically, as part of the broader Zionist project and as such, even if it were possible (which it currently is not), it is highly unlikely that Arabs would choose to become members and cohabitants.

In the case of the Buena Nujeidat/Kfar Kama/Kfar Tavor CCSP, Kfar Kama is one of only two Circassian villages in Israel. Circassians present a minority in Israel, who emigrated from the south of Russia in the late 19th century to avoid genocide in their traditional Caucasus homeland. They are well known for adapting to prevailing social and cultural conditions including taking on the dominant religion of the regions in which they have settled. In Israel, Circassians have maintained a largely neutral stance in relation to the conflicts between their Arab and Jewish neighbours. In addition to their native *Adyghe* language Circassians learn English, Hebrew and Arabic at school, which makes them ideal communicators between the diverse Israeli communities.

Following an interpretive mode of inquiry (Glesne 1999; Neuman 2003), findings from this research were derived by conducting observational research and semi-structured focus group discussions with the five international volunteer sports coaches. When relevant these observations were supplemented by comments made by volunteers working on other projects. For example, they reported on their impressions of the project management; the importance, challenges and level of local community involvement in staging the projects; and the social, cultural and psychological impacts and development witnessed. Finally, based on their impressions and experiences potential strategies for programme improvement were discussed. The transcribed discussions along with observational field notes and information gleaned from the diary memoirs of selected volunteers were used to build an extensive database out of which grounded empirical and theoretical insights were cultivated. These are offered as a series of critical themes drawn in chronological order from the data generated from both projects.

Findings: Kaukab/Nahalal/Shfraram

Breaking Down Barriers: getting to know 'the demonised other'

To begin with there was encouraging evidence that an increased awareness of 'the other' in his or her distinctive cultural context was having a positive impact on the participants' attitudes. This realisation comes neither automatically or instantly; the conditions that allow it to happen need to be engineered. As might be expected, on the first day of the project, as the children arrived in buses and cars at each project site, they gathered in separate Jewish and Arab groups, usually sitting quite far apart from one another. One of the first tasks of the coaches was to break them up into four coaching groups, mixed both in terms of community identity and football ability. In this way not only could contact across a sectarian divide be facilitated, but also, as teams emerged during the week in preparation for the finals day, no one team would dominate through an imbalance of skill. Once done, as the following diary extracts illustrate, it was not long before the volunteer coaches were able to notice barriers coming down:

> The divide was clear at the start and I felt like I had a real challenge ahead of me, but once the footballs were out the divide almost fully disappeared. It sounds very idealistic, but it's true!

Several of the Arab coaches explained that one of the things that they liked most about the F4P project was that it gave local children the opportunity to see what conditions were like in neighbouring Jewish and Arab communities. For each pair of communities, half of the practices take place in one town and half in the other. In terms of football at least Nahalal is unusual in as much as even though it is an exclusively Jewish community they do have a significant minority of Arab boys and coaches involved with the local football club. One of the Arab coaches worked in a Jewish town and he saw F4P as a vehicle through which the children could see for themselves the material effects of inequality:

> As someone who lives in the Arab sector and works in the Jewish sector I can see the difference, see that the kids in the Jewish sector get a lot more than the Arabs do. Today, for instance, most of the kids from Nahalal (a Jewish town) and even the bus driver couldn't tell where Kaukab is, even though it's only 25km from their homes. This project gives Jewish boys the chance to see what it is like to be an Arab in Israel and how to see how Arab children are living.

This enlightened outlook is shared by at least one of the children from his community, a remarkable 12 year-old whose father, a heart surgeon, was blown up by a suicide bomber in a shopping centre in the Jewish town of Afula. His father survived the blast but lost the sight of both eyes. Despite this trauma, the blinded surgeon had managed to impress up on his son a forgiving attitude. Speaking of the bombing the boy explains:

> It changed my life, for all days it's changed, but my father does not hate the Arabs, he just hates the terrorists. They are not the same, and I too do not hate the Arabs, just the terrorists.

Later, at the end of the project on the day of the finals one of the authors met the boy's father who made a point of coming up and embracing him, thanking him for 'doing this marvellous thing' for his son. This was a humbling experience. Other parents who were on the fringes of the project for most of the week were equally supportive and insightful. As one father watching his son play explained:

> It is not a common thing that Arabs and Jews come together, it doesn't usually happen. But we believe in living together (gestures towards his wife who is also watching) and I want to believe things like this will help.

Their generation

The coach co-ordinator for Nahalal claims to be on good terms with his Arab neighbours and wants to promote more contact with them, particularly for the sake of the children:

> I think it is very important for people to participate in co-existence projects, particularly in areas like this where you have more Arabs, more Arab villages. And I believe that we must start with the children at this age (gestures towards

the 9–11 year-olds playing behind him) in order to find a solution for the Arab-Israeli conflict, problems between Arabs and Jews. Then, eventually, this will reach the older ones, the others.

Of course this project will not solve all of the problems, but the contribution of such projects in making, the children meet each other and talk to each other may help to create a different kind of dialogue. What adults do is blame each other all of the time. We always think of ourselves and we know nothing about the other side. Something we 'adults' don't have, we don't have such channels of communication. So maybe through this project those kids – the next generation of adults – will be able to create a different kind of dialogue before being influenced by the opinion of adults.

Some of the children who take part in the project also seem to understand this, as one Jewish boy from Nahalal commented, 'It's good to bring the young Jewish and Arab kids closer together because the grown-ups are already at war. So that the next generation of kids when they grow up will respect each other and be able to live in peace'. A new friend he had made through the project from the neighbouring town of Kaukab had a less sophisticated, but nonetheless important interpretation of the situation he found himself in: 'I have heard, what I have been told, is that the Jews are not nice, but now I realise that they are nice!'

The performance pragmatic

While the co-existence theme which is a big part of the rationale for projects like F4P seems to be borne out through many of the views outlined above, there are other, more practical reasons why a Jewish community like Nahalal might open itself to Arab participation in its football teams. At all age levels they have one of the most successful amateur clubs in the region. One of the reasons for this is that the club is not ethnically exclusive. One of the local coaches was an émigré ex-professional footballer from Ukraine. He had a clear view of this:

> Football is very important for Arabs and recently there is a boom for football in the Arab sector. Arab kids who join the team contribute a lot toward its success because football is a popular game and in order to succeed you should have the will to succeed. Arab kids, who sometimes come from distressed backgrounds, are eager to succeed and contribute more to the team than kids who have spent more time playing computer games. It doesn't mean that all the Arab players are poor and all the Jewish players are rich, but in the Arab villages you don't have the big variety of activities as you would in a Jewish city or village.

Put crudely, in the Ukrainian's view, the relative deprivation of the Arab sector in Israel produces 'hungry' athletes who are more willing to make the kind of sacrifices that it takes for sporting success than their more cosseted Jewish counterparts: an unscientific observation perhaps, but something that has been axiomatic for professional sport as long as it has been played. While this – the performance pragmatic – should not be ignored, there is a view that no matter what the motivations are for any given initiative, up to a point, if it can lead to more opportunities for positive and mutually beneficial, cross-community contact, in the long term the interests of co-existence must be enhanced.

Maintaining the balance

Not everything was so positive at the Shfaram/Kaukab/Nahalal project, however. As the week went on it became clear that there were considerably less Jewish participants than their Arab counterparts: a pattern that was emerging across many other CCSPs. This, thought one of the volunteer coaches, was undermining the project's objectives:

> I was very disappointed at how few Jewish kids we had. This makes it a bit difficult to properly integrate the two communities. It might make the football coaching easier, but that's not the point is it? I feel very upset that we will not have the chance to rally work hard to build these relationships and disappointed that the those who didn't come will not have the chance to meet others from different communities.

This may be partially explained by the point made above by the Ukrainian coach: the Jewish boys have more things to do already in their school vacation time and have the facilities to do them (when F4P takes place). Thus F4P is not such a treat as it might be for Arab boys. While this may account for some of the problem, there is also an underpinning dynamic at work which is to do with power relations between the two communities. In Northern Ireland, for instance, it was always easier to get Catholics involved in community relations activities than their Protestant counterparts (Sugden 1993). Broadly speaking, this was because for the Protestant majority – traditionally the community with the most power – any initiative that promoted the interests of the less powerful Catholic minority was viewed with suspicion as part of the thin end of a fat wedge that would eventually undermine their ascendancy. It cannot be ruled out that the same dynamic is at work in Israeli society. Nevertheless, more positively, it is important to note that year-on-year the numbers of Jewish communities taking part has grown from none in 2001 to 20+ in 2010.

Speaking a common language

This is related to another issue that emerged: the problem of language and translation. The F4P model required that each coaching group had approximately 12 mixed Arab and Jewish children with a European coach-leader and two local assistants (Jewish and Arab) who would help with both coaching and translation. Hebrew is taught in all of Israel's schools, Jewish and Arab, but Arabic is taught in Arab schools only. English is the preferred 'foreign' language in both sectors;

although in practice there is wide variance in the children's fluency. The coaching was conducted in English, hence the need for translation. In practice, quite often Hebrew emerged as a dominant mode of communication. This was partly because of the situation in schools but also because of the assertiveness of Hebrew translators in comparison to their Arab counterparts. This was commented upon by one of the UK coaches:

> The Jewish translators appeared to take the lead and always translate first. This is something to think about and be conscious of. Translators should feel they have equal status and take on equal responsibility and no language should dominate within the session. This may have been because the Arab coaches knew that the Arab children understood Hebrew and that this would speed things up, but it is something that we will need to watch in future.

The problem of translation was compounded by the fact that in 2004 the coaching manual had only been translated into two languages: English and Hebrew. This was largely determined by financial considerations – there was only enough money to pay for the translation and printing of manuals in two languages – linked to the linguistic skills of the children that we were dealing with. Nevertheless, while there may indeed have been practical reasons for the dominance of Hebrew, because of the significance of language in terms of the politics of cultural reproduction, if the project is to succeed in progressing its co-existence agenda – one based upon inclusiveness and equality of citizenship – this issue of translation in the manual and coaching sessions had to be addressed. By 2008 the manual had been translated into all three languages, including Arabic.

Competition and values

Another problem identified by the volunteer coaches was a tendency for the local coaches to be too competitive, particularly when the project moved towards the final stages. This is what two of the volunteer coaches recorded in their diaries:

> At times during the day I got quite stressed with some local coaches as they weren't controlling their teams and didn't seem to have grasped the concept of the project. Some of the coaches must be made aware that the winning is not important but the values are.

Sport is inherently competitive and this can be one of its most enjoyable qualities. Of course if sport becomes too competitive – that is the quest for victory at all costs overrides the desire to take part in a balanced and equitable struggle for achievement – then any attempt to use sport to enhance positive social goals can be undone. A minority of the local coaches were too competitive, but to the credit of the European coaches they took measures to ensure that such behaviour did not go unchecked.

Significantly, of the Israeli coaches who had experienced the training week in the UK (and by doing so been tutored in a values approach to coaching football), none portrayed an over-competitive attitude once the project proper commenced. It is also gratifying to note that as the week wore on there were clear indications that the children themselves were getting to grips with the underlying rationale of the project, something that the international volunteers commented upon:

> It appeared that the values were really getting across to the children and they were embracing them. It was great to see this development. The values were evident in various moments throughout the day and it was hugely pleasing to see this as it was clear the values were not being lost in competition.

Changing volunteer perspectives

From its initiation in 2001 it has been absolutely clear that F4P has been a valuable, and generally positive, horizon-expanding experience for the overseas volunteers that have taken part. The vast majority of volunteers come from relatively comfortable middle class backgrounds and apart from holidays abroad in 'westernised' resorts, few of them had spent time in distinctive cultural settings. For them Israel was a place they knew only through its very negative coverage in the media. As two of the coaches put it before embarkation:

> I arrived at the airport at 7.30am, really looking forward to the trip; however I'm a little apprehensive about security in Israel. There has been very little spoken (by the programme leaders) about the trouble that goes on in Israel, but it's always at the back of your mind.

By the time they had returned their perspective tended to change as this comment illustrates:

> Israel isn't how I expected it to be. I kind of expected it to look quite deprived and poor – I know it's silly. It doesn't really feel like a place of conflict, just feels like an exotic country ... I feel really privileged to be here and part of the project. It's an experience that I'm never going to forget. It's a lovely place with lovely people, it's just a shame that the media portrayal of the country has negative effects on its reputation.

As would be expected, most of the communities that we worked with were eager to show themselves in the best possible light to their overseas guests and the students recognised this. Many of our hosts avoided talking about the political context – as if it was a taboo subject. Some preferred to offer a more rhetorical approach to peace and reconciliation. Something not lost on the student volunteers:

> It has been very eye-opening at times and extremely interesting. I am glad to have been to a politically unsettled country and experienced first-hand some

of the issues. Although admittedly we have been wrapped in cotton wool somewhat.

There is little doubt that the international volunteers accrue huge interpersonal advantages – social capital – from taking part in horizon-extending projects such as Football 4 Peace (Kay 2009). Even more can be gained through ensuring that their experiences facilitate and benefit – empower – the learning and life opportunities of the local groups with whom they work. This is greatly enhanced when the volunteers treat their engagement as a holistic educational experience, beforehand learning as much about the context within which they will be embedded and embracing local cultures as fully as possible when they are in the field.

Findings: Buena Nujeidat/Kfar Kama/Kfar Tavor

Training

The international volunteer sport coaches reported experiencing problems with local support staff members who had not been sufficiently trained in the F4P method, but who were nevertheless put in charge of some of the football and team-building sessions. They complained that such *ad hoc* staffing arrangements did not provide an environment conducive to social development through sport. It was observed that some of the locals had either not experienced one of the F4P training camps or if they had, had not bought into the underpinning values. As one volunteer explained:

> Some local coaches were only involved because they needed another person to manage a team. Ariel and another person from the community were brilliant football coaches but they did not understand the purpose of F4P, the values of trust, responsibility etc. So all they wanted to do was play football. They were even telling the children to move the cones closer together to make the goal smaller, so that it was harder for the opposite team to score. So they were basically telling their team to cheat.

In order to prevent these issues from happening in the future, the interviewees recommended the strategic inclusion of compulsory cascade training sessions during the pre-project stage. Often at the European training event it was mainly the Israeli community leaders and official representatives who were present, not the actual sport coaches. The interviewees suggested a change of focus towards 'the people who are actually running the sessions, rather than the "bosses". [That] would be helpful to get the values of F4P across'. Building on this argument, another volunteer stressed the importance of educating local coaches for reasons of project continuity and overall sustainability, suggesting that 'obviously after we (the internationals) go, these guys are going to be the ones carrying on to coach football throughout the year'. A further suggestion was made by an English coach, who recommended a separate training workshop to be staged onsite in Israel, which could include and prepare the entire group of local community coaches.

Overall, a strategic change from 'informing the community leaders' towards 'training the trainers' was expected to have long-term benefits, as local coaches would be empowered through additional technical know-how and further understanding of socio-cultural teaching methods. A volunteer summed up:

> This means that [in the long run] you would not have to explain all drills to the locals, as they would already have the experience. So when the football side is tight, they can then focus more on the social aspects. So if they were taught the drills before at the training camp and they have the manuals etc., you can then focus more on specifics such as when to point the 'teachable moments' out, when to focus on social issues etc.

Role models and leadership

Many interviewees reported on the importance of having community-based role models who support the children during their sport and social activities. Particularly in the cultural off-pitch sessions, role models were identified as the key to social engagement, participation and development:

> There was no Jewish role model involved in the dancing. The cultural off-pitch activities were pretty much run by the Arabs and Circassians only, and there was no Jewish representative leading something or doing something, which would have been important for the Jewish kids. Say, if you are a Jewish kid and you watch people that have nothing to do with you, and your leaders are not there, you just switch off.

Role model support was considered important from both a moral and integrative perspective, particularly in situations where cultural differences are strongly observable. One volunteer explained that despite efforts from the international coaches, the Jewish children 'were reluctant to join the others and dance. Even if they got up for a minute, their friends were not there and so they sat down again. It was hard without Jewish coaches or role-model support' (FG: 233–6).

In other examples, Arab and Circassian community leaders presented great role models and encouraged the children to (literally) join hands with others. They assisted in building social bridges and it became obvious that in many instances their behaviour was mirrored by the youngsters. Unfortunately, it was not just positive behaviour that had an impact on the children, as one international coach explained:

> If the coaches start arguing like they did a couple of times yesterday, everything that you have done is just lost... The kids start to leave the group circle wanting to join them, they were looking into their direction and it was hard to connect and talk with them. The adults are role models and if they don't behave, the whole week's work is just lost.

According to the interviewees, a pre-requisite for success in inter-community development is the commitment and leadership of dedicated individuals who 'make things happen' by providing a sport framework conducive to social development. Dedicated leaders organise the necessary equipment and 'go the extra mile' to allow projects to prosper. The Kfar Kama project coordinator was identified by many of the international coaches as the prototype of a committed leader who was able to make a real difference:

> Yesterday Felix had asked Murad if we could have more equipment for the separate stations. We got there today and we normally only needed two bags of balls, some bibs and cones, but today he had organised four bags of balls, four bags of bibs and four sets of cones. He was insisting on keeping them together, so I guess he must have borrowed them from somewhere else. But he got the stuff and we had an amazing amount of equipment, which allowed us to run the drills quicker and smoother. We asked Murad on Monday if he could organise materials to paint flags for the teams. He hadn't thought of this before, so we just asked him and he agreed. Within 24 hours we got the papers and he already got the paint etc. So the leader of the project was very committed and keen and he was able to find ways to organise everything we were asking. I think he is amazing: he's running around, always observing things, trying to help and improve and manage as well as he can.

The importance of commitment and leadership becomes clear when looking at those instances where cooperation and dedication was lacking. If commitment is not there, things can go wrong and any type of social development may be undermined, as two international coaches explained:

> While we were both energised to do things, trying to work things out and the local translators were sitting around the edge, they were on the phones and playing between themselves. Sometimes they even left and we asked 'What you are doing?'. We did not get any answer and felt a bit lost.

On the pitch it could be observed that those local translators and support staff who engaged enthusiastically with the children during activities, were able to achieve their social and educational goals more efficiently. One of the international volunteers pointed out the difference in two local translators who showed a varying degree of passion towards the F4P project and its goals:

> Kfir came to help and… I did not feel as if he was translating my words with the emphasis that he should. When Mashour came to help in between, the kids seemed to pick up a lot more information. So it is important to communicate the values and examples with energy and enthusiasm.

In addition to those people that were actively involved in the sport activities, the coaches highlighted that enthusiasm and commitment are qualities also needed from people *around* the peace project. Interestingly, some interviewees mentioned that in cases where there were no adult role models available, some of the children stepped in and took the role of 'quasi role models' for their peers:

> One thing that impressed me was one kid who translated everything for me and got many others involved, so there were small leaders among the kids who I pointed out as role models later to everyone. And once the kids realised they get the praise for their behaviour, they continued with it. So this boy helped me as a role model to get the values across.

Structure and programming

During the week-long training sessions, local and international coaches tried to find the best structure and style to control and educate children on the one hand, and to keep them entertained and excited on the other. From an operational perspective, it took the coaches some time until they had identified the best set-up to achieve both these goals. While on days one and two the international coaches were responsible for all individual on-pitch activities and football games, on day three operational structures were changed and more responsibility was transferred to the local coaches:

> It seemed to be a good idea to divide the field into different stations and have one of the Israeli translators responsible per station. So with your kids you walk around the stations and each time there is an Israeli coach who can explain the game on their own… If things went wrong, you could stop the game and interfere and explain things again, but that was not even needed. It was a good learning process for the translators/coaches, too. It increased their responsibility in running the games and their ability to do it properly.

The increase in responsibility for the local translators – acting as support coaches – had positive impacts on their self-assurance and levels of confidence. Respondents praised this outcome and commended the locals for their willingness and commitment to learning:

> Today, the on-pitch was just brilliant. The structured circle set-up worked really well and everyone knew what they were doing. It gave the translators a lot more onus, because they stayed at their station and were able to explain the drill and values to the kids who came along. So they knew what values that drill was focusing on and we were able to run things a lot better and quicker and I believe the kids enjoyed it a lot more, too. So it went really, really well.

Overall, it was argued that this change in programming made the activities and changeovers 'a lot smoother, just because you had that structure, you had those four stations. The kids knew exactly where they would go … and it was easy … They didn't even have a chance to misbehave'.

Wider community involvement and ownership

The international coaches recommended an extension of the educational and social foci of F4P beyond the practical work with children alone. This suggestion builds on the experiences made at this year's project, where there was insufficient information provided to parents, friends and families who were therefore unable to engage and prepare children for the F4P project activities.

In particular the Jewish groups from the Lower Galilee region seemed ill-informed about the social purpose of F4P. In contrast, Arab supervisor Mashour had told the parents of the Buena Nujeidat community in advance about what F4P stands for and what it wants to achieve. According to the interviewees, this proactive and inclusive approach made a big difference to the success of the project:

> Mashour got the phone numbers of all children from his Buena Nujeidat community to explain the project to all parents. Apparently there are a lot of projects out here like summer camps and other football projects ... So Mashour called all the parents and explained to them in a short phone call the values of the project. He argues that this often makes a difference and that families therefore decide to come to F4P.

Considering the delicate political situation in Israel, personal contact was considered important to building trustful relationships between the community supervisor, the parents and their children. Personal conversations about the purpose and social value of F4P may have been the key to convincing parents to send their children to the project. However, while Mashour was successful in recruiting a large number of children, he was not able to convince a lot of parents to contribute and become actively involved in the F4P program.

Active involvement of parents and supporting families is something the international coaches would like to see, as the F4P idea could be expanded and leveraged to the wider community. Indeed, one of the other 2009 F4P inter-community projects in the Upper Galilee region had already managed to include parents into the official program, providing them with a chance to become part of the F4P-family:

> When I was speaking to Yossi in Upper Galilee yesterday, he was saying that on the final day before the festival the parents from both his partner-communities are invited to come and see the final training. Also, they are required to bring fruits and some of the drinks to contribute to the success of the day.

Despite the overall support for the inclusion of parents into the program, one volunteer remarked that parents could also be a potential problem-factor for the overall success of the project. Clearly, the young man's comment needs to be taken into account when planning for future events:

I could see the parents' presence as more of a problem than actual help. Just the fact that they have the wrong pre-conceptions before the project ... So it might be an advantage to get the kids away from the parents, just so you don't have that negative influence... I mean, it clearly depends on what kind of parent it is, some might be very helpful, while others may be discouraging. It could be either way...

Making a difference?

It would be pointless to pretend that there do not remain enormous social and political divisions and inequalities among the communities in which F4P works. It would be equally foolish to think that, taken in isolation, a small initiative like F4P can change history in Israel, but as one of the parents from Nahalal pointed out, it can make a small but nevertheless valuable contribution:

Of course alone it won't help make peace, the problem is too big, and it's difficult today for Jews and Arabs to make peace because of everything going on around. But I think that this project and projects like it, not only in football, but in everything, in music, and in other sports, when you meet together, it's more than just playing football. It will teach the children that we are all children the same, who like to be happy, who like to love who are just the same as us.

Discussion

Using Israel as an example for intergroup tensions and conflict, the aim of this research was to investigate the management and implementation strategies employed and/or recommended for the successful delivery of inter-community sport projects in divided societies. Several broad critical themes emerged from the re-examination of the 2004 and 2009 data. Firstly, in the context of Israel's complex, confrontational, and volatile contemporary political history, the very fact that communities such as the ones featured were prepared to get together to support a project like F4P gives great encouragement to those who believe in a peaceful road to co-existence and reconciliation. In no small measure was this attributable to the fact that both children and their elders had come to believe that the future of Israel and its relationship to its Palestinian constituencies rested with tomorrow's and not today's generation of leaders.

Secondly, over time, the gradual change of emphasis from top-down to bottom up project development and delivery, with increasing importance being assigned to training the trainers, was viewed to be a huge factor in the sustainability of the F4P initiative. The increasing strength and application of the values-based training curriculum and its multi-layered implementation was one of the key differences between the 2004 and 2009 projects. There does, however, remain room for improvement. It was argued that all local volunteers need to be fully briefed and strategically prepared for the sport projects, so that they can fulfil their roles as supporting change agents. Ideally, this process should not be implemented *ad hoc*, but during the pre-project phase. An *ex ante* approach to social development should provide locals with a first insight into event planning and inter-cultural management, and with an opportunity to learn from management experts. For example, pre-project community workshops and cooperative coaching sessions under a 'train the trainers' approach could be conducted to transfer valuable management skills, technical knowledge and overall control to community members. For this to work, the international sport coaches need to be willing to transfer responsibilities to the locals facilitating a 'bottom-up' management approach (Moscardo 2007; Murphy 1988). In their attempts to empower communities, they could follow the philosophical principles of Schulenkorf's (2010a) 'Model for Community Empowerment', which focuses on gradually reducing external dominance and increasing local control over time.

Thirdly, when staging inter-community projects in disadvantaged communities, the commitment and leadership of key individuals is a crucial factor for achieving positive social development. Going beyond Kay's (2009) and Meier and Saavedra's (2009) argument that sport can be an agent of personal change and development, this research shows that not sport *per se*, but the active involvement of passionate community leaders and change agents makes a strong contribution to positive intergroup development, cooperation and inclusive change. This implies that the conditions (e.g. downplay of competition and the focus on social values) and context of the event (e.g. combination of foreign experts and community support) are important success factors, particularly in a tension-laden environment.

Local community members and role models should have a responsibility in the operational management of sport-for-development projects. While previous studies have highlighted the importance of key individuals sharing their knowledge and experiences to excite youth about professional/élite sport development (see e.g. Green and Houlihan 2005) this study shows that in a challenging multi-cultural environment adequate role model support is needed to encourage children to even participate in any type of interactive activity. It seems fundamentally important for peace projects to involve key individuals as role models, or – otherwise – build on self-confident children to take up this role instead. For project organisers and development coaches, the alternative of empowering children to become role models for their peers is an interesting direction to consider. However, further empirical work needs to be conducted to investigate the potential of local youth in supporting projects, in order to prevent them from being overwhelmed or inundated.

Fourthly, there were also insights gained regarding the actual programming of sport-for-development projects. This study suggests that with only a limited number of local volunteers facilitating communication and group activities, the set-up and structure of activities need to be flexible. For example, instead of a generalist approach to on-pitch and off-pitch training and support, it was recommended that local volunteers should become specialists in one particular activity for the day. Operationally, this requires a change from locals being in charge of one particular *group* during the day to supervising one particular *training station*. This adjustment is likely to facilitate a smooth running of activities, as it transfers the responsibility to locals who are able to act with confidence as experts in their particular field.

Fifthly, while Kay (2009) had shown that sport projects can provide people from disadvantaged communities with increased self-confidence derived from increased body-confidence, this study shows that people increase their self-confidence through applying teaching skills and technical sport knowledge. This finding ties in with the community empowerment strategies proposed by different development advocates, who have tried to grow capacities of local talent in areas such as education (Grootaert *et al.* 2002), tourism (Heenan 1978; Hinch and Delamere 1993), sport (Coalter 2007; Kidd 2008; Lawson 2005; Skinner *et al.* 2008; Vail 2007), or festivals and event management (Misener and Mason 2006; Moscardo 2007). However, in contrast to previous work this study highlights the importance of interpersonal and inter-community cooperation and dedication in advancing capacities in the context of a divided society. Moreover, as we have seen, there is little doubt that the international volunteers accrue huge interpersonal advantages – social capital – from taking part in horizon-extending projects such as Football 4 Peace. Even more can be gained through ensuring that their embedded experiences are educationally and culturally holistic and work to facilitate and benefit – empower – the learning and life opportunities of the local groups with whom they work.

Finally, in order to benefit from social development on a wider scale, project organisers need to strategically focus on the wider community to grow and leverage individual projects while at the same time ensuring that pro-rata levels of recruitment from Jewish and Arab Communities are maintained. While Burnett (2006) and Stidder and Haasner (2007) highlighted that a) active participation in sport can be successful in reducing distance between *participating* people and groups, and b) experts can support local parties with community-building knowledge and educational activities *at* projects, this research found that a stronger focus *around* events needs to be designed to make a significant contribution to overall inter-community development efforts (see also Schulenkorf and Edwards 2010). Here, the challenge for maximising social outcomes is to transfer the positive atmosphere of the project beyond the borders of the sport arena. To achieve growth and leverage, project organisers and communities could, for example, focus on more involvement from the parents, wider families, friends and finally their communities into project-related support activities or more structured community exchange programs. In other words, a strategic shift towards social leverage requires what Chalip (2004, 2006) describes as a focus beyond the planning of direct social impacts to achieve lasting social outcomes for communities. Sugden (2010) has shown, this is best achieved by building durable partnerships, first at the level of community, then through durable alliances with a network of other key stakeholders in the surrounding policy communities for sport.

Conclusion

Overall, it becomes obvious that international development agencies, local communities and change agents are becoming increasingly aware of sport and events' social potential. However, we argue that our understanding of this phenomenon still has some distance to travel. For example, despite an increase in practical development projects around the world and the empirical evidence that sport and event projects can be a successful starting point and catalyst for social development (Burnett 2006; Gasser and Levinsen 2004; Stidder and Haasner 2007), not many studies have investigated their social, cultural, psychological and educational long-term outcomes. Given earlier discussion, long-term development studies are recommended to assess the sustainability of social outcomes, and the overall contribution of sport and event projects in the inter-community development process.

Full details concerning the methodology of F4P, including the rationale for having girl's/women's-only projects, can be found in the book *Football for Peace? The Challenges of Using Sport for Co-Existence in Israel* (Sugden and Wallis 2007). The theoretical model that underpins F4P is explored in the journal article, *Critical left realism and sport interventions in divided societies* (Sugden 2010).

References

Allen, W. E. D. and Muratoff, P. (1953) *Caucasian Battlefields: History of the Wars on the Turco-Caucasian Border 1821–1921,* Cambridge: Cambridge University Press.

Ateek, N. (1989) *Justice and Only Justice*, Maryknoll, NY: Orbis.

Burnett, C. (2001) Social Impact Assessment and Sport Development: Social spin-offs of the Australia-South Africa Junior Sport Programme, *International Review for the Sociology of Sport*, 36(1), 41–57.

Burnett, C. (2006) Building Social Capital through an 'Active Community Club', *International Review for the Sociology of Sport*, 41(3–4), 283–94.

Chalip, L. (2004) Beyond impact: a general model for host community event leverage, in Ritchie, B. and Adair, D. (eds) *Sport tourism: Interrelationships, impacts and issues*, 226–52), Clevedon: Channel View.

Chalip, L. (2006) 'Towards Social Leverage of Sport Events', *Journal of Sport and Tourism*, 11(2), 109–27.

Christenson, J. A., Fendley, K. and Robinson, J. W. (1989) 'Community Development', in Christenson, J. A. and Robinson, J. W. (eds) *Community Development in Perspective*, 3–25), Ames, IA: Iowa State University Press.

Coalter, F. (2007) *A Wider Social Role for Sport: Who's keeping the score?*, Abingdon, Oxon: Routledge.

Coalter, F. (2010) 'The politics of sport-for-development: Limited focus programmes and broad gauge problems?', *International Review for the Sociology of Sport*, 45(3), 295–314.

Darnell, S. C. (2007) Playing with Race: *Right to Play* and the Production of Whiteness in 'Development through Sport', *Sport in Society*, 10(4), 560–79.

Dowty, A. (2008) *Israel/Palestine*, Cambridge, Polity.

Gasser, P. K. and Levinsen, A. (2004) 'Breaking Post-War Ice: Open fun football schools in Bosnia and Herzegovina', *Sport in Society*, 7(3), 457–72.

Glesne, C. (1999) 'Meeting Qualitative Inquiry', in Glesne, C. and Peshkin, A. (eds) *Becoming Qualitative Researchers: An introduction* (2nd edn, 1–17), New York: Longman.

Green, M. and Houlihan, B. (2005) *Élite Sport Development: Policy Learning and Political Priorities*, London; New York: Routledge.

Grootaert, C., Oh, G.-T. and Swamy, A. (2002) 'Social capital, education and credit markets: empirical evidence from Burkina Faso', in Isham, J., Kelly, T. and Ramaswamy, S. (eds), *Social Capital and Economic Development*, (85–103), Cheltenham, UK: Edgar Elgar Publications.

Gschwend, A. and Selvaranju, U. (2007) *Psycho-social sport programmes to overcome trauma in post-disaster interventions*, Biel/Bienne: Swiss Academy for Development (SAD).

Heenan, D. A. (1978) 'Tourism and the Community: a Drama in Three Acts', *Journal of Travel Research*, 16(4), 30–2.

Hinch, T. D. and Delamere, T. A. (1993) 'Native Festivals as Tourism Attractions: A Community Challenge', *Journal of Applied Recreation Research*, 18(2), 131–42.

Ife, J. W. (1995) *Community development: creating community alternatives – vision, analysis and practice*, Melbourne: Longman Australia.

Kay, T. (2009) 'Developing through sport: evidencing sport impacts on young people', *Sport in Society*, 12(9), 1177–91.

Kidd, B. (2008) 'A new social movement: Sport for development and peace', *Sport in Society*, 11(4), 370–80.

Kramer, R. M. and Specht, H. (1975) *Readings in community organization practice* (2nd ed.), Englewood Cliffs, NJ: Prentice-Hall.

Kunz, V. (2009) Sport as a post-disaster psychosocial intervention in Bam, Iran, *Sport in Society*, 12(9), 1147–57.

Lawson, H. A. (2005) 'Empowering people, facilitating community development, and contributing to sustainable development: the social work of sport, exercise, and physical education programs', *Sport, Education and Society*, 10(1), 135–60.

Levermore, R. and Beacom, A. (eds) (2009) *Sport and International Development*. Houndmills: Palgrave Macmillan.

Meier, M. and Saavedra, M. (2009) 'Esther Phiri and the Moutawakel effect in Zambia: an analysis of the use of female role models in sport-for-development', *Sport in Society*, 12(9), 1158 –76.

Midgley, J. (1986) *Community Participation, Social Development and the State*, New York: Methuen.

Miles, M. and Huberman, A. (1994) *Qualitative data analysis: an expanded sourcebook*, California: Sage Publications.

Misener, L. and Mason, D. S. (2006) 'Creating community networks: Can sporting events offer meaningful sources of social capital?', *Managing Leisure*, 11(1), 39–56.

Moscardo, G. (2007) 'Analyzing the Role of Festivals and Events in Regional Development', *Event Management*, 11(1–2), 23–32.

Murphy, P. (1988) 'Community-driven tourism planning', *Tourism Management*, 9(2), 96–104.

Naparstek, A. J., Dooley, D. and Smith, R. (1997) *Community Building in Public Housing*, Washington, DC: US Department of Housing and Urban Development.

Neuman, W. L. (2003) *Social research methods: qualitative and quantitative approaches* (5th edn), Boston and London: Allyn and Bacon.

Said, E. (2002) *The End of the Peace Process*, London: Granta.

Schulenkorf, N. (2010a) 'The Roles and Responsibilities of a Change Agent in Sport Event Development Projects', *Sport Management Review*, 13(2), 118–28.

Schulenkorf, N. (2010b) 'Sport events and ethnic reconciliation: Attempting to create social change between Sinhalese, Tamil and Muslim sportspeople in war-torn Sri Lanka', *International Review for the Sociology of Sport*, 45(3), 273–94.

Schulenkorf, N. and Edwards, D. (2010) 'The Role of Sport Events in Peace Tourism', in Moufakkir, O. and Kelly, I. (eds) *Tourism, Progress and Peace*, (99–117), Oxfordshire, UK: CABI International.

Skinner, J., Zakus, D. and Cowell, J. (2008) 'Development through Sport: Building social capital in disadvantaged communities', *Sport Management Review*, 11(3), 253–75.

Spaaij, R. (2009) 'The social impact of sport: diversities, complexities and contexts', *Sport in Society*, 12(9), 1109–17.

Stake, R. (1995) *The Art of Case Study Research*, California: Sage Publications.

Stidder, G. and Haasner, A. (2007) 'Developing outdoor and adventurous activities for co-existence and reconciliation in Israel: an Anglo-German approach', *Journal of Adventure Education and Outdoor Learning*, 7(2), 131–40.

Sugden, J. (1993) *Sport, Sectarianism and Society in a Divided Ireland* (with Alan Bairner), Leicester University Press.

Sugden, J. (2006) 'Teaching and Playing Sport for Conflict Resolution and Co-Existence in Israel', *International Review for the Sociology of Sport*, 41(2), 221–40.

Sugden, J. (2010) 'Critical left-realism and sport interventions in divided societies', *International Review for the Sociology of Sport*, 45(3), 258–72.

Sugden, J. and Haasner, A. (2010) 'Sport intervention in divided societies', in Tokarski, W. and Petry, K. (eds) *Handbuch Sportpolitik*, (332–42), Schorndorf: Hofmann-Verlag.

Sugden, J. and Wallis, J. (2007) 'Football for Peace? The Challenges of Using Sport for Co-Existence in Israel', Oxford: Meyer and Meyer Sport.

Uruena, N. (2004) ‚Citizen participation as a means of controlling corruption at the local level in Colombia‘, Unpublished MSc Thesis, Oxford, Oxford University.

Vail, S. (2007) 'Community development and sports participation‘, *Journal of Sport Management*, 21(4), 571–96.

Whitfield, G. (2006) *Amity in the Middle East*, Brighton: The Alpha Press.

8 Sticks and stones may break my bones, but words will never hurt me?

Challenging racial stereotypes in physical education and school sport

Sid Hayes and Daniel Burdsey

First came rugby (never rugger) – the noble game, the rite of passage to manhood, a good marriage, the professions and freemasonry. Next, and nowhere near at all, came other sports – frivolous wastes of time – and, in the case of gymnastics, a source of refuge for the skinny, the fatty bookworms, the asthmatic and effeminate. My hatred of rugby spread to other sports. I hated the physical intrusion of slapped congratulations and the embarrassment of the team talk. I despised referees – those pompous, puffed up officiators of bad laws that gave strangers carte blanche to kick, hurl missiles, dance around, taunt and humiliate me. I hated sports' body odour, trite philosophies and false camaraderie. And I always will.

Redwood F (2003)
'Why I hated school PE', in *PE and Sport Today*,
Spring 2003, Optimus Education

Introduction

In November 2011, the retrial into the murder of the black teenager, Stephen Lawrence, in south-east London in 1993, provided a stark reminder that race and racism remain prominent features of British society. In this context, sport is widely perceived to be one of the social spheres in which most advancements towards racial equality have been made. Although few individuals would completely deny that racist incidents still occur on the playing field (see below) and in the stands, these are seen as sporadic, spontaneous occurrences caused by the highly-charged, competitive nature of professional sport and/or emanating from individual prejudices (Müller *et al.* 2007). In short, the idea that racial inequality in élite sport is ingrained and permeates many of its structures and institutions is widely shunned (Burdsey 2011).

Thus it came as a surprise to many – both inside and outside of sport – that, within two weeks of each other, two incidents of racist abuse (one of which, at the time of writing, has not been proven and is awaiting verdict in a criminal court) occurred at the highest level of domestic professional football – the FA Premier

League – in the month of October 2011. Luis Suarez (Liverpool) was formally charged with racially abusing Patrice Evra (Manchester United) by the Football Association in November 2011, yet immediately issued an appeal. The Football Association still found him to be guilty, issuing a 115-page document explaining their findings which resulted in an eight match ban. John Terry of Chelsea will undergo a court trial in July 2012, having been accused of making a racist comment to Queens Park Rangers' Anton Ferdinand. These incidents preceded the arrest of a fan in the FA Cup 3rd round tie between Liverpool and Oldham Athletic for racially aggravated public order offence in relation to one of the players from Oldham Athletic, Tom Adeyemi. Predictably, the incidents regarding Terry and Suarez led to months of claim and counter-claim, with many figures within the professional game speaking out on behalf of the various players involved in the controversies. Others were drawn – often at the prompting of press conference journalists – to engage in broader debates about the continuing significance (or not) of race in English football: some of which was progressive and, indeed, relatively radical; some of which was, in our opinion, misguided, ill-advised and offensive. Either side of these episodes, football has also seen the use of social networking media, e.g. Twitter, by 'fans' as a means of abusing, often racially, (current and former) professional footballers of black or 'mixed ethnicity' backgrounds (including James Vaughan, Louis Saha, Micah Richards, Shola Ameobi, Mark Bright and Stan Collymore). As mentioned previously, political debate on this issues has been significantly contested with claim and counter claim among the political parties. Shadow Minister for Public Health, Diane Abbott, became the latest politician to become embroiled in discussion about the appropriateness, or otherwise, of language she used on Twitter with regards to white people. This occurred in January 2012 and ultimately resulted in her issuing an apology for any offence caused.

As youngsters, we were both frequently informed – by parents and teachers – that 'sticks and stones may break my bones, but words will never hurt me', as a means of responding to the unkind comments of others. Yet, if we are to learn anything from the above episodes, it is that verbal comments can be just as upsetting, damaging and dehumanising as other forms of racism.

Consequently, this chapter is designed to act as a reminder that even though a number of advances have been made in eradicating many of the more blatant articulations of racist discourse and practice, covert and subtle forms of racism continue to exist. These manifestations have become increasingly difficult for many observers to recognise and deal with accordingly. The challenge for those involved in physical education and school sport is to be aware of the multifarious ways in which racism manifests itself in these contexts and to ensure that they respond appropriately towards challenging discriminatory behaviours and epithets.

These questions raise some contentious issues that the PE profession has to navigate in its attempt to deliver race equality, and which we will address in this chapter. In order to engage effectively with race and racism in school PE and sport we need to clarify some conceptual frameworks and provide a social and historical context. We therefore begin the chapter with a discussion of the ways in which key concepts such as race and racism have been understood. Then we give a brief overview of the debates around, and nature of, contemporary racism in the UK. This is followed by a discussion of the relationship between race and racism in education, before we examine how it affects school sport and PE. We conclude by looking at the importance and potential of Initial Teacher Training in contributing to genuinely social inclusive PE and sport curricula.

Personal reflections – Sid Hayes

Interest in this area of study arrived part way through my career. As a pupil I was relatively unaware of the phenomenon associated with stereotypes and ethnicity. It was not until I embarked on my teacher training course that race issues in relation to sporting performance were addressed, albeit at a somewhat superficial level. I was schooled into the genetic explanation of sporting performance by selected 'racial groups' in certain sports and it seemed very plausible at the time. With the simplicity of the argument and the media evidence in the form of national television coverage of football and athletics, etc., there seemed little reason to question its logic. It was not until I embarked on further study programmes that I was exposed to alternative viewpoints and began to question the folklore explanation of sporting performance by certain ethnic groups. I was also fortunate to work in an inner city environment as a teacher of physical education where I could be reflective with regards to my perceptions and expectations of pupils from minority ethnic backgrounds in PE and sport. It was whilst at this secondary school that I came across viewpoints of colleagues who were also seeking explanations for sporting performance in the field of genetics associated with race. Whilst I had and still have the utmost respect for the work of all my colleagues during my teaching days in schools, I did sense that there were some mixed views surrounding expectations, in the sporting arena, of pupils from different ethnic backgrounds. It was such perceptions that have motivated me to research into this area further. My present position as a teacher trainer allows me some reflective time relating to this issue, and it still appears that the question of ethnicity in relation to education, and specifically in the area of PE and sport, is under-represented as a discussion point.

Personal reflections – Daniel Burdsey

On a work visit to the Channel Islands in 2011, I was fortunate enough to be invited to observe one of the editors of this collection, Gary Stidder, teach a physical education lesson with a group of a dozen, male, Year 12 students. Much to my surprise, there was no running, minimal noise, and a notable absence of sweating bodies crashing into each other. Instead I witnessed an hour of problem-solving, co-operative learning and young people thoughtfully navigating their way through the spaces and obstacles of the gymnasium. As I helped Gary put away the materials after the session, I was drawn to make the following observation to him: 'If *this* is what physical education is, I don't think that I've ever experienced it'. It would certainly be incorrect to say that I didn't enjoy 'PE lessons' and school sport. Indeed, I feel particular fondness for my junior school years. Growing up in Brighton meant that in the summer term literally *every* day included a game of stoolball – a popular Sussex sport – after morning break, while having frequent handball sessions still seems relatively innovative for 1988. Secondary school was a different matter altogether though. While there were positive experiences (such as my actual GCSE Physical Education classes), my abiding memory of 'Games' is of unsupervised, large-sided football matches, endurance activities (the dreaded cross-country run) and military style drills. The benefit of hindsight has done little to change my perception at the time that these activities were designed to antagonise, domineer, humiliate and exhaust us. Physical? Definitely. Education? Not for me. Attending schools with very few minority ethnic pupils in a city with an overwhelmingly white population meant that race was not something we considered at the time. Yet, looking back, it was this very *absence* of multicultural exposure which meant that our experiences of school sport were intrinsically racialised, influencing the games we played, the opportunities we were afforded and the privileges we held.

Understanding race and racism

A common distinction made by many writers is to distinguish – chronologically and conceptually – between biological and cultural racism. Where racial characteristics, such as skin colour and physicality, are invoked to justify discrimination, it is said to be *biological* racism. Where cultural characteristics, such as religion and language, are foregrounded in the process of excluding social groups, it is said to be *cultural* racism. Biological racism, it is argued, evolved in the seventeenth and eighteenth century. Some see this as an attempt to rationalise the practice of slavery, while others regard it as an explicit belief in the notion of racial hierarchy. Either way, it developed subsequently to justify the expanding British Empire in the nineteenth century (Fryer 2010).

The experience of the Nazi-inflicted Holocaust during the Second World War, however, made biological racism politically unacceptable. This was evidenced in the UNESCO statement of 1950. Advances in genetics also rendered the idea of biological races scientifically invalid. Rather than resorting to a biological rationale, many scholars have argued that racism subsequently began to operate predominantly through the medium of culture, whereby culture is mapped onto nations to constitute national cultures (Barker 1981; Short and Carrington 1998; Gilroy 2004). Accordingly, cultural racism manifests itself in the declaration that different ethnic groups – however they are defined – are culturally distinct, with each group having their own incompatible lifestyles, customs and ways of seeing the world. In addition, attempts to mix the cultures are perceived to lead to inevitable social breakdown. In stark political terms, cultural racism is often employed to defend the notion of a monocultural white and Christian British identity, with the aim of excluding those who are deemed to be different or 'alien'.

It can also be seen, for example, in the growing anti-Muslim sentiment in the UK over the last decade. This phenomenon, termed 'Islamophobia' (Runnymede Trust 2000), has become increasingly widespread, particularly following the terrorist attacks of 11 September 2001 (on the USA) and 7 July 2005 (on London), manifesting itself in discrimination, abuse and violence towards Muslims (as well as those conflated with/confused as being Muslim) (Abbas 2005; Allen 2010; Kundnani 2007).

It is important not to overstate the difference between the two forms of racism, nor to overplay the shift from a crude biological racism to a cultural one. For example, anti-Jewish and anti-Irish sentiment at the turn of the twentieth century was often cloaked in cultural terms (Panayi 2010), while – 19 years after the murder of black teenager Stephen Lawrence in south-east London – members of minority ethnic groups continue to live under the threat of racist violence. Further evidence of this violence is evidenced through the fatal shooting of Anuj Bidve, a 23 year-old Indian student, in Salford. Although no formal trial has yet taken place, Greater Manchester Police are investigating the nature of the murder to see if there was any racial motive to the killing. Though conceptually distinct, in reality biological and cultural racism tend to interface, to produce 'a matrix of biological and cultural racism' (Cole 1998: 39). Perhaps what is most important to recognise is that, conceptually, the notion of *racisms* in the plural now provides us with the most insightful way of accounting for the multiple forms of racialised privilege and disadvantage that characterise contemporary Britain in the early twenty-first century (Garner 2010).

As Britain emerged as an increasingly multicultural society in the post-war period, the concept of ethnicity began to replace race as a means of identification and categorisation. Whereas race categorised people according to their assumed fixed biological make-up, ethnicity emphasised the fluidity of identities based on culture, history and practices (Hesse 2000). In the context of cultural racism, however, the dynamic and processual meaning of ethnicity has undergone a process of racialisation, leading to the development of what Paul Gilroy (1987) has called 'ethnic absolutism' – the process of fixing cultural identities so as to be seen as innate rather than socially constructed. As Malik argues (1996: 104), 'though the political use of racist science was discredited, its conceptual framework was never destroyed. The discourse of race was reformulated, but the concept never disappeared'. The fixing of cultures, so that they effectively come to represent races, reflects a stubborn persistence in the belief of race, even if it is articulated through the language of ethnicity, nation and culture. This problematic status of race as 'biologically meaningless, although still socially explosive' (Rose 1998: 37), explains the traditional placing of the word in inverted commas. However, a recognition of this fact, along with acknowledgement that other concepts such as gender are also social constructions, means that the practice of putting 'race' in inverted commas is no longer as common.

An initial definition of racism, then, is that it exists where a group of people is *discriminated against* on the basis of *racial* and/or *cultural* characteristics that are held to be *inherent* within them as a group. Such a definition focuses on:

a) fixed racial/cultural differences
    and
b) discriminatory action.

The focus on the former identifies the process of stereotyping social groups on the basis of race and/or culture. Such stereotypical thinking becomes racist where it leads to, or feeds into, or sustains discriminatory practices against the targeted social group. Crucially, it highlights that racism is an expression of power whereby the disadvantaged position of subordinate social groups is reproduced (Bhattacharyya *et al.* 2002).

Race, racism and society

In the period following the publication of the Macpherson Report in 1999 – the investigation into the murder of Stephen Lawrence and the subsequent bungled investigation by the Metropolitan Police – there was a widespread sense of optimism that, at last, the political resolve existed to combat racism wherever it surfaced, be it on the streets, in the police force, or in any public body or organisation. However, on the whole, such expectations have not been met. Issues of race, racism, and national identity remain one of the most contentious areas of politics in Britain, especially under the return of a Conservative Prime Minister. While the electoral advances made by the British National Party following the urban unrest in the northern towns of Oldham, Burnley and Bradford in the summer of 2001 appear, thankfully, to have subsided for the time being, another pernicious threat can be found in the overtly racist and Islamophobic English Defence League.

The story of political responses to 'race relations' since the publication of the first edition of this collection has fundamentally been one of continuity and change. Between 1997 and 2010, New Labour displayed an inconsistent stance on race equality. Having overseen the Macpherson Inquiry and the introduction of the Race Relations (Amendment) Act 2000 – which meant that public authorities had a statutory duty to promote race equality – this government also introduced draconian legislation around immigration, asylum and the so-called 'war on terror'. Notwithstanding this, in contrast to the previous Conservative administrations, it would be fair to say that anti-racism became part of official discourse in the UK at this time. Yet numerous commentators, campaigning groups, activists and scholars have argued that, in practice, the Labour government did little to alleviate racial injustice and inequalities faced by Britain's minority ethnic communities (Schuster and Solomos 2004).

What is clear is that much of the New Labour discourse around ethnic diversity and racism was articulated through the notion of 'community cohesion' (Cantle 2008), and focused predominantly on migrants, asylum seekers and Muslims (Kundnani 2007). Indeed, the Nationality, Immigration and Asylum Act, introduced in the wake of the 2001 riots, was widely condemned as racist, as it combined an exclusive notion of British citizenship, targeted at South Asians, with a battery of controls to stop (certain groups of) migrants entering the UK.

The thinking underpinning this controversial piece of legislation was made explicit by David Blunkett's statement that 'we have norms of acceptability, and those who come into our home – for that is what it is – should accept those norms' (cited in Mahamdallie 2002: 4). In targeting migrants seeking a better life in Britain, Blunkett simultaneously recast many South Asians who were either born in Britain or who have lived in the country for decades, as foreigners and, therefore, to be tolerated only if they become 'more English'.

Perhaps tellingly, as the Labour government reached the end of its administration, in January 2010, Communities Secretary, John Denham, stated that 'focusing on somebody's race or ethnic background to explain their achievements or opportunities is far too simple' (cited in Travis 2010). Detailing the social changes that Britain had undergone during his party's tenure, he spoke instead of the salience of individuals' class status in underpinning contemporary inequalities, adding that 'we must avoid a one-dimensional debate that assumes all minority-ethnic people are disadvantaged' (cited in Sparrow and Owen 2010). Life under the current coalition government shows little sign of improvement – arguably unsurprising given Prime Minister, David Cameron's 2011 declaration that 'state multiculturalism' had 'failed' (BBC 2011). At the present time, issues around racism and policing, the criminal justice system, immigration and education – and, let us not forget, sport – remain particularly prominent.

Race and racism in education

Current discriminatory ideologies and practices are rooted in history. For example, a legacy of British colonialist ideologies of race and empire, which posited 'non-white' people variously as the inferior, threatening, and exotic 'Other', was influential in framing young black people in the 1950s and 1960s as 'a problem'. Anxiety amongst many white parents led to a policy of dispersion in the 1960s to ensure that minority ethnic children did not constitute more than 30 per cent of the school population (Blair and Cole 2002). This 'monoculturalist' approach to education sought to make all newcomers socially and culturally British. The idea was both to prevent 'a lowering of standards in schools' and to ensure rapid assimilation of the children into the "British Culture"' (Blair and Cole 2002: 63).

It was during the 1970s that 'the imagery of violence and decay became synonymous with those inner-city localities in which black migrants had settled and established themselves' (Solomos 1993: 135). An important factor in this was the 'moral panic' about mugging in the early 1970s, which was constructed as a new 'black juvenile' crime, and perceived by the public as constituting a major social problem (Hall *et al.* 1978). In response, there was a growing sense of frustration within the black communities and an increasingly antagonistic relationship between black youths and the police, reflecting 'a deep crisis in the relationship between these communities and the state, especially the police' (Witte 1996: 59).

Racial stereotypes of black youngsters not only as 'disruptive' but as physically threatening abounded in the media and official reportage of the riots that erupted across Britain in the early 1980s. Instead of understanding the riots as an expression of extreme frustration and anger caused by lack of decent employment opportunities, police harassment and poverty, the perception emerged that black youths were 'trouble'. As Blair and Cole (2002: 64) comment, 'the view which carried into the classroom was that black children were not only disruptive, but violent'. The notion of the physically able but educationally inferior black child was established. With it emerged an educational discourse of 'underachievement', which placed the 'failing' black pupils with low 'self-esteem' under the spotlight in the search for explanations and solutions.

Ironically, the first official recognition that racism was adversely affecting the education of black children came with the Rampton report in 1981 – the year of the riots. This report, however, was not received well by the right-wing Thatcher government, especially in the wake of the riots, and so the Prime Minister commissioned another study with a brief to cover all pupils from minority ethnic backgrounds. The Swann Report, *Education for All* (1985), while confirming the findings of the Rampton report, made its mark more for its recommendation that children in all schools should be educated for life in an ethnically diverse society. The belief that underpinned the Swann Report was that if all children, but especially white children, were taught about different cultures, then prejudice and racism would be undermined. This represented a real shift from a 'monocultural' approach to education, based on the concept of assimilation, to multicultural education. Though multiculturalism is a complex and multi-layered term (Hesse 2000), we concur with Waller *et al.* (2001) in defining multicultural education as the acceptance of cultural difference and the attempt to forge a greater understanding of diverse cultures.

The principles underpinning multicultural education and the practicalities of its effective implementation in the school setting have stimulated extensive debate within educational research over the past few years. With developments in multicultural education, it was necessary to develop further the understanding of racism to account for the continuing inequalities in experiences and attainment. Gillborn (1998) argued that the a definition of racism based on a degree of intentionality – that is where racially discriminatory action is conscious and deliberate – is a necessary component but not by itself sufficient. It doesn't account for the 'possibility of "unintentional" or institutional racism, where individuals and organisations act in ways that are discriminatory in their *effects*, though not in intention' (Gillborn 1998: 43). The salience and credibility of this observation was confirmed with the publication of the Macpherson Report in 1999, which identified institutionalised racism as a key issue in combating racial inequalities. The report defined institutional racism as:

> The collective failure of an organisation to provide an appropriate and professional service to people because of their colour, culture, or ethnic origin. It can be seen or detected in processes, attitudes and behaviour which amount to discrimination through unwitting prejudice, ignorance, thought-lessness and racial stereotyping which disadvantage 'minority' ethnic people.
>
> (Macpherson Report 1999: 321)

Following the publication of the Macpherson report, a range of British institutions have been subject to accusations of institutional racism, including the police force, the army, the legal profession, the National Health Service, and of course the educational system. Indeed, long before Macpherson, many writers had identified institutional racism within the educational system (Gillborn and Gipps 1996).

A key report by Gillborn and Mirza (2000), however, gives an insight of where progress has and has not been made. Before we look at the report, an important caveat to consider is that 'progress' is narrowly interpreted here as attainment in GCSEs. It thus leaves out a number of important other factors relevant in understanding racial equality in schools, such as the qualitative experiences of pupils from minority ethnic backgrounds and the type and structure of subject provision. We will return to these other factors when reviewing the impact of race on school PE and sport. Gillborn and Mirza (2000) confirm that the 1990s saw a dramatic improvement in the proportion of pupils completing their compulsory schooling with five or more GCSE higher grade passes (A–C) or their equivalent. Of the principal ethnic groups looked at: White, Indian, Pakistani, Bangladeshi, African-Caribbean, all are now more likely to attain five higher grades than ever before. This rising overall profile notwithstanding, there are less encouraging trends.

Considerable differences in attainment exist between ethnic groups, suggesting that pupils of different ethnic origin do not experience equal educational opportunities. African-Caribbean, Pakistani and Bangladeshi pupils are less likely to attain five higher grade GCSEs than their White and Indian peers. Indian pupils achieved the largest improvement in performance. Indeed, during the period from 1997 to 1998, the gap between Indian pupils and White pupils was erased. Bangladeshi pupils had also improved at the same rate as White pupils, thus leaving the pattern of inequality intact. While Black and Pakistani pupils have improved, however, it is not enough to close the gap with their white peers; in fact the gap has widened. Gillborn and Mirza conclude that 'African Caribbean and Pakistani pupils have drawn least benefit from the rising levels of attainment: the gap between them and their white peers is bigger now than a decade ago' (Gillborn and Mirza 2000: 14). Furthermore if we examine the issue of exclusions from school, once again there are some serious concerns with regards to minority ethnic groups. The rate of exclusion for African-Caribbean pupils is three times greater than for their white peers. The reasons for such an imbalance are complex but, generally speaking, research demonstrates the ways in which representations of some groups are socially constructed and, in the case of minority ethnic pupils, they are often constructed based on stereotyped assumptions about aggression (Bhavnani, *et al.* 2005). Such social constructions of various ethnic groups can see pupil referral units containing a significant number of pupils from these groups which contributes to patterns of labelling.

Disturbingly, in one large urban local education authority cited in the report, the experience of schooling proved detrimental to black pupils:

> At the start of their compulsory schooling black pupils are the highest attaining of the main ethnic groups in the LEA; recording a level of success

20 percentage points above the average for the authority. At Key Stage 2 pupils in the same group are attaining below the LEA average and in their GCSE examinations they attain 21 points below the average.

(Gillborn and Mirza 2000: 16)

Encouragingly, one of the most important findings to emerge from the report is that for each of the main ethnic groups there is at least one LEA where that group is the highest attaining. Gillborn and Mirza (2000: 9) conclude that:

It suggests that even for the groups with the most serious inequalities of attainment nationally, there are places where that trend is being bucked. The significance of this finding should not be overlooked and is a reminder of the variability of attainment and the lack of any necessary or pre-determined ethnic ordering.

Gillborn and Mirza (2000: 9)

The report, in common with most other studies on educational achievement (Abbas 2002; Haque and Bell 2001; Gillborn 2008), does not give any clues as to levels of attainment by ethnicity in PE. It would be interesting to see if the under-attainment of black pupils is replicated or contradicted in PE. It would also be useful to know how pupils of Indian and Pakistani origin fare in PE given their contrasting experiences of attainment more generally. A further issue that requires examination is the relationship between ethnicity, gender and social class. Most studies of school PE and sport focus on the impact of racial ideologies on the experience and delivery of school PE and sport, and, given the differential experiences of Britain's ethnic minorities, we would expect to see that ideologies of experiences of racism are expressed in a diversity of ways.

Race and racism in school sport and physical education

It is clearly the case that pupils of African-Caribbean background are not performing as well in schools as their White and Indian counterparts. Indeed, young people of African-Caribbean origin are over-represented in suspensions and expulsions from school and in units for pupils with emotional and behavioural difficulties (Gillborn and Gipps 1996). Assumptions about the supposed disruptive, aggressive and violent natures of youths from African-Caribbean backgrounds have informed a number of strategies intended to contain such behaviour. For example, many of the testimonies of successful black sportsmen of the 1970s and early 1980s recalled how they were encouraged by their teachers to concentrate on sport at the expense of their academic studies (Cashmore 1982). Such personal accounts were further exemplified by a study conducted by Carrington and Wood (1983) that illustrated how school teachers used school sport as a tool of social control over black pupils. By encouraging them to do well in PE and play school sport – physical activities in which black pupils were seen as most likely to excel – it was felt that their self-esteem would improve. Furthermore, the teachers would be better able to secure their peaceful compliance in the classroom by threatening to prevent black pupils from access to sport.

What these studies show is the need to situate the experience of PE and sport in its context, because they clearly illustrate how success in sport can be the consequence of racial ideologies. As Back and Solomos point out (2009: 230):

> ...[r]acist discourses need to be rigorously contextualised. This means that racism needs to be situated within specific moments. The effect of a particular racist discourse needs to be placed in the conditions surrounding the moment of its enunciation.
>
> Back and Solomos (2009: 230)

Hoberman's *Darwins Athletes* (1997) has reminded us of the importance of this approach with his devastating, though ultimately flawed, analysis (see Carrington and McDonald 2001: 10–12, for a critique) of the deleterious impact of black athletic success in the USA. The sub-title of his book neatly encapsulates his argument: 'How sport has damaged black America and preserved the myth of race'. For Hoberman, the over-emphasis on achievement in sport may be reflected in success at school level but, for the vast majority of young blacks, it will not lead to success in professional sports. Furthermore, such a 'sports-fixation' directly contributes to an anti-intellectualism in the black community and black under-achievement in schools.

The theoretical significance of this observation is that it is naïve to correlate racism simply to levels of exclusion from sport and low attainment in PE. It may well be those high levels of attainments in PE and success in school sport are related to processes of racial stereotyping. An adequate understanding of racism, then, should not only refer to negative impacts and characterisations, but should also include 'seemingly positive characteristics':

> [n]egatively evaluated characteristics include such instances of biological and intentional racist discourse as 'black children are not as clever as white children', but excludes such seemingly positive though biological statements as 'black children are good at sports'. While this latter assertion can lead to individual and/or group short-term enhancement (an unmerited place in the school football team for the individual or enhanced status for the group as a whole in an environment where prowess at sport is highly regarded), it is potentially racist and likely to have racist consequences. This is because, like most stereotypes, it is distorted and misleading and typically appears as part of a discourse which works to justify the channelling of black children into sport, rather than academic activities.
>
> (Cole 1998: 41)

Hayes and Sugden (1999) showed how the PE profession still considers some aspects of performance in PE and sport by ethnic groups as being founded in racial ideology. They challenged this notion and identified the racial stereotypes this may reinforce, and may be implicated in the under-achievement of black pupils:

The physiological mythology surrounding blacks in sport seems deeply entrenched within the physical education profession. This evokes a set of beliefs on behalf of teachers and pupils which maintains a mutually reinforcing and vicious circle.

(Hayes and Sugden 1999: 105)

While racial ideologies help to explain the over-representation and narrow focus on sport amongst youngsters of African-Caribbean background, a different set of racial ideologies frames the discussion of the lack of participation of South Asians in sport generally and school sport specifically (Burdsey 2007). For example, Fleming's research (1991, 1995) on South Asian male youth and sport has highlighted how the existence of stereotypes about Asian physical frailty and cultural priorities have adversely impacted upon the school-based experiences of Asian male youths. His research showed that rather than bringing different communities together, sport and PE instead provide an opportunity for the dominant ethnic group, the white pupils, to racially bully and abuse South Asian pupils. The South Asian pupils in turn adopted various coping strategies such as avoiding school sport and internalising the stereotypes. Fleming outlines the different ways that racism is experienced and responded to according to the religious, class, and linguistic backgrounds of the pupils. Such differences in cultural responses, however, should not lead to a preoccupation with the differences in cultural backgrounds, as 'the preoccupation with cultural difference is a diversion and a distraction from the most fundamental issue – the pervasive impact of racism in all its guises' (Fleming 1994: 172).

Without a critical understanding of the nature and development of stereotypes, PE teachers are more vulnerable to such myths, especially when they seem to be confirmed by the limited number of role models from the South Asian community in high profile sports such as football (Bains and Patel 1995; Burdsey 2007; Johal 2001). As with pupils of African-Caribbean background, success in some sports can actually serve to perpetuate racial ideologies. As a result, the successes of some South Asians in activities like cricket and badminton serve to bolster ideas that they are good only at sports that require limited or no contact. Pedagogically, the concern is that as Fleming (1995) suggests:

Perceived aptitude for a particular sport became the basis on which many schools focused their PE curricula to accommodate a large South Asian population in the school. That is to say, emphasis was placed on those activities that were considered popular with south Asian and other ethno-cultural groups, invariably cricket and hockey. Indeed, assertions based upon 'natural ability' which has been overwhelmingly rejected elsewhere has become prominent as an expedient rationalisation of the situation. Some south Asians have internalised the self-image and even 'swallowed the myth' themselves.

Fleming (1995: 40)

The gender aspects of ethnicity were focused on by Benn (2000) in her research on South Asian females. Benn notes the difficulties that occur when cultural norms conflict with traditional practices in a PE department. For example, dress codes are often considered as indicators of standards within departments, which can be problematic. The adherence to a specific form of dress attire in PE and sport in schools is felt to be appropriate by professionals in terms of its health and safety in practical activities. This conflicts, however, with a cultural norm shared by many South Asian, especially Muslim, girls that requires them to cover most parts of the body and to avoid public nudity, even amongst members of the same sex. This clearly poses challenges during practical mixed-sex classes as well as in the pre- and post-lesson environment in the changing rooms, and points to the importance of Initial Teacher Training in preparing PE teachers for the challenges of delivering an equitable and just educational experience for all pupils.

Conclusion: the importance of Initial Teacher Education

One vehicle which might be considered as an area in which a number of the issues discussed in this chapter might be addressed is the training process for teachers, particularly newly qualified teachers. Although there are now a number of routes through which to gain your qualified teaching status, the standards that need to be demonstrated are consistent across these routes (Hayes *et al.* 2008). With this in mind it may be interesting to examine in a little more depth the role of Initial Teacher Education (ITE), specifically the experiences of those teachers from a minority ethnic minority background in their training processes. A recent study by Flintoff (2008) highlighted a number of issues in relation to the ethnicity of people studying to become a PE teacher which seem to replicate some of the experiences that pupils have in schools. Three of the black male students had experienced assumption-making stereotypical comments in relation to their ethnicity. An example of one of the students is given below, where the student states:

> Obviously you just get normal things that happen in everyday life, but nothing … Well, if we're playing, in our practical activities, like before anyone' seen me play, I'm getting picked first, so like … When we was doing athletics. No one had ever seen me run at this uni [university] because I did boxing and you don't see anyone running and no one off my class ever went to boxing. But we were doing athletics and I was just assumed to be the fastest for 100, so I had to get videoed.
>
> (Flintoff 2008:52).

Swimming also received a significant mention in the study as being an area of the curriculum where there was a degree of discomfort and stereotypical implications afforded to students from different ethnic backgrounds.

Gaine (2001) argues – correctly in our opinion – that 'schools that recognise "race" and ethnicity as issues are more likely to be successful in serving minority pupils' needs than a "colourblind" approach' (2001: 119). Although racial equality is accepted as an ideal in education, it is not clear how far it is embedded in the structures of school provision and in professional practices. This makes it even more important that newly qualified teachers are aware of equity issues and inclusive practices. As Tomlinson and Craft acknowledge, 'if such matters are not addressed in initial teacher training they are unlikely in future to be addressed anywhere' (1995: 10). There is evidence, however, that 'neither initial nor in-service training pays sufficient attention to race and racism issues' (Richardson and Wood 2000: 35). It is an observation that is confirmed by our investigations into the amount of time spent on multiculturalism and ethnicity on undergraduate courses taken by trainee PE teachers. As expected, all of the institutions we contacted covered issues of multiculturalism and ethnicity, because they are required to do so by the Training and Development Agency (TDA). Most of the institutions were able to show that they satisfy TTA requirements by showing that they were being covered *somewhere*, albeit for just a couple of hours within a full degree programme. Only a small minority went beyond this tokenistic approach, with evidence of a more sustained and developmental engagement with the issues.

Trainee PE teachers need to have a sound sociological understanding of how race, ethnicity and racism operate within society, schools and in the curriculum, and an awareness of the Equality Act 2010 in order to understand their professional role in this area of practice. This is not just a question of technique that can be left to 'professional practice', based on a superficial understanding of different cultures. What we are advocating is the incorporation of anti-racist education that encourages teachers to:

> Engage in 'critical reflection' to question their own practice and that of their schools, with a commitment to working within a morality of social justice and egalitarianism and a concomitant determination to raise issues of racism and anti-racism within the classroom, the school and society.
>
> (Waller *et al.* 2001: 166)

It is a call for teachers to become more self-reflexive so that they understand the complex dynamics of racism and multiculturalism, and can deliver PE and sport that eschews stereotyping and actively combats all forms of racism. To do anything less would mean our newly qualified teachers would continue to be ill-prepared to question established structures of provision, unable to challenge entrenched stereotypical thinking and, therefore, culpable in perpetuating a culture of racial inequality in school PE and sport. One could take the view of FIFA President, Sepp Blatter, where a handshake would suffice in order to undo any racial wrongdoing. We, however, feel that a more in depth and concerted approach is required to challenge racism in its many forms.

We would like to thank Ian McDonald for his contribution.

References

Abbas, T. (2002) 'The Home and the School in the Educational Achievement of South Asians', *Race, Ethnicity and Education*, 5(3), 291–316.

Abbas, T. (ed.) (2005) *Muslim Britain: Communities Under Pressure*, London: Zed Books.

Allen, C. (2010) *Islamophobia* Farnham: Ashgate.

Back, L. and Solomos, J. (2009) 'Introduction: Theorising Race and Racism', in Back, L. and Solomos, J. (eds) *Theories of Race and Racism: a Reader* (2nd edn), London: Routledge.

Bains, J. and Patel, R. (1995) *Asians Can't Play Football*, Midlands Asian Sports Forum.

Barker, M. (1981) *The New Racism*, London: Junction Books.

BBC (2011) 'State Multiculturalism has Failed, says David Cameron', www.bbc.co.uk/news/uk-politics-12371994

Benn, T. (2000) 'Towards Inclusion in Education and Physical Education', in Williams, A. (ed.) *Primary School Physical Education*, London: Routledge.

Bhattacharyya, G., Gabriel, J. and Small, S. (2002) *Race and Power: Global racism in the twenty-first century*, London: Routledge.

Bhavnani, R. Mirza, H. S. and Meetoo, V. (2005) *Tackling the Roots of Racism: Lessons for success*, Bristol: Policy Press.

Blair, M. and Cole, M. (2002) 'Racism and Education', in Cole, M. (ed.) *Education, Equality and Human Rights*, London: RoutledgeFalmer.

Burdsey, D. (2007) *British Asians and Football: Culture, Identity, Exclusion*, London: Routledge.

Burdsey, D. (2011) 'That joke isn't funny anymore: racial microaggressions, colour-blind ideology and the mitigation of racism in English cricket', *Sociology of Sport Journal*, 28(3), 261–83.

Cantle, T. (2008) *Community Cohesion: A New Framework for Race and Diversity (Second Edition)*, Basingstoke: Palgrave.

Carrington, Ben and McDonald, I. (2001) *'Race', Sport and British Society*, London: Routledge.

Carrington, Bruce and Wood, E. (1983) 'Body Talk: images of sport in a multi-racial school', *Multiracial Education*, 11(2), 29–38.

Cashmore, E. (1982) *Black Sportsmen*, London: Routledge and Kegan Paul.

Cole, M. (1998) 'Racism, Reconstructed Multiculturalism and Antiracist Education', *Cambridge Journal of Education*, 28(1), 37–48.

Equality Act (2010), London: HMSO.

Fleming, S. (1991) 'Sport Schooling and the Asian Male Youth Culture', in Jarvie, G. (ed.) *Sport Racism and Ethnicity*, London: Falmer Press: 30–58.

Fleming, S. (1994) 'Sport and South Asian youth: the perils of false universalism and stereotyping', *Leisure Studies*, 13: 159–77.

Fleming, S. (1995) *'Home and Away': sport and South Asian male youth*, Aldershot: Avebury.

Flintoff, A. (2008) 'Black and Minority Ethnic Trainees' Experiences of Physical Education Initial Teacher Training: Report to the Training and Development Agency', Carnegie Research Institute Leeds Metropolitan University.

Fryer, P. (2010) *Staying Power: the History of Black People in Britain*, London: Pluto Press.

Gaine, C. (2001) 'Promoting Equality and Equal Opportunities: school policies', in Hill, D. and Cole, M. (eds) *Schooling and Equality*, London: Kogan Page.

Garner, S. (2010) *Racisms: an Introduction*, London: Sage.

Gillborn, D. (1998) 'Racism and the politics of qualitative research: learning from controversy and critique', in Connolly, P. and Troyna, B. (eds), *Researching Racism in Education: Politics, Theory and Practice*, Buckingham: Oxford University Press.

Gillborn, D. (2008) *Racism and Education: Coincidence or Conspiracy?* Abingdon: Routledge.

Gillborn, D. and Gipps, C. (1996) *Recent Research on the Achievements of Ethnic Minority Pupils*, Ofsted Report, London: HMSO.

Gillborn, D. and Mirza, H. F. (2000) *Educational Inequality Mapping Race, Class and Gender*, Ofsted Report, London: HMSO.

Gilroy, P. (1987) *'There Ain't No Black in the Union Jack': the cultural politics of race and nation*, London: Routledge.

Gilroy, P. (2004) *After Empire: Melancholia or Convivial Culture?* London: Routledge.

Hall, S., Critcher, C., Jefferson, T., Clarke, J. and Roberts, B. (1978) *Policing the Crisis: mugging, the state, and law and order*, London: Macmillan.

Haque, Z. and Bell, J. F. (2001) 'Evaluating the Performances of Minority Ethnic Pupils in Secondary Schools', *Oxford Review of Education*, 27(3), 357–68.

Hayes, S., Capel, S., Katene, W. and Cook, P. (2008) 'An Examination of Knowledge Prioritisation in Secondary Physical Education Teacher Education Courses', *Teaching and Teacher Education*, 24: 330–42.

Hayes, S. and Sugden, J. (1999) 'Winning Through "Naturally" Still? An analysis of the perceptions held by physical education teachers towards the performance of black pupils in school sport and in the classroom', *Race, Ethnicity and Education*, 2(1), 93–107.

Hesse, B. (ed.) (2000) *Un/Settled Multiculturalisms: diasporas, entanglement, transruptions*, London: Zed Press.

Hoberman, J. (1997) *Darwin's Athletes: how sport has damaged black America and preserved the myth of race*, Boston: Mariner Books.

Johal, S. (2001) 'Playing their own game: a South Asian football experience' in Carrington, B. and McDonald, I. (eds) *'Race', Sport and British Society*, London: Routledge.

Kundnani, A. (2007) *The End of Tolerance: Racism in 21st century Britain*, London: Pluto Press.

Macpherson, Sir W. (1999) *The Stephen Lawrence Inquiry: report on the inquiry by Sir William Macpherson of Cluny*, Cmd 4262, London: HMSO.

Mahamdallie, H. (2002) 'Racism: myths and realities', *International Socialism Journal*, 95: 3–39.

Malik, K. (1996) *The Meaning of Race: race, history and culture in Western societies*, London: Macmillan.

Müller, F., van Zoonen, L. and de Roode, L. (2007) 'Accidental racists: Experiences and contradictions of racism in local Amsterdam soccer fan culture', *Soccer and Society*, 8(2/3), 335–50.

Panayi, P. (2010) *An Immigration History of Britain: Multicultural Racism since 1800*, Harlow: Longman.

Richardson, R. and Wood, A. (2000) *Inclusive Schools, Inclusive Society*, Stoke-on-Trent: Trentham.

Rose, S. (1998) *Lifelines: biology, freedom, determinism*, London: Penguin.

Runnymede Trust (2000) *Commission on the Future of Multi-Ethnic Britain*, www.runnymedetrust.org/meb/TheReport.htm

Schuster, L. and Solomos, J. (2004) 'Race, immigration and asylum: New Labour's agenda and its consequences', *Ethnicities*, 4(2), 267–300.

Short, G. and Carrington, B. (1998) 'Reconstructing Multicultural Education: a response to Mike Cole', *Cambridge Journal of Education*, 28(2), 231–4.

Solomos, J. (1993) *Race and Racism in Britain* (2nd edn), Basingstoke: Macmillan.

Sparrow, A. and Owen, P. (2010) 'Minister: ethnic minorities "no longer automatically disadvantaged"', *The Guardian*, 14 January.

Swann Report, Cmnd 9543 (1985) *Education for All: the report of the Committee of Inquiry into the education of children from ethnic minority groups*, London: HMSO.

Tomlinson, S. and Craft, M. (1995) 'Education for All in the 1990s', in Tomlinson, S. and Craft, M. (eds) *Ethnic Relations and Schooling: policy and practice in the 1990s*, London: Athlone: 1–11.

Travis, A. (2010) 'John Denham's subtler approach to race and class carries new risk', *The Guardian*, 14 January.

Waller, T., Cole, M. and Hill, D. (2001) 'Race', in Hill, D. and Cole, M. (eds) *Schooling and Equality*, London: Kogan Page: 161-85.

Witte, R. (1996) *Racist Violence and the State*, London: Longman.

9 Physical education and social class

John Evans and Alan Bairner

I am completely useless at all PE and sports, I hated it at school with a passion and the humiliation I suffered at every session stayed with me forever. I was the last to be chosen by the team captains, I was bright enough to understand why (I was useless, why would they want me as a member of their team, I was a handicap!), no one wanted to be my partner. I was told that it was the taking part that counted – they must have thought I was really stupid, have you ever heard of a sportsman not aiming to win? I particularly hated team games and cross-country running (always came in last!). As I got older I tried to avoid it wherever possible. I was good at other things of course, music and academic aspects were my thing but I do remember how awful the whole games/PE thing was. As a teacher, I always remembered that and never ever let that happen to any child in my care (I always picked teams and partners and allowed no discussion about it!).

www.netmums.com/coffeehouse/general-coffeehouse-chat-514/
coffee-lounge-18/584895-who-hated-sports-days-pe-school.html
Accessed 11 July 2011

Form is temporary; class is permanent

Why should physical educationalists be concerned with social class? Is talk about class any longer relevant to today's practitioners of PE, sport and health (PESH)? If class is inscribed in formal education through the practices of PESH then, what implications are there for the actions and identities of young people in and outside schools? To be sure, significant socio-economic change of the last 50 or more years has both obscured and eroded some of the more obvious and corrosive features of social class. For this, and a number of other reasons, it has become unfashionable across the social sciences to make too much of class (Bairner 2007). We will however, argue that class still matters in the lives of young people, determining both their opportunities and outlook on life. It is enacted in education and PESH not only through the configuration and distribution of cultural capital *qua* academic qualifications and (physical) 'ability' but also via the allocation of symbolic value to these and other social processes, and in all kinds of schools (Fitz *et al.* 2006). Indeed, we would like to suggest that class, more than any other social category, forces us to think again about the nature of 'ability' and how it is recognised, configured and distributed, to whom, where and why in PESH. It ought also to be intimately connected to what we do either as teachers, coaches or health practitioners, in addressing these issues in the names of social justice, education and, not least, PESH.

It has been argued (Evans and Davies 2006) that class is not to be thought of simply as a discursive artefact, a category, or construction of either governments' or academics' classificatory schemes, to be embraced as an add-on with other crucial social categories of race, gender and age. But rather, a visceral reality, constituted by a set of affectively loaded, social and economic relationships that are likely to strongly influence, if not determine and dominate, people's lives. These involve dynamic processes within and across many social sites or fields of practice (Bourdieu 1986) particularly in families and schools. Commenting on the issue of racial and ethnic integration in contemporary British society, Younge (2005: 23) argues, 'A decent job with a decent income is still the best path out of the crudest forms of racism and fundamentalism. Polls and studies show a link between wealth and the propensity to integrate'. Much of the debate in the United States and beyond in the wake of Hurricane Katrina, concentrated on the extent to which African Americans were most seriously affected. The fact is though, that poor people in general were the victims. That the overwhelming majority of those affected in New Orleans were black demands additional analysis, however, this should not detract from the reality that poor whites were equally damaged and that class was the single most important factor as to whether one was able to escape from the hurricane or not.

Social and economic relationships are increasingly consolidated, organised and reshaped ethereally through the use of various technologies (websites, mobile phones and the like). They are not just processes in which orientations to the body are nurtured, expressed, some rejected others assimilated, affirmed and endorsed – but locations of opportunity and cost where physical and intellectual capital is distributed and legitimated and sometimes withheld. It is class that has long (maybe even more in Britain and, specifically, England than elsewhere) guided our views of 'others' as of more or less value; and led us to pass judgement on their food, drink, clothes, houses, shapes, the way they treat their children and even their pets. For many, 'let not thy children be or become working class', remains a mantra, as evident/pertinent now as it was some half century ago:

> The English attitude toward Education has been somewhat similar. The moment they could afford it, ambitious parents have relieved their offspring of the need to travel the educational road in the standard vehicles provided by public instruction, and entrusted them to the private school – in the conviction that these would convey them faster and further and to altogether more advantageous points *d'appui* for their pilgrimage through. It might be merely a matter of sending the small tradesman son to the local grammar school, where he would pick some Greek, a few intonations in his speech, and clerkly ambitions for his future …
>
> (Lewis and Maude 1953: 186)

The quality of the system of English private (including public, 'private' and grammar) schools is the result of concentrating boys and girls, mainly from the middle classes, in one set of schools. The schools in part reinforce, in part correct, and in part build upon the product of the middle class home; and for that very reason they have the power to convert limited numbers of children from other than middle-class homes into middle class personalities.

(ibid.: 195)

The notion that 'the middle class' (which itself needs to be treated as a differentiated category) offers more civilised, refined, disciplined and altogether better values than do the working classes, remains deep-rooted in the public psyche, particularly of those peddling such views. Such claims, as distasteful now as they were over 50 years ago, continue to nurture class envy, prop up highly unequal and differentiated forms of schooling – the better public (fee paying) schools seen (correctly because of their rich resourcing) as offering routes to not only bright economic futures, wealth and health but also distinction and separation from the purportedly less disciplined, aspirationally deficient, irresponsible, culturally impoverished working class.

Useless middle-class soccer kids consoled with promise of nicer lives

▨ 5th October

After a severe thrashing from yet another tough looking school, the bruised and demoralised middle class boys from St Jude's felt like giving up altogether.

The team of eleven-year olds had just lost 12–0, with several of the boys coming off in tears because their opponents had 'barged past them', 'been too rough' and 'kicked the ball hard on purpose'. But at the end of full time, Jack Randle the team coach and father of hapless goalkeeper Timmy, gave the miserable squad an uplifting team talk… 'you may have lost 12–nil today against this big bunch of bullies, but lets get things in perspective. You're going to have much nicer lives than them. They're going to be poor. You are all going to get well paid jobs in a warm dry office. They are going to have to lift heavy things in the rain for a pittance. One day, some of those eleven year old thugs laughing over there may develop poverty-related diseases or become drug addicts from their time in prison. Who are the losers, boys: them or you?'

(O'Farrell, 2009: 110, 'The News Before it Happens' www.rbooks.co.uk)

Figure 9.1 O'Farrell's (2009) spoof news of item 1

As O'Farrell's (2009) spoof news items highlight, schools are not just contexts in which orientations to the body are rehearsed , but platforms for opportunity and cost (see below).

Yet, for all its impact on our daily lives, class has become something of a forbidden topic in PE research (and wider areas in PESH), somewhat overtaken by others (gender, race, sexuality) in the conceptual fashion parade. It just does not seem to cross, or even surface as an explanatory category in some people's minds. This silence arises partly because class had been sanitised and obscured in wider public discourse, educational policy and practice, occluded by a language of 'lifestyle', 'partnerships', 'disadvantage' and 'social exclusion'. It is, therefore, not surprising that when identifying inequalities in education all too few teachers or students name the problem directly in terms of social class (Lynch and Lodge 2002: 55). Yet, to look at gender, age, or ethnicity, among others, without mention of class is like talking about football without mentioning pitch dimensions, size of the goal mouth, or the weight and shape of the ball (Evans and Davies 2006).

Talking class

Despite claims made by some that 'class no longer matters' (and as mentioned, very often it does not for the ideologically cushioned folk making the claims), facts around health, longevity, opportunity and wealth tend to speak for themselves and have powerful bearing on people's lives (www.archive.official-document 02/02/2006). In health, as in PE and sport, being 'middle class' offers massive advantage if your goal is either to achieve healthy longevity or perform in top level sport.

> According to a report leaked last week, more than a third of British competitors at the London Olympics in 2012 will hail from private schools – a staggering number when you consider that only 7 per cent of children are educated in the independent sector. But consider this, too: a full 58 per cent of athletes who won Gold at the 2004 Olympics in Athens were educated at private schools, including a good few from the super-elite public schools such as Eton.
>
> (Syed 2010, 1)

So, again, we might ask: why and how is this so? If an explanation is required, need we look further than the example of Wellington College in Berkshire, England, annual fees for attendance at which are around £30,000 in a country in which the average wage is £25,000 a year? The school has 16 rugby pitches, two floodlit astroturf pitches, a state-of-the-art sports hall, 22 hard tennis courts, 12 cricket pitches, an athletics track, two lacrosse pitches, six netball courts, a shooting range, and a nine-hole golf course (Benn 2011). Compare this with Lilian Baylis Technology School in south London – 'a good school with outstanding features' according to Ofsted – where about 75% of pupils receive free school meals, and a far higher percentage of pupils than the national average have special educational needs (Benn 2011). It is little wonder that Olympic success may seem infinitely more accessible when the future is viewed from Wellington's 400 acres of English countryside than from Kennington Lane in inner-city London. (But contrast this with the 'hungry-for-it'/skint family footballer myth mentioned elsewhere in this chapter).

Given such contrasting educational circumstances, would anyone now claim that the 'middle classes' are more 'naturally gifted', inherently (genetically) better endowed with more 'talent' (sporting and academic) than the rest of the population, as did leading politicians Lewis and Maude (1953) over half a century ago? Their analyses of class offering:

> A critical survey of the history, present condition and prospects of the middle classes, from whom come most of the nations brains, leadership and organising ability ...
>
> (Lewis and Maude 1953)

Or, are the 'middle classes' simply better equipped, by virtue of upbringing in relatively richly resourced families and schools, to access resources (knowledge, skills, values and opportunities) required to display, or perform, the 'ability' or 'talent' which bring recognition and 'success' in education, sport, health (sic) in and outside schools? If so, how is PESH implicated in processes of this kind?

Down memory lane

PE and school sport have always mattered greatly in the process of schooling; they have signified and celebrated, elevated and excluded, laid down the rules of belonging to our gender and class faction. Indeed our personal experiences as school children offer some testimony at least to how class once was enacted powerfully and explicitly in different kinds of schooling intended to produce distinctive kinds of experience, identity and outcome. Some years ago, for example, Evans (1988) reported:

> It seems like an aeon since, as a small, cold, blue-kneed schoolboy, I took (or more precisely, was taken) to the rugby field at my Welsh valley grammar school. There I learned not only the act of running leaning sideways without trying, such was the incline of the pitch at the time, but also to dread and fear the violence of The Game as much as the possibility of revealing such cowardice to my teachers, peers and friends. Worse still in a school where rugby ruled, my distaste for The Game was matched only by my delirious attachment to that other boys' sport – soccer – a game ruthlessly religiously outlawed by the culture of my school. To play soccer was to go looking for trouble, to court instant ignominy and invite the status if deviant. It was, especially if one had the ability to play The Game, a denial of ones' duties, a betrayal of one's school, friends, community and country. After all it was The Game that celebrated our school's and county's status, that demarcated the boundaries and announced the qualities of our subculture and our precise class position. It was The Game that would help us mingle with the posh and

the proletariat, that told us we were the 'tidier' (the more respectable) within our working class. Just down the road, four miles away, the unfortunates in their secondary modern, who had unluckily failed to master the massive meritocratic hurdle, the hated eleven plus, could play the commoner game – soccer – a game of no passion, no quality, requiring no courage or character. And for all we knew and cared, in our sister single sex grammar, as in the coeducational secondary modern, girls into sport didn't go.

Bairner's experience offered evidence of similar class distinction and reward:

> PE or gym as we called it, with considerable childish amusement when we came to be taught by a new teacher whose name was also Jim, was a relatively inconsequential part of our lives in the selective grammar school in a small town in central Scotland. Two classes a week during which nothing much happened and certainly nothing that appeared classed in its meanings or implications. The twins with muscular bodies who could walk on their hands were undeniably middle-class but that alone cannot explain the animosity which the handful of boys from working-class families felt towards them. After all, the middle-class pupils hated them as well! Sport, however, was a different matter altogether. In an area traditionally renowned for producing talented footballers, including John Thomson and George Connelly of Celtic and Scotland and Jim Baxter of Rangers and Scotland, to name but three, boys at our school were denied the opportunity to play our favourite game. Instead we learned to play rugby union. Even at the time, it was obvious to us that this was part of a wider agenda to enhance our social standing. But this project backfired spectacularly when we visited Edinburgh's merchant schools (George Heriot's, George Watson's, Daniel Stewart's) and saw what real middle-class education looked like. More sobering still was the realisation that often they would ask their second fifteen to play our firsts and so on down the fixture list. In rugby, as in life, we were beneath them. Even further above us were the really posh schools such as Edinburgh Academy, Tony Blair's *alma mater* Fettes College, and Glenalmond in Perthshire against whom we were not even allowed to play.

PE and school sport, then, have always mattered greatly in the process of schooling, in the UK; albeit differently configured in Wales, Scotland, Ireland, and England and elsewhere; they have signified and celebrated, elevated and excluded, laid down the rules of belonging to our gender and class faction. But is it still so? Visit that same Welsh valleys school today, some 40 or so years on and one finds not a selective all boys grammar but a thriving co-ed comprehensive. And, remarkably, given 'the authority' once afforded the game; where once stood rugby posts, soccer posts stand proud, with girls and boys freely playing on previously boys own, hallowed terrain. Soccer – the lesser game – given equal footing, perhaps even privileged over rugby, finding place in the curriculum alongside many other cultural forms. In Bairner's old school, once a grammar now also a comprehensive, football is dominant, as it is in many schools throughout Scotland, in keeping, one might argue, with popular demand. One consequence of this, however, is that today Scottish rugby is less socially mixed than at any time since the end of the Second World War with damaging implications for the national team's level of performance and unleavened by any concomitant gain in terms of Scotland's status in world football. So, how are we to read such turns of events? As seismic shift in cultural tastes, reflection of the dissolution of intra-class and gender hierarchies and differences, evidence of the democratisation of social life and sport both in the Principality (Wales) and elsewhere? Or, chimera; greater opportunity and choice hiding, while reconfiguring old class and cultural hierarchies beneath the surface appearance of new allegiances and a diversification of sport and leisure interests within the UK? So, again we ask, does social class still matter? Does PE and school sport play a part in the production and reproduction of social hierarchies and inequalities; if so, in what way? Are young people faced with equal opportunities to engage in whatever sport they chose? Have they the 'mobility' and opportunity to chose and access physical activity and leisure opportunities (and by extension, to be healthy) both in and outside schools. After all, 'mobility is a resource to which not everyone has an equal relationship' (Skeggs 2004: 49; Morley 2000, in Sheller and Urry 2006: 211). If social class no longer matters, then how might we explain the classed patterns reported above in health, Olympic sport and indeed in participation in physical activity outside schools?

Intersections

Of course, class alone is not the only identity that matters, and class analysis should necessarily embrace all other social processes and identities with which class always and inevitably intersects (for example, ethnicity, gender, age and sexuality) to generate associated injustices and opportunities (Azzarito, *et al.* 2005; Flintoff *et al.* 2008). But in every case class gives these identities a particular edge (Connolly 2006). Ignore it and all kind of superficial claims can be made, for example, that in terms or academic qualification girls are no longer an educational issue, that what matters most is the educational underachievement of boys, or conversely that, in PESH, boys are not an issue, it is girls that matter, in need of special resources and attention to get them into exercise in and outside school. Invoke class and the fashionable fallacies of such claims are soon revealed, for not all boys, or all girls are advantaged or disadvantaged in education and PESH and, in that which occurs, class conditions and mediates. In the last instance it is the most important determinant of opportunity and identity, both in and outside schools. And we are unlikely to appreciate the complexity of class reproduction through the allocation of physical and symbolic capital unless we adopt relational perspectives, not only between gender, class and ethnicity but, critically, between families, labour processes and schools (Fitz *et al.* 2006). Having done that, we then need to foreground them against a landscape both saturated with policy and pervaded by media (e.g., books, TV, websites) which increasingly reach into and regulate every aspect of our lives[1].

Class configurations in the discourse of PESH

Much of the interest in social class within the PESH and wider educational research communities, historically, has emanated from social mobility and social reproduction theories (Fitz *et al.* 2006; Green *et al.* 2005a, b)[2] while, more recently, 'the politics of identity' (or, broadly, 'post structuralism') has reinvigorated and supplemented such concerns. The politics of identity is primarily concerned with the social re-production of class interests through the discursive production of identity, while the politics of opportunity draws attention to recognition, selection and distribution of dispositions (called 'ability') through the practices of families and schools. In our view, both the politics of identity and opportunity and distribution are required in any analyses of education if the story of class is to be adequately told. As Lynch and Lodge (2002) remind us however, the problems for many groups, such as women and ethnic minorities (e.g., in school PESH) are not simply problems of recognition (of identity) but also problems of redistribution of opportunity, resource, obligation and responsibility. Indeed, we might consider that class differences and opportunities to achieve in PESH are established long before children get to school.

Family dynamics and the economics of class inequality: the ability to pay for physical 'ability'

It is evidently the case that some sections of the population in the UK are much better able than others to research and take advantage of the education and physical education opportunities (e.g., informal and privately-funded early learning provision such as '*Tumbletots*', or activity and sport based summer schools) available outside schools in order to invest their children with academic, social and physical capital (see Vincent and Ball 2007; Reay 1998, Reay *et al.* 2008; Gillies 2007; Evans and Davies 2010). Drawing on his previous work with Caroline Vincent, Ball (2009) for example, points to a number of factors that facilitate middle class families' retention of their educational social position which apply equally well to achieving recognition as being 'able' and reproducing high participation levels in sport and health related behaviours once outside schools. For example, their decision-making strategies are less likely to be constrained by factors such as a lack of resources and disincentives, the need to work unsocial hours, earn immediate income, attitudes to debt and absence of experience or familiarity with role-models than many families in lower socio-economic groups. Moreover, some, but not all (see Reay *et al.* 2008) middle-class parents seek out opportunities to maintain educational social advantages for their children, including using resources to ensure that they are able to develop correct forms of embodiment, 'in so doing, they may limit the opportunities available to working-class children, for instance, inflating the costs of accessing physical culture' (ibid. 8). These conditions may have long been prevailing contingencies of inequality in PE, sport and health, but in contemporary culture *increasing* amounts of the 'work of learning' in order to become appropriately embodied

– slim and active and/or physically literate in physical activity and sport – is and has to be done outside school, in and around the home, as part of what Evans and Davies (2010) have called the *'corporealisation of childhood'*. As Ball (2009) noted with reference to academic credentials, 'access to much of this "learning work" costs time and money and demands particular sorts of energy and social resources borne more realistically by some sections of the population than others'. Again, there is nothing new in this; historically different social classes have always invested heavily but differently in particular forms of physical capital for their offspring. However, as more and more people (are expected to) aspire to a common set of sport and/or health behaviours, itself to be regarded as a democratisation of interests (normatively configured as taking action to eat properly, exercise and lose weight), we may well have exacerbated inequality and highlighted that *deficits* not *differences* that underlie it in terms of sport and health outcomes.

As in education generally, increasingly demanding strategic and navigational skills are needed to access and manage children's learning and acquisition of physical culture/capital out of school, as sport/activity routes become more formal and complex. Parents in the UK now operate within a market in educational services which is no longer simply a matter of choice and competition between educational institutions and the different forms of PE/sport which they provide. For example, in England, between specialist sport colleges, private and mainstream state schools there exists 'a diffuse, expanding and sophisticated system of goods and services, experiences and routes – publicly and privately provided' (Ball 2009: 8). In such terms the acquisition of corporeal capital is now provided by a combination of transmissions at school, in families and those 'bought in' from the market. Access to these things simply and fundamentally may depend upon the amount of economic capital available to families to exploit the opportunities available, in a culture where there is now 'a seething and swarming of official discourse around parenting' (p. 9), exacerbated by a plethora of media and public policy messages intended to convey to parents that they and their offspring face imminent danger and 'risk', not just of being subjected to lowered educational standards and of 'falling behind' in the educational marketplace but also of falling prey to contemporary maladies, such as obesity, drug abuse, deviant behaviour, and so on, unless they take steps to intervene actively to counter them (Evans *et al.* 2005). As Vincent and Ball's (2007) research attests, even good schools and teachers are no longer considered to be worthy of trust *on their own* to deliver advantage and effective social reproduction. In Ball's terms, 'the prudential parent' (ibid. 8) can 'no longer take on trust either state services or, indeed, their own intuitive parenting as adequate in providing the kind of childhood which will ensure their child opportunities, advantages, happiness and well being'. The 'good parent' must be both prepared and willing to 'enact responsibilities for their child through their engagement with the market' (ibid. 9). Given this climate, it is not at all surprising that increasingly parents seek, but only some are able to secure, physical educational opportunities for their children through a mix of state and private institutions. And given that parents seek out such opportunities to maintain social advantages for their children, so too a new generation of specialist childhood PE/sport advisers and services have come into play and thrive on the commercial exploitation of their anxieties. Such service may 'offer advice while fuelling fears' (for example, in relation to diet, exercise and obesity), giving rise to a new form of inequality, 'the inequality of dealing with insecurity and reflexivity' (Beck 1992: 98; cited in Ball 2009, 9).

So again we ask of schools and PESH within them, do they simply build upon or interrupt processes such as these? Do they actually reduce 'ability' differentials between children, i.e. alter or improve the physical literacy levels which children bring to schools, particularly of those who cannot access opportunities for physical education/activity pre- and alongside school? Or simply build upon and expand them? Are schools inevitably destined to both differentiate and consolidate simultaneously, i.e., making people/pupils different (by invoking categories of 'ability' or performance) while creating the illusion that they are all much the same? Does PESH, through its practices of sieving and sorting, of privileging particular body orientations through the curriculum, 'preserve structural relations between social groups but change structural relationships between individuals to create the impression of general and probable movement' (Bernstein 1996: 11, quoted in Fitz *et al.* 2006: 11).[3]

Reconfiguring social reproduction: health and the embodiment of class difference

Class analyses have recently focused on how contemporary health imperatives around obesity and weight, shaped by education policies within a 'performative' education culture (see Ball 2004), not only help sustain social class hierarchies but also generate alarming corporeal disorders deeply damaging to some young people's wellbeing and health (Evans *et al.* 2005). Of importance here, however, is that in this discourse certain categories of the population risk being labelled 'deviant' or 'aberrant' for not being either willing or able to achieve or engage with these inherently 'good things' – achieving correct weight and shape (see Campos 2004; Evans *et al.* 2005). Echoes of an earlier age when juvenile courts reached into the private lives of youth and disguised basically punitive policies in rhetoric of 'rehabilitation' (Platt 1971) reverberate in this discourse. Its proponents believe that 'youth' and their parents and carers need protection and correction from their inclinations to eat badly and exercise too little. Thus they endeavour to reach into and control many aspects of their lives. Obesity discourse and the many health policy initiatives it has spawned in the UK and elsewhere, readily embraced by PE and health professions, can be seen as latter day versions of 'child saving' crusades, their goal not only to rescue a population 'at risk' but regulate 'deviant' populations by announcing and (re)establishing acceptable social norms (be thin, exercise, eat the correct foods). Its contemporary form reflected in threats to remove children from purportedly aberrant, non-compliant, fat-inducing working-class (or single parent) families, for example, as expressed in the views of Tam Fry, Chairman of the Child Growth Foundation, cited by Smith (2008):

In 99% cases, obesity is so avoidable. Letting a child get fat is a form of abuse as there's a possibility they could die before their parents. It's important they are taken out of their homes and put under 24-hour surveillance from doctors and nurses. We have no hesitation in removing a severely undernourished child from their home. We should be as concerned when they are seriously overweight. The blame is not always entirely on the parents. In this case where were the health professionals to intervene early? Going into care is a last resort. But if your kid is obese, do something. Apart from the name-calling they will suffer, do you want a death on our hands?

Extreme caution should, of course, be exercised when reading such claims, as in almost every instance they are either erroneous, misleading, confused or wildly exaggerated when appraised against available primary research evidence in the obesity field (see Gard and Wright 2005, Gard 2011; Campos *et al.* 2006; Evans *et al.* 2005). Our point here is simply that the medicalisation of contemporary social/ health and education policy serves certain socio-political purposes. It not only sanctions ever more intrusive and ubiquitous control especially over working-class people's lives but also the opinions of those now privileged in popular culture (including PE teachers, fitness experts' and other health practitioners) to laud the virtues of their particular lifestyle (active, diet conscious, ever mobile and 'healthy') while denouncing others (e.g., pupils or colleagues) either as aberrant or less worthy as culture or class. Just as in the eighteenth and nineteenth centuries health crusaders were driven by far more than concern for children's ill-health, addressing what they perceived as the risks posed by inadequate or irresponsible working-class or aberrant middle class behaviour to the wider social order. Given the potentially damaging effects of obesity discourse on the lives of children, one might consider, for example, is it right that children in schools should be weighed and measured given the inaccuracies of the BMI and potentially damaging effects it can have on the attitudes of children toward their own and others' bodies. Should PE teachers (endowed with middle-class attitudes, platitudes and propensities toward excessive exercise, and often exponents of the slender body ideal) be permitted to engage in 'health education'? If so, how are they to do so in ways that avoid hurting pupils (eroding their sense of value and worth) with the reductively damaging message of obesity discourse – that health equals slenderness, dieting and exercise for weight loss?

PESH cannot compensate for society

The question we now pose, then, is whether PESH has also become an element in what others have called 'the technology of seduction', not only helping create the illusion that we live in a classless society but that it is itself a classless activity trading in promises and illusions of what people can, and ought to, achieve. If this is so, we need to ask: whose images and what cultural values are reflected and rejected in the policies and practices of PESH? Is PESH education or social control? Addressing these questions presses us to ask: What constitutes 'education' and 'educability' in PESH, *and* how are children's opportunities to experience

Parents to be notified if their children are working class

8 November

A New initiative from the Department of Children, Schools and Families will see their parents notified by letter if their children are considered to be at risk of growing into working-class adults.

The controversial intervention follows a series of concerns about children eating unhealthy diets, not being encouraged to read at home, being allowed out late at night, breaking the law and generally appearing a bit unkempt or failing to wear a single item from Mini Boden. Professor Sir Piers Cockburn (Oxon) warned that 'Unless steps are taken now large numbers of our pupils could leave school unable to sustain dinner party conversation about the Tuscan countryside or the benefits of organic vegetables. The only circumstances in which children should be out late at night is if they are queuing up to buy the latest Harry Potter book dressed as a wizard. However the idea has been slammed as 'nanny state intervention gone mad' by some educationalists who fear that schools will become stigmatized for not doing enough to encourage pupils to listen to *The Archers* or browse around antiques shops in Richmond. 'Children are all different and we should accept that some may get the bus to school rather then be driven in a large people-carrier listening to storybook tales', said one teacher. 'Children mustn't be made to feel second class, just because they are going to be poor and exploited for the rest of their lives'.

The government has also revealed that it may publish league tables detailing the percentage of proletarian children in each school, so that parents can make an informed choice before sending their children into an environment with kids who 'may have had fizzy drinks for breakfast'. But ministers have admitted that writing letters to working-class parents may not be that effective in the short-term. 'We accept that they are unlikely to read any letters we send them anyway. We are thinking of putting a big warning on the side of crisp packets instead'.

(O'Farrell, 2008: 121, 'The News Before it Happens' www.rbooks.co.uk)

Figure 9.2 O'Farrell's (2009) spoof news of item 2

these things framed (limited or facilitated) by the restrictions and nuances of their material conditions of existence? Discussion on these matters might also help readjust our focus toward *principles* rather than content (on how, why or when, we teach, rather than on what). For too long the PESH profession has generated sterile, dichotomised debates of a 'which is better' kind, e.g., sport education or multi-activity PESH, Teaching Games for Understanding (TGFU) or traditional techniques, dance or gymnastics and the absurd belief that each and any one of these modes is inherently less 'social', i.e., sexist, racist, ablest, homophobic, etc., than another. Instead, we should be together asking how each of these modes is socially encoded, arises from and reflects particular social class relations, conditions, distributions of power and control; how each will be read and received in specific contexts of opportunity, by specific social groups, with specific needsand resource to access them. In short, we should always be considering the role of PESH in a wider politics of schooling, if our accepted aim is to advance the possibilities for achieving comprehensive (inclusive) ideals.

None of the above analysis is to suggest that some social injustices have not been eroded through education and PESH over recent years, but it is to say that (radical

Surgeon Perfects 'Class-Change' Operation

<u>7 February</u>

Private health practices using the latest surgical techniques have successfully carried out the first operation allowing the patients to permanently alter their social class.

But critics say the procedure is unethical, and that in some cases the operation can go tragically wrong. After Reginald Smythe's class change operation, friends say that they 'don't know whether he is a chav or a toff'. 'He drinks decaffeinated cappuccino, but with five sugars'. Reg is stuck with a bizarre accent , which swings wildly between upper class and cockney, meaning that the only job open to him is becoming an alternative comedian.

(O'Farrell, 2008: 9, 'The News Before it Happens' www.rbooks.co.uk)

Figure 9.3 O'Farrell's (2009) spoof news of item 3

measures apart – see spoof news extract above) education can not compensate for society and that, without better understandings of the way in which class is inscribed in educational practices, we are unlikely to set meaningful or realistic agendas either for research or policy and practice in schools and PESH.

Conclusions

If nothing else the above analysis reminds us that PESH should always be studied by looking at the social forces that induce, maintain and legitimate its variety of forms. PESH reflect and endorse particular class interests not least with its emphases on élite sport performance and corporeal perfection (Evans and Davies 2005; Evans *et al.* 2005). It defines particular body pedagogics, practices which give meaning and value to 'the body' (particular bodies) in time, place and space. Privileged students, those with an extended experience (through early and supplementary learning outside school) of specific forms of linguistic, cognitive, social interaction *and embodied disposition*, and with the resources to access them, have structures of perceptions that inform their successful navigation of schools' constellation of meanings and message systems. These resources are, to a large degree, acquired tacitly, outside education's domain but actualised within the privileging practices of the school. The experience in working-class schools is very different. Writing about the United States but in terms that are readily applicable elsewhere, Finn (2009: 175) argues that:

working-class schools expend nearly all their energy on preparing students to improve their lot by individual advancement – border crossing which reinforces the meritocracy myth – while, in fact the route to acquiring social rights for a vast majority of their students is collective struggle, not individual advancement.

Indeed, in Finn's opinion, 'individual advancement depends in many cases on the collective uplifting of entire classes of people' (p. 175) – hence, ironically, the irresistible rise of that most individualistic of social groups, the middle classes.

Perhaps one of the key implications for policy and practice in PESH arising from this analysis is that, simply because it is possible to statistically and conceptually (as in this book) separate out 'the effects' of say, gender from class and also ethnicity, it still does not mean that, for example, gender differences can actually be addressed in isolation from class and ethnicity. As Connolly's (2006) research demonstrated, given the ways in which gender identities are so intertwined with and mediated by social class and ethnicity, there can be no singular programme of intervention (for example, around health and exercise) that will be appropriate and applicable to all boys and girls. Different boys and girls have vastly different experiences of education depending on their social class and ethnic backgrounds, and, we add, their location. Class does not mean the same thing in Merthyr Tydfil as it does in Dunfermline, Manchester, London, Adelaide or Mumbai. Indeed, recent class analysis 'emphasises the interactions of space and social networks in class formation and reproduction' (see Ball 2006: 7). Given this, the message of our narrative must be that, if we take sufficient cognisance of class and how body pedagogies reflect class and cultural interests, then we might begin to arrive at a more reasoned, nuanced and realistic attitude (see, for example, Tinning 2002) toward what can be achieved in the way of social justice (and related health and 'ability' concerns) in and through the practices of PESH. At one level this is to recognise that we need more targeted or 'situated' solutions, both in and outside schools, to issues, such as 'ability', exercise levels and obesity; at another, it is to underline the need for continuing respect for the fact that both agency and structure matter if we are to change for the better the conditions (for example, of health) of peoples' lives. If the Jamie Oliver school dinner TV series revealed anything at all, for example, it showed that in order to change attitudes and behaviour toward food, one had to change not only the content (for example, raising the quality of turkey twizzlers) of provision but also the structure of opportunity (setting new boundaries, applying greater regulation, limiting choice) while making greater investments of resource. The challenge in the changing environment is not only, as Critser (2003; 167) stated: 'to go back in time but to engineer physical activity and healthy eating back into the lives of individuals in a way that is compatible to their socio cultural values'. It is also to act on views that require neither moralising behaviour (for example, around weight), nor pathologising those who cannot, because of the conditions of class, easily reach preferred ideals. If nothing else this means that education, not weight control, should be the driving concern of a culturally enlightened PESH.

It is futile to measure the success of PESH by levels of physical activity and exercise in which people engage or health and fitness they achieve once outside or having left school because it can, at best, only partially determine such things. We do not judge RE teachers on the numbers of people who go to the mosque or church on Sundays or want to become ministers, rabbis, imams or nuns but we do expect children to have a religious education and to be able to recognise the difference between ideas, faith and knowledge, to recognise that religion has as great a capacity to uplift the spirit as to ruin lives. Of course physical educationalists should be concerned with the wellbeing of the general population; of course PESH should be concerned with levels of exercise, fitness, talent and health but not if a focus on the 'projected identities' of children and young people, that is to say, on what they might do or become, either after they leave or outside school, is at the expense of attention first being given to 'ability differentials' and the nature and quality of pupils' immediate educational experiences in PESH and the wider school environment. Moreover, we must frame our activities in the light of what we know of the part played by PESH in reproducing persisting levels of failure and success in schools which, in the UK, by the way, still leaves some 40 per cent of school leavers with either few, or no, qualifications to speak of, at all. In the absence of such focus, PESH will, at best, be thought of both as a second class subject and an opportunity for the physically 'gifted and talented', with overtones of palliative distraction for the academic failure of disaffected youth. For even them, as with the academic curriculum, its unattainable aspirations, promises and mantra (get fit, stay fit, be healthy, be a sporting star) may seem at first attractive but ultimately shallow when it is realised that it simply cannot deliver on these functional ideals; fool's gold for the many, gold dust for the few.

It is perhaps too much to expect that a social and economic citizens' rights movement of the type called for by Patrick Finn (2009) might emerge in PESH. It is arguably even less likely that were such a movement to emerge, the struggle would be fought out within working-class school classrooms as Finn demands. Nevertheless, PESH can and should imbue all pupils with physical and cultural capital, it should try to alter and impact attitudes toward who plays what and when, it should challenge racism, sexism, homophobia and leave as many as possible with a lasting desire to be fit, stay healthy, develop and learn. At the same time, it must acknowledge that it has little capacity alone to alter the structural conditions which determine people's opportunities to achieve many of these things, we should repeatedly ask, how does PESH contribute to the overall educational experience of children? What forms of activism can or should PESH teachers engage in across the curriculum, in wider structures and processes of schooling (play times, meal times, etc.) and in the wider community, if their chosen project is effecting education and social change? Does PESH connect with the physical cultures and class conditions that regulate people's lives, does it offer children and young people the 'ability' in the form of confidence, competence and control of their bodies' potential to deal with them effectively?; or, merely help reproduce the patterns of success and failure (whether defined in levels of participation or achievement levels), along class lines that stubbornly persist in and out of schools?

Notes

1. The media (TV, press, webpages, written, visual, digital) have become powerful agencies of socialisation. It has increasingly significant bearing on what and who we think we are. TV, for example, will inform you of the merits of a Jamie Oliver dinner, tell you what to wear while eating it, where your house should be located and how you should care for your garden, dogs and kids, as well as how much to exercise and how thin you should be. What it won't do, however, is determine whether or not you can achieve any of these things, no matter how much you might desire them; or, how much exercise you can do, how long you will live, and the quality of your health care; in a way that the labour process and your experience of school undoubtedly will.

2. This research ethic has influenced policy thinking in education for many years, and is reflected in much of the policy research on sport and PE. The success of PE or sport programmes has been perceived largely in terms of either how many people by class, race or gender, take part in physical (extra curricular) activity inside, outside and after school, or in terms of how active they are, or how fit they become. A recent overview by Green, *et al.* (2005), for example, reported that patterns are quite complex, showing some erosion in class differences involving blurring of boundaries as to who does what and when, though patterns tend to be as clear as ever in later life as to who get involved in physical activity and who enjoys better health. What all these studies show, however, whether in education, PE, sport, or health, is that neither targeted nor universal policy initiatives have blunted the close associations between social origin, educational attainment and subsequent employment prospects in a changing labour market and, concomitantly, in leisure and health prospects, despite marginal gender differences in the size of effects on opportunity and attainment in all of these things. The question remains as – what would need to be done to achieve such ends.

3. Like Oliver (2006) we emphasise that even if we do use 'weight' as a proxy for other more serious, class-based, problems we would still not want to make it the focus of health or education policy and practice either in or out of school. This is largely because the inappropriate use and definition of the terms 'overweight' and 'obese' have such damaging consequences for peoples' lives, including, for example, their employment opportunities, whether they are considered fit parents, insurance costs, and so on (see Oliver 2006: 34). Furthermore, as Oliver and others (Gard and Wright 2005) have pointed out, current 'weight' standards (which have dubious scientific rationale) not only damage the self image of the many who cannot possibly attain them, particularly if they are poor, female or a minority (see Oliver: 34), and of those that can, and do so (some to the point of starvation: see Evans *et al.* 2005); they also have more pernicious and wide-reaching effects, for example, compelling doctors to tell their patients they are sick (when they aren't), health workers to tell parents their newborn children are too fat when they are not; and convincing millions that they should starve themselves with crash diets and other strategies of weight loss in the pursuit of 'health'. In essence, 'current designations of "overweight" and "obese" may cause all sorts of unfair, unhealthy, and unnecessary behaviours on the part of the Americans (and British) who have been led to think they need to be thin in order to be healthy' (Oliver 2006: 34).

References

Azzarito, L. and Solomon, M. A. (2005) 'A Reconceptualisation of Physical Education: The intersection of gender/race/social class', *Sport, Education and Society*, 10, 1: 25–49.

Bairner, A. (2007) 'Back to basics: class, social theory and sport', *Sociology of Sport Journal*, 24 (1), 20–36.

Ball, S. (2004) 'Performativities and fabrications in the education economy: towards the performative society', in Ball, S. J. (ed.) *The RoutledgeFalmer Reader in Sociology of Education*. London: RouledgeFalmer.

Ball, S. (2006) Education Policy, CeCEPS Launch Education Policy, Institute of Education, London, 1 March.

Ball, S. (2009) 'New class inequalities in education: Why education policy is looking in the wrong place! Education policy, civil society and social class', Paper presented at the Centre for Research in Social Policy Conference, 22–23 January, University of Loughborough, Loughborough, UK.

Beck, J. (2009) Appropriating professionalism: Restructuring the official knowledge base of England's 'modernised' teaching profession, *British Journal of Sociology of Education*, 30, No. 1: 3–15.

Benn, M. (2011) Our education system has never been so divided, *The Guardian*, G2, 17 August, 6–9.

Bernstein, B. (1996) *Pedagogy, Symbolic Control and Identity. Theory, Research, Critique.* London: Taylor & Francis.

Bourdieu, P. (1986) 'The forms of capital', in Richardson, J. (ed.) *Handbook of Theory and Research for the Sociology of Education*, New York: Greenwood Press.

Campos, P. (2004) *The Obesity Myth*, New York: Gotham Books.

Campos, P., Saguy, A., Ernsberger, P., Oliver, E. and Gaesserg, G. (2006) 'The Epidemiology of overweight and obesity: Public health crisis or moral panic', International Journal of Epidemiology, 35, 1: 50–60.

Connolly, P. (2006) 'The effects of social class and ethnicity on gender differences in GCSE attainment: a secondary analysis of the Youth Cohort Study of England and Wales 1997–2001', *British Educational Research Journal*, 32, 3–23.

Critser, G. (2003) Fat *Land. How Americans became the fattest people in the world*, London: Penguin.

Evans, J. (1988) 'Body matters: Towards a Socialist Physical education', in Lauder, H. and Brown, P. (eds) *Education in Search of a Future*, London: The Falmer Press, 174–92.

Evans, J. and Davies, B. (2005) 'Endnote: The embodiment of consciousness', in Evans, J., Davies, B. and Wright, J. (eds) *Body Knowledge and Control. Studies in the Sociology of Physical Education and Health*, London: Routledge.

Evans, J. and Davies, B. (2006) 'Social Class and Physical Education', in Kirk, D. O'Sullivan, M. and Macdonald, D. (eds) *Handbook of Research on Physical Education*, London: Sage.

Evans, J. and Davies, B. (2010) 'Family, class and embodiment: why school physical education makes so little difference to post-school participation patterns in physical activity', *International Journal of Qualitative Studies in Education*, 23(7), 765–84.

Evans, J., Rich, E. and Allwood, R. (2005) 'Disordered eating and disordered schooling: what schools do to middle-class girls', *British Journal of Sociology of Education*, 22, 2, 123–43.

Finn, P. J. (2009) *Literacy with an Attitude. Educating working-class children in their own self-interest*, 2nd edn, Albany, NY: State University of New York Press.

Fitz, J., Davies, B. and Evans, J. (2006) *Educational Policy and Social Reproduction*, London: Routledge.

Flintoff, A., Fitzgerald, H. and Scraton, S. (2008) 'The challenges of intersectionality: researching difference in physical education', *International Studies in Sociology of Education*, 18(2), 73–85.

Gard, M. (2011) *The End of the Obesity Epidemic*, London: Routledge.

Gard, M. and Wright, J. (2005) *The Obesity Epidemic: Science Morality an Ideology*, London: Routledge.

Gale, T. (2005) 'Towards a Theory and Practice of Policy Activism: Higher education research in the making', President's Address, AARE 2005, Education research. Creative Dissent: Constructive Solutions. International Education Research Conference, UWS Parametta.

Gillies, V. (2007) *Marginalised mothers: Exploring working-class experiences of parenting*, Abingdon: Routledge.

Green, K., Smith A. S. and Roberts, K. (2005) 'Social class, young people, sport and physical education', in Green, K. and Hardman, K. (eds) *Physical education: Essential issues*, London: Sage. 180–97.

Independent Inquiry into Inequalities in Health Report www.archive.officialdocuments. co.uk/documents/doh/ih/part/ih/part1b.htm (accessed 02 February 2006).

Lewis, R. and Maude, A. (1953) *The English Middle Class*, London: Pelican Book.

Lynch, K. and Lodge, A. (2002) *Equality and Power in Schools*, London: RoutledgeFalmer.

Morley D. (2000) *Home Territories: Media, mobility and identity* Routledge, London.

Oliver, J. E. (2006) *Fat Politics. The Real Story Behind Americas' Obesity Epidemic*, Oxford: Oxford University Press.

O'Farrell, F. (2009) *The news before it happens*, www.rbooks.co,uk.

Platt, A. (1971) The rise of the child-saving movement, in Cosin, B. R. (eds) *School and society: A sociological reader*, London: Routledge and Kegan Paul in association with the Open University.

Reay, D. (1998) *Class work: Mothers' involvement in their children's primary schooling*, London: RoutledgeFalmer.

Reay, D., Crozier, G., James, D., Williams, K., Jamieson, F. and Beedell, P. (2008) 'Re-invigorating democracy? White middle-class identities and comprehensive schooling', *Sociological Review*, 56(2), 238–56.

Sheller, M. and Urry, J. (2006) 'The new mobilities paradigm', *Environment and Planning A*, 38: 207–26.

Skeggs, B. (2004) *Class, Self, Culture*, London: Routledge.

Smith, M. (2008), 'Put the kids on a diet – or they go into care', *Daily Mirror*, 24 March, p. 21.

Syed, M. (2010) 'The Olympics: You need brass to go for Gold', *The Times*, 10 February, 1. http://women.timesonline.co.uk/tol/life_and_style/women/the_way_we_live/article 7020963.ece.

Tinning, R. (2002) Towards a modest pedagogy: reflections on the problematics of critical pedagogy, *Quest*, 54, 3, 224–41.

Vincent, C., and Ball, S. J. (2007) 'Making up the middle-class child: Families, acquisition and class dispositions', *Sociology*, 41(6), 1061–77.

Wright, J. and Burrows, L. (2006) 'Re-conceiving ability in physical education: A social analysis', *Sport, Education and Society*, 11(3), 275–93.

Younge, G. (2005) 'Please stop fetishising integration. Equality is what we really need' *The Guardian*, 19 September, 23.

10 Inclusive learning and teaching through accredited awards in physical education within a 14–19 curriculum framework

Gary Stidder and James Wallis

Okay I'm in year 7. Not popular. One friend who hates PE as much as I do. So long story short. It started in games when we were doing hockey and I'm rubbish at it. So I didn't try and all the girls were picking on me telling me that I couldn't do it and I was pathetic and stupid. So because they thought I was so stupid then I would act like it. So I put my stick on the floor and stood there. The teacher told me to pick it up but I didn't care what she thought I hated her and she hated me. So I got a yellow card and was sent out the class. The teacher caught up with me at lunch and said 'Detention tomorrow lunch time'. But she didn't tell me where. So I didn't show up so when she saw me in the dinner line she said 'I'm giving you another yellow card because you didn't show up to detention'. And I said I didn''t know where it was so she got annoyed and started shouting at me so I just walked off. It was half-term and the next topic in games was football. That day I forgot my shoes. So guess what she did? She told me to wear one tiny little shoe and one really big shoe. I swear I wanted to kill her. I couldn't walk I had blisters over my feet and everyone was telling me to run when I couldn't I really don't want to do games or PE again. She's so horrible she really is.

http://uk.answers.yahoo.com/question/index?qid=20110306080218AA4gCz0
Accessed 11 July 2011

Introduction

Since our previous chapter in the first edition of this book (Stidder and Wallis 2003) externally accredited courses in physical education for 14–19 year old pupils in the UK have continued to gain support amongst teachers at an unprecedented rate. Whilst the numbers of pupils who take the General Certificate of Secondary Education (GCSE)[1] examination course in physical education has remained relatively stable over the past five years, the introduction of other accredited types of courses in physical education and dance have added to the range of accredited courses in physical education available to pupils. As you will see in this chapter there is now a vast range and an eclectic mix of accredited awards available for pupils aged 14–19. Golder (2010) has highlighted the fact that many of these qualifications in physical education have been introduced as part of a 14–19 curriculum as all young people in the UK are now required to stay in education or training until eighteen years of age from 2015. This has only served to reflect the evolving nature of physical education as a subject and the UK coalition government's attention to raising academic standards. It is therefore our intention to specifically examine the place of compulsory accredited awards in physical education for all pupils aged 14 to 19 within an inclusive framework.

Our own experiences of physical education lessons in the latter part of our compulsory schooling were purely recreational. At the beginning our own penultimate year of secondary school we were provided with 'options' with regards to the types of physical activities we wished to pursue during the one-hour lesson devoted to physical education each week. These choices of activities usually meant that the boys played five-a-side football whilst the girls played netball. Neither of us learnt how to swim at school nor were we provided with any opportunities to try new or different activities. If we were lucky our physical education teacher would take the lesson, otherwise they were usually supervised by other non-specialist teachers from other departments. Accredited courses in physical education didn't exist at the secondary schools we attended and the situation was no different at the local sixth form college. It now seems quite ironic that we both went on to study physical education at university and have pursued our respective careers in this area of academia. Like other chapters in this book, our personal and professional experiences of physical education have provided the impetus for writing this chapter and are a result of critical self-reflection on contemporary practices in the subject. Consequently, our experiences as teacher–educators in higher education have led us to explore possible curriculum developments within Key Stage 4 and beyond and a framework within which all pupils can enhance their learning. It is on this basis that a broad and balanced accredited physical education curriculum is suggested at the expense of 'core'[2] non-accredited programmes which we believe are better suited to the needs and interests of all pupils after the age of 14.

Nearly ten years after the writing of our original chapter (Stidder and Wallis 2003) the provision of 'core' non-accredited physical education in many UK schools still does not meet the needs of many 14–19 year old girls and at least some boys. Curriculum developments and trends in physical education have shown, however, that non-examination or 'core' programmes of physical education after the age of 14 are fast becoming the exception rather than the rule in secondary schools with more schools than ever providing accredited forms of physical education and dance in place of 'core' programmes (Ofsted 2009). The situation has been similar elsewhere in the UK as highlighted by the Scottish Executive (2004):

> While physical education was offered to all pupils in the 5–14 age range, for those pupils not pursuing a national qualification in physical education beyond age 14, there was concern about a drop in participation in non-certificated, or what is often termed 'core' physical education programmes.
>
> (Scottish Executive 2004: 21)

While the number of pupils who opt for the study of physical education for national qualifications is very healthy and steadily increasing, the number of pupils involved in non-certificated or "core" physical education in secondary schools is declining. Many pupils in the post-14 school environment opt out of physical education, and some schools no longer provide this option for the senior students, unless they are pursuing the subject for a national qualification.

(Scottish Executive 2004: 29)

Our own research evidence suggests that a move towards compulsory accredited programmes of physical education are in the best interests of all pupils and are far more inclusive to a broader population of pupils (Stidder and Wallis 2005, 2006).

Accreditation in physical education

There is recognition that the continued growth of accredited physical education courses is a reflection of the value that teachers place on accredited forms of learning (Ofsted 2009). This is part of a process referred to by Green (2008: 88) as the 'academicization' of physical education that has been apparent for over a quarter of a century, whereby there is increasing emphasis on the theoretical study of physical activity and sport in both absolute and relative terms (that is, in relation to, and sometimes at the expense of, practical activities). Green (2008) has shown how the increase in the numbers of 14–16 year old pupils taking GCSE and 16–19 year old students studying Advanced level physical education has surpassed virtually all other subjects and within a 13-year period has witnessed a growth rate of 221 per cent at GCSE and 2863 per cent at A level. Green (2008) has referred to this dramatic growth as an 'explosion' and represents a step-change in the way physical education is organised at Key Stage and post-16. Similarly, there has been a rapid increase in the numbers of pupils following alternative forms of traditional 'core' physical education such as leadership awards which now account for over one hundred and forty thousand young people aged between 14 to 19 (Sports Leaders UK 2011). In this respect Ofsted (2009) found that most secondary schools offer 14–16 year-old pupils GCSE physical education and other accredited physical education awards in order to broaden the choices open to pupils, as many schools prefer a more vocational approach to physical education where pupils are assessed as performers, leaders or officials through accredited courses. Much of the impetus for this has been the result of increasing concerns amongst physical education teachers that pupils who only take 'core' non-accredited physical education receive less than one hour per week of physical education (40 minutes of activity) and there is little connection in the way physical education is organised in Key Stage 3 and what is offered in Key Stage 4 'core' physical education (Ofsted 2009).

There is an overwhelming educational rationale for introducing compulsory accredited awards in physical education compared to 'core' non-accredited programmes based on equity and inclusion. Ofsted (2009), for example, have identified that the use of non-specialist staff in 'core' physical education lessons at Key Stage 4 is more common than in any other secondary year, especially in games teaching, and this is sometimes unsatisfactory as pupils tend to be supervised rather than effectively taught.

A small minority of the (PE) lessons seen were taught by non-specialist (PE) teachers, often deployed with core Key Stage 4 students, or by external coaches. Generally, these lessons were satisfactory rather than good, mainly because either the teacher's knowledge of the requirements for the physical education National Curriculum or knowledge to support progression in learning was weaker.

Ofsted (2009: 33)

Other researchers (Green 2008) have also commented that these types of practice are commonplace:

Physical education departments in England and Wales have always been inclined to make use of non-specialist teachers – especially in activity choice or 'option' PE for upper school pupils.

Green (2008: 50)

Moving to compulsory accredited courses for all pupils can ensure that physical education staff do not have to teach any other subject and therefore the quality of teaching can often be of a higher standard as all pupils are exclusively taught by a physical education specialist (Stidder and Wallis 2005, 2006). Further evidence from Ofsted (2009) has shown that pupils in core lessons at Key Stage 4 had insufficient time to study an activity in depth. Pupils often had limited choice and lacked alternative curriculum pathways to suit their interests. At one school inspected Ofsted (2009: 40) noted that:

All students have access to two hours of high quality physical education at Key Stage 3 and Key Stage 4 within the core physical education curriculum, while GCSE students receive an additional two hours. The addition of GCSE dance, the BTEC First Diploma in Sport and the Junior Sports Leaders award broadens the curriculum further. Different pathways for success as student's progress through the school, including leadership, vocational and traditional academic routes of accreditation, help to ensure that all students are included.

Ofsted (2009: 40)

Since the introduction of the GCSE examination in physical education in 1986 the number of entries has expanded rapidly. In 1988, 18,000 pupils took the first GCSE in physical education (Carroll 1995) and by 2008 that number had risen to just below 200,000 (JCQ 2008). Similarly, courses such as national governing body awards (NGBA) and sports leadership qualifications have grown in popularity amongst pupils aged 14 to 19. For example, the increasing number of schools showing interest in accredited physical education courses has resulted in many schools re-designing their physical education curricula at Key Stage 4 and the number of pupils achieving alternative awards in physical education, compared to examination courses, at the end of Key Stage 4 has increased significantly (Ofsted 2009).

The unprecedented growth of accredited awards in physical education and the increasing number of candidates engaged in such courses has been a response to professional accountability, which has continued to have an impact on the teaching profession in general. Furthermore, increased opportunities in vocational courses and sports-related occupations have also contributed to the expansion of accredited physical education courses in secondary schools and provided further justification for their place within the secondary school curriculum. The number of schools moving away from 'core' non-accredited programmes of physical education can have a very beneficial effect on curriculum design and has the potential to improve pupil achievements in an increasing number of schools. Ofsted (2009) suggested that the best work observed in Key Stage 4 physical education is often seen in examination classes, and that the teaching of examination groups tends to be better than in the 'option' classes traditionally offered to pupils. In this respect, non-accredited courses rarely have fully planned outcomes and standards are often poor compared to examination classes. Furthermore, pupils' achievements are highest when they are following an accredited course and the links between informal and formal assessment in examination lessons is stronger than in core physical education lessons where the assessment of non-examination pupils is often neglected. The latest inspection evidence (Ofsted 2009: 54) reported that:

> Few of the secondary schools continued to assess students beyond Key Stage 3, unless they were on examination or accredited courses, and therefore they had no records of students' progress in core Key Stage 4 physical education or beyond.

Furthermore, Ofsted (2009: 58) clearly highlighted the weaknesses in providing core non-examination physical education at Key Stage 4.

> There was good continuity of learning between Key Stage 3 and examination courses in Key Stage 4, including the use of prior learning to set realistic challenges and targets. This was particularly effective in preparing students to select and follow the appropriate accredited course, including national governing body awards, for their ability and interests. However, the lack of assessment in core Key Stage 4 lessons meant students taking only core lessons made less progress and not all were challenged to reach their full potential.
>
> Ofsted (2009: 58)

The growth of GCSE examination courses in physical education

Since the publication of the first edition of this book in 2003 the success of GCSE physical education has been acknowledged and recognised as a key innovation in the development of contemporary physical education (Golder 2010; Grout and Long 2009; Green 2005, 2008) and has made a significant contribution to the learning process and understanding of pupils (Stidder and Wallis 2006). Green

(2008) has shown that the percentage of candidates entered into a GCSE in physical education had risen more than any other subject between 1997–2007, representing a 31 per cent increase over ten years. Our research shows that numbers have declined since 2007 but whilst the top GCSE full course subject was Mathematics with 762,792 candidates in 2009, Physical Education was just below tenth place, behind Art (188,193). Interestingly, subject choice by gender showed that physical education was the third most popular subject amongst boys (64.7%) behind Economics (70.4%) and other technologies (92.8%), outnumbering girls by two-to-one (35.3%).

The GCSE short course has become increasingly popular within schools and these types of arrangements may provide a better structure for the large majority of pupils who have a limited amount of timetabled curriculum physical education each week. This provides a qualification with fewer activities in a shorter period of time (a highly motivating factor for some pupils) and has been increasingly introduced to pupils in year nine of secondary schools. Much of the impetus for these developments has arisen as many pupils find the theoretical aspects of GCSE physical education particularly challenging.

Table 10.1 GCSE Physical Education results 2007–2010

	2007	*2008*	*2009*	*2010*
GCSE PE Full Course	155,625	149,068	136,631	123,907
GCSE PE Short Course	29,378	31,697	32,073	29,080
Applied Double Award	823	1,205	1,181	1,247
Applied Single Award	2,137	3,005	3,538	3,110
Entry level certificate	12,388	12,455	12,107	11,291

Source: Joint Council for Qualifications (JCQ)3

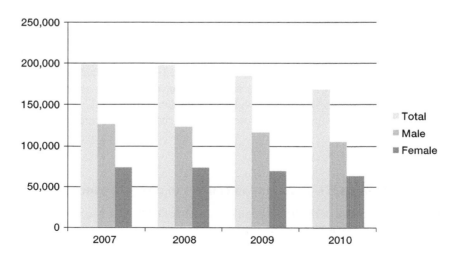

Figure 10.1 GCSE Physical Education results 2007–2010

Table 10.2 Total numbers of pupils taking a GCSE in Physical Education (all UK candidates)

	2007	*2008*	*2009*	*2010*
Total	198,391	197,430	185,530	168,680
Male	126,462	123,471	116,178	104,986
Female	71,129	73,959	69,352	63,694

GCSE Dance

An audit of dance provision in English schools in 2006/07 conducted by the Youth Sports Trust showed that performance in GCSE Dance was relatively good with GCSE attainment in Dance above the national average level at Grades A*–C. Entries for GCSE Dance were showing growths with the numbers of entries between 2005 and 2007 increasing by 28 per cent overall, and by 55 per cent for boys, and by 27 per cent for girls. There was, however, a strong gender bias with girls still making up 94 per cent of all GCSE dance entries. Post-16 A-Level pass rates in performing arts were broadly comparable with other subjects. Furthermore A-Level entries in performing arts 2004–2007 had risen by 34 per cent with girls showing the largest increase. However, there does seem to be further emerging patterns of gender bias in entry trends at A-Level where girls are making up a growing proportion of all those entered. Consequently the proportion of entries by girls has risen from 67 per cent of all A-Level entries in 2004 to 72 per cent in 2007

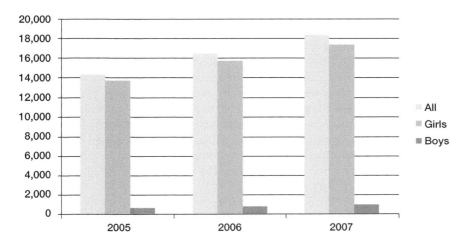

Figure 10.2 GCSE Dance results 2005–2007

(Youth Sport Trust 2008: 57, Source: DCSF)

The rise of Sports Leaders Awards

In 1994 the Central Council for Physical Recreation (CCPR) launched the Junior Sports Leadership Award (JSLA) in response to teachers who called for a nationally recognised leaders' award for pupils under the age of sixteen. Following the success of the JSLA older pupils were able to progress to the Community Sports Leadership Award (CSLA), the Higher Sports Leadership Award (HSLA), and General and National Vocational Qualifications (GNVQ). Since our previous analysis of the numbers of pupils undertaking sports leadership qualifications through sports leaders UK there have been significant advances in the types of qualifications now offered and increased numbers of pupils taking them from the age of 14. This has been confirmed by Ofsted:

> Opportunities to take leadership qualifications have increased substantially. In 2007/08, just over two thirds of the 28 schools visited were offering a range of qualifications such as sports leaders, young football or basketball leaders and young dance leaders. Students involved in these courses could not praise the opportunities highly enough to inspectors. One commented to an inspector: 'It has helped me become more confident, not just in physical education but in my other subjects too. I am more willing to ask questions and give input to class discussion.
>
> Ofsted (2009: 31)

Many of the sports leader's awards now available to pupils have the potential to be integrated into Key Stage 4 physical education teaching without any added time required and cause minimal disruption to core physical education lessons. It can also be an alternative for, or complementary to, GCSE physical education courses and may be more appropriate for pupils who find theoretical aspects of examination physical education more difficult. In addition, many National Governing Bodies (NGBs) such as the Amateur Swimming Association (ASA) and the English Table Tennis Association (ETTA) provide a range of young leadership awards developed as 'bolt-on' extras to the level two award in community sport leadership. Pupils are able to apply leadership skills to specific activities that qualify them to assist in the delivery of sports-specific sessions. This has helped to prepare pupils for roles within sports clubs as paid or voluntary leaders, coaches and officials and prepared pupils for further intermediate and advanced awards. This point was highlighted by Ofsted (2009: 30) as an aspect of good practice in secondary schools.

> In all the secondary schools visited, students had opportunities to complete sports leader, dance leader or national governing body awards. The majority of these students subsequently become involved in organising and running inter-form or inter-house competitions and clubs for younger pupils. They also make a good contribution by running festivals of sport, tournaments and clubs in partner primary schools. In a few of the secondary schools visited, students had been elected physical education prefects, sports council members

and house sports captains. Many of the students taking leadership awards acknowledged the opportunities to work together in teams, the gains in self-confidence because of the varied experiences and roles, and how this helped to prepare them for the future.

Ofsted (2009: 30)

Moreover, subsequent reports from Ofsted (2011: 5) confirmed that leadership courses in sport for pupils in the 14–16 range was having a considerable impact in secondary schools:

Growing numbers of pupils of all ages train to become young leaders and are helping to run clubs and competitions for others. SSPs provide a wealth of opportunities for young leaders to organise, officiate and support in sport which is having a beneficial impact on their personal organisation, attitudes and behaviour towards others.

Ofsted (2011: 5)

Based upon the increasing evidence of the rise in the numbers of young people taking sports leaders awards we have carried out further analysis which has shown almost a 200 per cent increase in the past ten years.

In the build up to the London 2012 Olympic Games Sports Leaders UK launched several new courses to add to their existing suite of leadership pathways. For example, the level two award in sports volunteering aimed at learners over the age of 13 is a practically-based award designed for pupils who 'traditionally fall through the educational net, giving them another chance to improve their

Table 10.3 UK Sports Leaders entries 2000–2011

Sports Leaders UK Qualifications	2000–2001	2001–2002	2009–2010*	2010–2011*
Level One Award in Sports Leadership	19,949	25,573	99,808	90,357
Level One Award in Dance Leadership	–	–	9,654	9,047
Level Two Award in Sports Leadership	–	–	–	7600
Level Two Award in Community Sports Leadership	24,989	27,253	35,395	32,463
Level Three Award in Day Walk Leadership	–	–	–	20
Level Three Certificate in Basic Expedition Leadership	2,735	2,549	2,324	1,665
Total Candidates	**47,673**	**55,375**	**147,181**	**141,152**

Figures as of 31 March 2011
Source: with kind permission of Sports Leaders UK (June 14 2011)

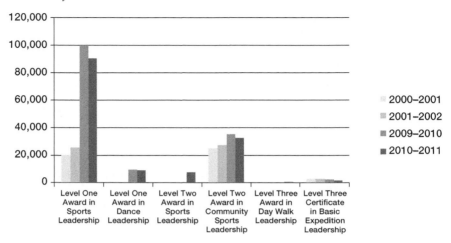

Figure 10.3 UK Sports Leaders entries 2000–2011

prospects' (Hammond 2012: 89). This enables pupils to develop volunteering skills that can be used as a community resource. Once achieved, pupils can progress to the level two award in community sport volunteering in which pupils are required to gain a First Aid certificate and an award from a National Governing Body of sport. These qualifications can be further developed through the level two award in assisting Basic Expedition Leadership consisting of 12 leadership hours and an overnight camping expedition.

Business and Technology Education Council (BTEC)

The Business and Technology Education Council (BTEC) is the UK body which awards vocational qualifications. Such qualifications are commonly referred to as 'BTECs'. The General Certificate of Secondary Education (GCSE) and the Business and Technology Education Council (BTEC) are both academic qualifications that are awarded in the UK. The main difference is that BTEC is awarded for vocational subjects, and the GCSE is awarded for a large number of other subjects. Some schools also offer the BTEC to students in the 14–16 age group , along with the GCSE. BTEC qualifications are undertaken in vocational subjects that include pathways for different types of pupils (academic, practically-able; disaffected). They are equivalent to other qualifications such as the GCSE (levels 1 to 2), A Level (level 3) and university degrees (levels 4 to 6). Examples of BTEC courses include certificates, diplomas and national awards on Health & Social Care, Business Studies, Engineering, Science, Information Technology, Media Studies, Travel & Tourism, sport, dance and outdoor education. These qualifications have equivalence on the DCSF School and College Achievement and Attainment Tables (SCAAT); a BTEC First Certificate has equivalence with 2 GCSEs graded A*–C and a BTEC First Diploma has equivalence with 4 GCSEs graded A*–C (www.edexcel.com/quals/firsts).

BTEC Sport Qualifications

The BTEC Level 2 First Sport qualification has been developed to provide education and training for employees in the Sport sector and give opportunities for Sport employees to achieve a nationally recognised Level 2 vocationally specific qualification. It provides full-time learners a better understanding of the Sport sector, which can help them to obtain employment in this sector or to progress to a Level 3 vocational qualification, such as the BTEC Level 3 National in Sport and gives learners the opportunity to develop a range of skills, techniques, personal skills and attributes essential for successful performance in working life. The value of BTEC qualifications in sport has been recognised as a major advancement in the physical education profession and has helped pupils otherwise excluded from physical education to achieve a nationally recognised award in sport. For example, Ofsted has stated:

> Students studying Business and Technology Education Council (BTEC) or sports leader courses are required to plan and run a sports festival for primary school students. They relished the opportunities to be good role models for physical education and sport and to work with younger students in local primary schools and in their own schools. The opportunities not only enhanced their self-esteem but also extended the range and number of activities in the schools in which they worked. In one outstanding school, a larger than average school drawing from a wide rural area, the impact was exceptional.
>
> Ofsted (2009: 31)

In the 16–19 age range this had also been equally effective in raising pupils' aspirations and achievements:

> All the schools in the survey with a sixth form offered A level physical education or BTEC Level 3 Sports Studies, or both. However, few of them provided intermediate or lower-level courses. Very few other sixth-form students had access to timetabled physical education provision, although most of them were offered an enrichment programme. Take-up of these opportunities varied considerably, either because involvement was not compulsory or access to provision was not an entitlement, or both.
>
> Ofsted (2009: 41)

Diploma in Sport and Active Leisure (14–19)

The Diploma in Sport and Active Leisure was introduced to schools in September 2010 and the result of the Tomlinson Report (2004). This course gives young people the opportunity to explore the sport and active leisure sector and designed to help them become more employable. The employer-endorsed content is up-to-date and relevant, reflecting the blend of knowledge, practical skills, communication and team-working skills needed to progress to further study or employment in the sector and beyond. Huggett and Manley (2010: 30) suggested the rationale for the new 14–19 diplomas in sport and leisure was that it might provide a unified system of diplomas better suited to 14 to 19 year-olds and help them to become better engaged within an education system that promoted equity between academic and vocational programmes. At the time of writing it is premature to make any conclusive judgements about the impact of these diplomas other than to say that they are in a state of flux with regards to changes in government policy. Suffice to say that provisional figures from the Joint Council for Qualifications (2011) for the number of candidates that achieved principal learning at level two in sport and active leisure was 27 (10 male and 17 female) whilst at level one there were 15 candidates (14 male and one female).

1st4Sport Level 2 Certificate in supporting learning in physical education and school sport

This qualification has been developed in partnership with the Association for Physical Education (AfPE) providing learners with guidance on further opportunities, including how to contribute to physical education and school sport (PESS) programmes as a sports leader, coach and teaching assistant. The skills may be used by learners in working in other sporting environments, under appropriate guidance. The level two certificate aims to provide learners with an introduction to a number of roles through an engagement with physical education and school sport (PESS), including teaching, activity leadership and coaching for young people. At the time of writing it is too early to tell the extent to which this type of accredited award has appeal to 16–19 year-old learners.

(www.1st4sportqualifications.com)

Exemplar approaches – specialist sports colleges 'leading the way'

In response to the disaffection shown by some pupils in physical education, many sports colleges now offer these types of accredited awards during core physical; education time. This approach has raised achievement levels in Key Stage 4 compared to the activity choices traditionally offered to pupils (Ofsted 2009). Many more young people now have the opportunity to gain leadership qualifications and accredited awards, for example, as all pupils at these colleges must follow an accredited course in physical education at Key Stage 4 suited to their individual needs (Ofsted 2009). Moreover, the majority of specialist sports colleges offer additional opportunities for pupils to obtain awards such as The Duke of Edinburgh Award and national sports governing body awards and have provided more appropriate experiences for pupils across a full range of educational needs (Ofsted 2009). Accredited courses and packages of alternative physical education qualifications based on pupil ability and needs arguably gives much greater motivation to pupils at key stage four. Below are examples of how specialist sports colleges involved in 'partnership' training have introduced a range of accredited course for pupils in Key Stage 4.

At the Coopers' Company and Coborn school in Essex, the physical education department has developed their Key Stage 4 programme by moving towards wholesale accreditation for all pupils aged between 14 and 16. The school became a Sports College in 2000/2001 and subsequently the Head Teacher in consultation with the physical education department decided to make it compulsory for all pupils to take GCSE physical education. In 2011 370 pupils were following either the GCSE physical education or dance course through the Edexcel examination board. One hundred and ninety year ten pupils choose either the full or short in physical education or dance and are provided with five hours of curriculum time over a two-week timetable (three one hour practicals and two one hour theory sessions). One hundred and eighty seven year eleven full course, short course and dance pupils receive four hours (two one hour practical and two one hour theory sessions). In year eleven the practical lessons are based on the activities the pupils have selected for GCSE with full and short course candidates taught together. Dance is taught within the drama faculty rather than within the physical education department due to space and timetabling issues. All year ten and eleven pupils follow a pathway in either physical education or dance.

A similar picture is apparent at The Seaford Head Community School in East Sussex where The GCSE in Physical Education is provided alongside BTEC certificates and diplomas in sport, dance and outdoor education as well as sports leaders awards and national governing body awards. This is regarded as a core subject with the delivery of all components of the course to all pupils whereby pupils elect two courses from the range of options on offer. All pupils select two options as part of their 'core' physical education during key stage four. These include the BTEC first certificate in sport taken either in year nine, ten or eleven and worth two GCSEs, BTEC Sport or Outdoor Education, a GCSE in physical Education (Double Award) or a Sport Leaders UK level one award.

At the Dorothy Stringer High School in Brighton all year nine pupils are provided with additional opportunities to obtain awards such as The Duke of Edinburgh Bronze Award and national sports governing body awards which have provided more appropriate experiences for pupils across a full range of educational needs. Accredited courses and packages of alternative physical education qualifications such as this based on pupil ability and needs arguably gives much greater motivation to pupils at Key Stage 4 and therefore allow all pupils to gain the qualifications that are best suited to their ability.

In the context of a 14 to 19 physical education curriculum, accredited forms of learning for all pupils in physical education can provide pupils with opportunities to engage in other aspects of sports development through which they could gain school and community recognition as well as credit towards a vocational diploma as part of their wider activities and extended projects, and could be considered as more appropriate for certain types of pupils. This has been endorsed by Ofsted (2009):

Students in Key Stage 3 benefit from opportunities for leadership built in throughout the curriculum, while Key Stage 4 and post-16 students are able to gain academic and vocationally based accreditation such as GCSE physical education, a BTEC Sport Diploma and A level physical education. In addition, students undertake the Duke of Edinburgh Award and the Junior and Community Sports Leaders awards. There are also opportunities to experience sport in different cultural settings through international sports tours, and to take part in outdoor and adventurous experiences, such as mountaineering and orienteering expeditions.

Ofsted (2009: 40)

With this in mind, accredited forms of teaching and learning in physical education and dance within a 14 to 19 framework could be viewed as being an integral part of future developments in physical education and appears to sit naturally within the government's vision for a 14–19 curriculum. In this respect, accredited courses can potentially be a quality means of teaching physical education for all pupils at Key Stage 4 and beyond as it aims to promote vocational training and leadership through which achievements are acknowledged and formally accredited outside of the formal conventions of the academic curriculum. In this respect we have highlighted below what a fully inclusive physical education curriculum might look like, hypothetically, within a 14–19 framework for all pupils. Whilst we recognise that some schools may not have the capacity or resources to offer a vast range of accredited courses in physical education we suggest that schools consider what might be appropriate for their pupils in the context of their particular circumstances as shown in Figure 10.4 opposite.

Much of what we discussed this chapter has focused on the abandonment of non-accredited 'core' programmes of physical education in favour of accreditation for all pupils and we have provided a rationale to support our views. Whilst we recognise that many physical educationalists have extolled the virtues of such an approach to teaching and learning, there is not universal acceptance and the merits are not unequivocal with regards to the scoring, grading, quantifying and measuring of pupils' performance, or the need to continually assess in a subject that has its roots in personal development and qualities that do not convert well to levels of attainment or grade descriptors. Such an unprecedented growth, however, suggests that the academicisation of physical education has gained increasing popularity amongst pupils and can be viewed as a 'new orthodoxy' (Reid 1996, cited in Green 2008) amongst teachers.

Golder (2010) has also shown how the strong emphasis by the current UK coalition government to extend opportunities for 14–19 year-old pupils has focused on academic, applied and key skills qualifications which will allow pupils to pursue their particular talents whilst maintaining a focus on basics. Through this pupils may take a range of academic and vocational courses that provide them with a 'passport' to higher education through the achievement of an 'overarching' diploma. As a result, physical education teachers can now expect to teach theoretical, practical, applied and leadership work through a range of courses. In this respect, Golder (2010) has acknowledged that physical education departments can enhance opportunities, broaden skills and raise standards of all pupils through the introduction of accredited awards and therefore meet the aims and objectives outlined in the 14–19 proposals.

■ GCSE PE Full Course

■ GCSE PE Short Course

■ GCSE PE Games/Dance

■ Level 1 Sport Leadership

■ Level 1 Dance Leadership

■ Level 2 Sport Leadership

■ BTEC Diploma Games

■ BTEC Diploma Outdoor
Education

■ BTEC Diploma Dance

■ Duke of Edinburgh Bronze
Award

■ National Governing Body
Young Leader Awards

■ Diploma in Sport and
Active leisure

■ A Level Physical Education

■ Level 2 certificate in
supporting learning in PE

Figure 10.4 An inclusive 14–19 physical education curriculum

Now that there seems to be a clearer direction with regards to the future of the education system in the UK we have also considered whether vocational courses in physical education are more appropriate for particular pupils. Vocational education has been identified as being at the heart of the education system and vocational awards and other forms of accredited learning in physical education would seem to be most appropriate in this respect. Likewise, an emphasis on accredited forms of sport education (Siedentop 1994) as part of Key Stage 4 physical education would be another viable alternative to 'core' non-accredited physical education. It provides pupils with experiences outside of traditional forms of participation whereby they learn to become informed spectators, officials, managers, record keepers and administrators and gain recognition for their achievements whilst displaying the fundamental values and virtues of physical education.

The previous line of thinking amongst education policymakers means that there may have been very positive reforms for physical education departments with the above structures in place. The introduction of the revamped 'English Baccalaureate' however, makes no such provision and data published in the House of Commons Select Committee report 2010–12[4] showed that physical education as a curriculum subject should not be considered when measuring school league table positions. We strongly believe, however, that compulsory accreditation in physical education should be an essential component of a pupil's overall education but must not reduce the essential values of physical education or jeopardise longevity in physical activity post-compulsory schooling. Our research suggests that accredited awards at Key Stage 4 and beyond can be taught in such a way as to maintain the humanistic values of physical education whereby pupils gain as much from the personal and social benefits of physical education as they do from accredited forms of learning. On this basis, physical education has an opportunity to utilise its potential in developing appropriate and appealing forms of physical activity beyond the age of 14, based upon individual needs and pupil choice.

Conclusion

Compulsory accredited awards for all pupils has much potential for improving pupils' learning in physical education within the established 14–19 age-range. Whilst we do not profess to have all the answers for an inclusive 14–19 physical education curriculum, we do recognise the need for innovation and change from more conventional 'core' non-accredited programmes of physical education in schools. It is still our contention that a range of accredited awards in physical education can provide opportunities for all pupils to engage in worthwhile lifetime activities whilst gaining relevant and appropriate qualifications that are applicable within the world of sport and leisure as well as local communities. Equally, our suggestions are a response to the changing nature of teachers' work in schools and the evolution of the role of the contemporary physical education professional.

Notes

1   The General Certificate of Education (GCSE) is taken by most UK pupils between the ages of 14–16 across a range of subjects including Physical Education.
2   Core physical education refers to the statutory provision of physical education that all schools must provide pupils aged 14–16 in secondary schools by law. Core physical education is usually taught as a non-accredited component of pupils compulsory 14–16 schooling.
3   The **Joint Council for Qualifications** commonly referred to as **JCQ** is a council acting as a single voice for the seven largest qualification providers in the UK offering GCSE, GCE, AEA, Scottish Highers, Entry Level, Vocational and vocationally-related qualifications: AQA, City & Guilds, CCEA, Edexcel, OCR, SQA and WJEC.
4   The Education Select Committee report (2011) included reference to a YouGov poll conducted for *The Sun* in January 2011 which asked which subjects should count towards a "school's league table positions". The total results shown in the House of Commons Select Committee report did not include physical education whilst Dance achieved eight percent response from those surveyed.

References

Carroll, R. (1995) 'Examinations in Physical Education and Sport: Gender differences and influences on subject choice', in Lawrence, L., Murdoch, E. and Parker, S. (eds) (1995) *Professional and Developmental Issues in Leisure, Sport and Education*, Brighton, LSA Publications: 59–71.

Golder, G. (2010) '14–19 Accredited Qualifications' in Capel, S. and Whitehead, M. (eds) (2010) *Learning to Teach Physical Education in the Secondary School: A Companion to School Experience*, London, RoutledgeFalmer: 234–51.

Green, K. (2005) 'Examinations: A 'new orthodoxy' in physical education?' in Green, K. and Hardman, K. (eds) *Physical Education: Essential Issues*, London, Sage: 143–60.

Green, K. (2008) *Understanding Physical Education*, London, Sage, 78–97.

Grout, H., and Long, G. (2009) 'Teaching theoretical physical education', in Grout, G. and Long, G. (2009) *Improving Teaching and Learning in Physical Education*: 177–210.

Hammond, N. (2012) 'Sports Leaders UK', *Physical Education Matters*, 7(1), 89.

Huggett, C. and Manley, C. (2010) *Teaching Sport and Leisure 14+*, Maidenhead McGraw-Hill, Open University Press.

Joint Council for Qualifications (2008) 'Results 2008', www.jcq.org.uk

Joint Council for Qualifications (2011) 'Results 2011 – GCSE, Applied GCSE, Entry Level, Diploma', www.jcq.org.uk

MacFadyen, T. and Bailey, R. (2002) 'Examinations in Physical Education', in *Teaching Physical Education 11–18*, London, Continuum Press, 90–101.

Nutt, G. and Clarke, G. (2002) 'The Hidden Curriculum and the Changing Nature of Teachers' Work', in Laker, A. (ed.), The *Sociology of Sport and Physical Education*, London: RoutledgeFalmer, 148–66.

Ofsted (2009) '*Physical education in schools 2005/08: Working towards 2012 and beyond'*, April, Reference No. 080249.

Ofsted (2011) *'School Sport Partnerships: A Survey of good practice'*, June 2011, Reference No. 100237.

Scottish Executive (2004) *'The Report of the Review Group on Physical Education'*, Scottish Executive, June 2004.

Siedentop, D. (1994) *Sport Education: Quality Physical Education through positive sport experiences*, Human Kinetics.

Sports Leaders UK (2011) – www.sportsleaders.org with kind permission.

Stidder, G. and Wallis, J. (2003), 'Accreditation in Physical Education: Meeting the needs and interests of pupils at Key Stage Four', in Hayes, S. and Stidder, G. (eds) (2003) *Equity and Inclusion in Physical Education: Contemporary issues for teachers, trainees and practitioners*, London, Routledge: 185–209.

Stidder, G. and Wallis, J. (2005) 'The Place of Physical Education within the Proposed 14–19 Curriculum: Insights and implications for future practice (Part One)', *British Journal of Teaching Physical Education*, Winter, 36(4), 43–8.

Stidder, G. and Wallis, J. (2006) 'The Place of Physical Education within the Proposed 14–19 Curriculum: Insights and implications for future practice (Part Two)', *British Journal of Teaching Physical Education*, 37(1), 40–4.

The House of Commons Select Committee (2011) *'The English Baccalaureate'*, *Fifth Report of Session 2010–12*, vol. 1, 28 July, The Stationery Office.

Youth Sport Trust (2008) 'Audit of Dance Provision in English Schools 2006/07 – Final Report', Youth Sports Trust.

11 Sport policy, physical education and participation

Inclusive issues for schools?

Marc Keech

I guess for me it was a double hatred thing. Not only did the PE teachers bully me for being 'un-sporty' ... but also because I think they realised that I was never going to be the macho sort of guy they wanted to produce from that school. I got picked on because I was a very girly sort of boy and remember watching as another boy got beaten up and called a poof and a f*&^ing queer by one male PE teacher. Ah the good old days of the late 1970s! ... NOT! I wonder what they'd make of me now?

http://uk.answers.yahoo.com/question/index?qid=20071115092019AA5mRs5
Accessed 26 August 2010

Introduction

Since 6 July 2005, when Jacques Rogge, President of the International Olympic Committee, announced that the Olympic Games would be hosted by London in 2012, there has been an unprecedented focus on domestic sport policy. The centrality of schools to the development of young people's sporting opportunities in the local community has meant that schools have reflected, with varying degrees of success, on how to extend and link their provision with the support of, and to, local agencies, especially local clubs. As the editors of this book have explained in their introduction, physical education and sport are clearly not the same, but PE and sport have become assimilated into an increasingly significant but complex and 'overcrowded' (Houlihan 2000) policy network in which PE became the initial focus of engaging young people in physical activity and sport for a variety of reasons. For example, ten years ago, health was seen as a medium-term policy concern amongst a number of broader policy goals attached to or attributed to the then nascent PE and School Sport strategy (Keech 2003), but now, the increasing rise in obesity amongst young people has meant that PE has a more prominent role in combating childhood obesity. This chapter reviews the recent developments in PE and sport policy in England with particular reference to PE and sport as elements of broader policy concerns. As with other contributors to this book the discourse for the chapter is developed through my personal reflections, and as shown in Chapter 2 discourse analysis requires a deeply reflexive approach to recognise the rules of formation, and to understand the patterns of power relations, through 'self-conscious analytical scrutiny' (England, 1994: 82). Discourse analysis enables the problematising of policymaking processes, through examining the dialogue which has occurred in speeches, debates, documents and other forums, and enables the development of understanding about dominant and marginalised discourses. Former Prime Minister Gordon Brown called for, a 'united team effort' in the run up to the 2012 London Olympic Games to make sport a part of every child's day, building a greater sporting nation and a fitter nation. However, the chapter asserts that the language and discourse of recent policy has led to confusion, rather than clarification, when, in actual fact, little has changed.

Personal reflections and policy implications: creating a reflexive discourse?

I thought I would be a PE teacher until my similarities to a brick near the swimming pool ruled out any possibility. I still wonder what type of teacher I would have been. A couple of years ago, I found myself half a mile from my old secondary school and in a moment of unusual nostalgia thought I would revisit the site of my school sporting success. It was disconcerting to see only two remnants of the school, now a pleasant enough housing development on the outskirts of a sizeable city. The first remnant was the half-length artificial cricket wickets, partially overgrown, where a couple of others and I spent lunchtimes and evenings honing our techniques or, more memorably, acting as net bowlers for the Head of PE, needing batting practice ahead of and/or after his latest weekend failure. The second was a view of the top of the 'Goat Track' a fairly steep incline of about 600 metres that was and still is a public footpath, but more infamously known as the sadistic element of the school's cross-country course. One PE lesson stands out; a cross-country 'lesson' in which my class would run a shortened version of the course in one direction and, at the end, we would run the opposite direction but starting in timed intervals, with the last setting off first, the idea being we would all finish at the same time. Having finished first, the second run started with me waiting for everyone else to start and I set off, quickly passing the physically challenged, the social workers, lawyers, nuclear physicists and someone who now resides at Her Majesty's Pleasure, all victims of the 'Goat Track'. Ignoring the abuse, I chased down a couple of decent runners and won the second race too – a great lesson; I won twice!

And now, with competitive school sport at the forefront of the current policy agenda, I wonder if I would have been a teacher that embodied that winning mentality or whether I would have been sufficiently reflective to develop the broad and balanced PE curriculum needed to develop physical literacy and contribute to developing the health of young people. Despite everything that has been written, in this book and elsewhere, significant questions remain. What is school sport about? Why sport and not PE? Why do we want to encourage participation? What is the role of schools, our PE profession and their partners in provision? At the heart of the ongoing ontological and practical debates about the purpose of PE and school sport is the perpetual issue of whether politicians, and many others, understand what has to be achieved and the only consequence of that misunderstanding will be to get things wrong. The 'school sport' programme under the Labour government developed and broadened the foundation learning that takes place in physical education. It also became the nexus of three important policy sectors with complex and overlapping relationships: talent identification and development; education and raising standards and the development of school/community sport and health. The purpose of school sport has been to expand a broader experience not only of sports themselves but of physical activities associated with health and physical literacy. Outdoor activities, dance or parkour[1] engage young people, women in particular, through different methods to traditional team or individual sports, but the hardest question to answer, and one which all those involved terms of increasing participation in terms of making policy work in practice have grappled with for the last 25 years, is how to sustain these activities for broader health and social benefits, and lifelong participation. Within physical education lessons pupils engage in a range of activities including games, gymnastics, dance, swimming, athletics and outdoor education. In the UK, programmes of study and units of work provide the basis for teachers to plan their intended learning outcomes which allow pupils to select and apply skills, tactics and compositional ideas, acquire and develop these skills and evaluate and improve performance. School sport is the structured learning that takes place beyond the school curriculum (i.e. in the extended curriculum), sometimes referred to as out-of-school-hours learning. Again, the context for the learning is physical activity but with the publication of 'Creating a Sporting Habit for Life' (DCMS 2012) the latest youth (and community) sport policy document, one may be forgiven for feeling dizzy.

Coming around again: continuity and change in PE and (competitive) sport policy

When Labour came to power in 1997, after 18 years of Conservative government, it was easy for the former to point out the failings of the latter. PE and school sport were commonly agreed to be in a neglected state and the first national sport policy statement, inspired by former Prime Minister, John Major, *Sport: Raising the Game* (Department of National Heritage 1995) had so far had had little impact. Labour pointed to the dismal state of school sport when they acceded power, citing the sale of playingfields, poor facilities and a lack of infrastructure to develop participation, and it is true that PE and sport had been of marginal concern to policymakers up until the early to mid-1990s. However, Roberts (1996), Rowe and Champion (2000) noted that, contrary to popular observations, young people's participation in sport and physical activity had increased from the mid-1970s to the mid-1990s. But by the time Sport England was reporting in 2003, both the time spent participating in physical activity and the range of activities were found to have increased (for the years 1995–2002) – especially in out-of-school activities. Furthermore, participation in 'lifestyle' activities, such as aerobics and recreational swimming, had increased amongst young people and was seen as evidence that sport and physical activity amongst young people was not in decline; rather, that young people were engaging in activities without being members of clubs and participating in competition. Far from this being the death knell for competitive sport, Bloyce and Smith (2010) noted a number of studies which demonstrated that:

> The increasing desire amongst young people (and adults) in many cases to engage in more commercialised, individualised and flexible sports and physical activities rather than more regular, structured forms of involvement such as that required by a strong commitment to club-based sport, would appear consistent with the broader changes in the increasingly individualised lifestyles of participants.
>
> (Bloyce and Smith 2010: 60)

The Labour policy paper for sport, *A Sporting Future for All* (DCMS 2000, 2001), again reiterated the need to address the perception of decline in young people's participation in sport and physical activity. The period since 2003 witnessed similar focus on physical education policy, initially through the PESSCL (Physical Education, School Sport and Club Links) strategy 2003–08 (DfES 2003), and the PESSYP (Physical Education School Sport and Young People) strategy, initially scheduled by the previous Labour Government from 2008 to 2011, and which came to an end when the Coalition government took power in May 2010. Community and school sport were increasingly better resourced under Labour, and beginning to attract funding from other departments as the physical and mental benefits of physical activity became more widely recognised and demonstrably evidenced that increasing government intervention in education and sport policy facilitated a 'dramatic change in the political salience of school sport and PE' (Houlihan and Green 2006: 74). Funded to the tune of over £1 billion the PESSCLs strategy incorporated the School Sport Partnerships network. Partnerships were centred on specialist sports colleges, part of the specialist schools programme initiated by the previous Conservative government, which were linked to local secondary and primary schools and sports clubs. School Sport Co-ordinators, released from full-time teaching to develop out-of-school hours opportunities were critical in ensuring that more opportunities became reality to a wider range of participants (Flintoff 2003). By 2008, 90 per cent of 5–16 year-olds received two hours of PE and school sport a week, up from 25 per cent in 2003 (DCSF 2008). Gordon Brown, in one of his first policy announcements as Prime Minister, pledged in July 2007, to increase the target to five hours a week. In February 2008 he backed this by committing £775 million over the next three years, of which £100 million would be spent on promoting competition. The 2008–11 strategy sought to extend the amount of opportunity through what became known as the 'five-hour offer'. In addition to at least two hours per week of high quality PE and Sport in school for all 5–16 year-olds, all children and young people aged 5–19 would be offered opportunities to participate in a further three hours per week of sporting activities provided through schools, Further

Education Colleges, clubs and community providers (Sport England/Youth Sport Trust 2009). Nevertheless, the 2009–10 PE and School Sport survey reported that:

> Across Years 1–13, 55% of pupils participated in at least three hours of high quality PE and out of hours school sport during the 2009/10 academic year ... an encouraging increase of five percentage points in terms of the proportion of pupils in Years 1–13 taking part in three hours of PE and out of hours school sport. Participation levels are highest in Years 4–6, and also reasonably high in Years 1–3 and Years 7–8. They are at their lowest in Years 12 and 13. The 2009/10 survey found a very large increase in the proportion of pupils participating in intra-school competitive activities during the academic year – up from 69% (of Years 1–11) in 2008/09 to 78% in 2009/10. Like participation in intra-school competition in general, regular participation has also increased substantially over the last year – up from 28% of Years 3–13 in 2008/09 to 39% in 2009/10.
>
> (Quick *et al.* 2010: 4–6)

Since 2003 the identification of young people's 'needs' have become increasingly prominent in developing policy direction. Of particular concern to physical education and school sport has been the extent to which there has been a contribution to other policy priorities such as health, wellbeing and educational attainment. Bloyce and Smith (2010) confirmed previous predictions (Keech 2003) that as a consequence of responding to the changing policy priorities of, and conflicting pressures from, government, aspects of the provision of PESS have come increasingly to be characterised by a move towards a slight downgrading of delivering sport and physical activity programmes through PE to achieve sports-related outcomes, in favour of implementing strategies designed to achieve other non-sport government objectives (Bloyce and Smith 2010: 71). School Sport Partnerships did reinforce the popularity of the most widely available activities traditionally present in many PE curricula such as football, cricket, gymnastics, athletics and netball (IYS 2008a, b). But other alternatives also grew in popularity, such as boxing, golf, swimming. Outdoor activities, martial arts and dance have been made available to pupils as part of curriculum PE but, also increasingly, as part of extra-curricular time too. SSPs have been effective in enhancing both the amount of time available for pupils to engage in PE and school sport and the links between schools, community sports clubs, sports development units and specialist sports coaches. The number of competitions was also growing steadily, augmented by the appointment of a competition manager to each SSP as part of the five-hour offer. The latter, in particular, are said to have been effective in helping to increase the number and diversity of intra- and inter-school sports competitions and events but evidence remains patchy for, just as the impact of increased competitions was taking effect, the posts ceased to exist.

Policy as discourse and discourse as policy in PE and school sport

The examination of discussion, narrative or dialogue is the basic premise of discourse analysis and it involves examining communication in order to gain new insights. Policymakers and politicians tend to think within a discourse framework which reflects their own value systems and beliefs. For some, the starting point for a policy as discourse approach 'is a close analysis of items that do make the political agenda to see how the construction or representation of those issues limits what is talked about as possible or desirable, or as impossible or undesirable' (Bacchi 2000: 49). Reflections on the coalition's policy have been initially focused on the factors which permit an initial understanding on the developing discourse, the establishing of coalition policy to distinguish and differentiate from previous policy, the rationale for competitive school sport, the implementation of the National School Games and the development of a new strategy for youth and community sport.

Faced with an unprecedented deficit in the public purse and within days of coming to power, the Coalition government began a review of Labour's ambitious Building Schools for the Future project in as series of austerity measures. Plans for the rebuilding or refurbishment of hundreds of secondary schools were put on hold. In early July 2010, Secretary of State for Education, Michael Gove cancelled Building Schools for the Future, immediately suspending plans for 715 new schools and cutting funding for school swimming pools. Mr Gove later announced that he would abolish Labour's £162 million a year SSP network; the language of the press release is indicative of the policy change from the previous government:

> The Department for Education is ending the £162 million PE and Sports Strategy of the previous administration, to give schools the time and freedom to focus on providing competitive sport. In recent years there has been a decline in young people taking part in traditionally competitive sports such as rugby union, netball and hockey because teachers and school sports coordinators have been too focused on top-down targets. In fact the most recent School Sport Survey showed that only around two in every five pupils play competitive sport regularly within their own school, and only one in five plays regularly against other schools.
>
> After seven years and £2.4 billion investment from the Government and Lottery, the Department expects all schools to have embedded the good practice and collaboration developed over this time and to continue providing two hours a week of PE and sport. ... The Department *has lifted the many requirements of the previous Government's PE and Sport Strategy, so giving schools the clarity and freedom to concentrate on competitive school sports* [emphasis added].
>
> (DoE October 20, 2010)

Prime Minister David Cameron ordered a rethink of the controversial decision and Mr. Gove was forced to announce a temporary U-turn: money would be found to keep 'key elements' of the scheme going until the 2012 London Olympics. Mr Gove believed the SSP network had become overly bureaucratic and had failed to deliver increasing levels of competitive sport in schools. The answer, he surmised, was to free schools from the requirement to meet targets and allow them to manage their own policies in order to avoid: planning and implementing a centralised approach to sport, collecting information about every pupil for an annual survey, delivering a range of new government sport initiatives each year, reporting termly to the department on various performance indicators, conforming to a national blueprint for how to deliver PE and sport, and how to use their staff and resources, all of which were requirements for the PESSYP strategy. Free schools, therefore, will not have to follow the national curriculum, nor report back to government and may take their own decisions. All of a sudden, the analogy used in our Introduction of the dinosaur games teacher bearing one ball and bag of bibs became a stark reality. When considering the challenges facing sport policy in the UK, especially after the Olympic Games are over, developing increased participation and achieving a legacy for young people is an objective more difficult to achieve than all the other legacy promises combined. Using a six-week, time-limited mega-event to inspire young people to participate for a lifetime and ensure that adults return to, or increase, participation in sport and physical activity is an impossible undertaking. It may be possible to lever participation through the profile of the London 2012 Olympic Games to aid the rebuilding of PE and school sport infrastructure from 2003 until 2010, providing investment in the latter remains at appropriate levels. The partial reprieve of funding did little to lift the gloom of the long-term picture and caused the former Labour Minister for Sport, Gerry Sutcliffe to later lament:

> The Coalition noted that competitive school sport under Labour had declined. The number of children taking part in competitive sport, not just between schools but in schools, increased from 58% in 2006–07 to 78% in 2009–10. Sport was a cornerstone in tackling numerous key policy issues, such as obesity and related health issues, antisocial behaviour, educational attainment and citizenship. It was a genuinely cross-departmental priority. Interestingly, there was general cross-party consensus that Labour got it broadly right on school sport, and certainly cross-party support for school sport partnerships. There was no indication that Opposition parties had an alternative agenda.
>
> Within weeks, the Government [was] forced into a partial U-turn because of an unprecedented backlash against their proposals – lead not just by politicians, but by Olympians, sports bodies, sports journalists and the grass roots volunteer army. What we got was a cobbled together set of announcements that still leave the future of school sport in jeopardy. SSPs and school sports organisers have been told not to expect funding beyond August 2013. Those cuts will effectively mean an end to the infrastructure that supports the school sport network at the very time that we should be seeking to increase activity in the run-up to next year's Olympic and Paralympic games. What makes matters worse is that the Secretary of State

has removed the need for schools to collect data on pupils' progress. That will make it almost impossible effectively to monitor future participation rates and the effect of those cuts.

(Hansard 2011a: col. 203WH)

The School Games, the flagship government policy, already existed in the guise of the UK school games, which were and have continued to be supported to the tune of £10 million a year by the marquee sponsor, supermarket chain Sainsbury's. The emphasis on an annual competition, which is most likely to be beneficial to young people who already participate and/or who are at the élite end of their sport, and which was only formalised in 2010 as a replacement for the SSP network, is a desperately risky policy. Griffiths and Armour (2010) had already noted that whilst it was too late to establish anything new, embedding legacy ambitions within existing PE and school sport structures offered the most likely chance to obtain a legacy for young people's participation after 2012. The Children's Minister, Tim Loughton, rebuffed such thought: 'Young people's involvement in competitive sport remains disappointingly low. We aim to spark a competitive sport revolution by giving thousands of young people the chance to compete at the Olympic and Paralympic-style school sport competitions in 2012' (Vasager 2010: 3).

The School Games are made up of four levels of activity: competition in schools, between schools, at county/area level and a national finals event. Level one focuses on sporting competition for all students in school through intra-school competition. At level two individuals and teams are selected to represent their schools in local inter-school competitions. Level three has the county/area staging multi-sport School Games festivals as a culmination of year-round school sport competition and the culmination is level four – the Sainsbury's School Games finals: a national multi-sport event where the most talented young people in the UK will be selected to compete in our sporting venues (including the Olympic Park in 2012). Supporters of the School Games could point out the varied levels of activity and competition that are available to participants. The introductory level seems easily embedded in the practice of many schools, linking with curriculum enrichment activities and wherein existing individual or house rewards can be earned, providing, that is, that the school chooses to do so. Thereafter, the inclusive educational value of the Games can only lessen because of the nature of selection and whilst the selection of (many) additional teams, at varying levels of competition, can overcome some individual and practical barriers, the School Games already exhibit many of the problems of previous event-based policies such as in Active Sports, wherein the event, as an end, is perfectly plausible but there is no indication of exit routes or sustainability pathways into further participation. One of the 450 schools games organisers, who previously ran a successful School Sport Partnership in a major city, has countered the potential of the School Games claiming that the event will not lead to more competitions, but the reverse, because of the number of schools able to opt out of the process.

In January 2011, the Government announced a comprehensive review of the national curriculum. The review is likely to see a slimmed down curriculum for

PE and sport in schools. Although PE is likely to be retained as a compulsory national curriculum subject, there is no guarantee that the two-hour offer of the Labour Government, never mind the five-hour offer, will be retained. The quality and quantity of PE and school sport that is now being offered in schools has improved vastly in recent years and it is this point that has vexed many PE and sport development professionals. Having been told by one government that they were doing an important job well, to then be told by another government that they were not doing anywhere near as well as they thought has led to confusion, disgruntlement and disenchantment. The policy shift which led to the dismantling of the school sport system drew highly negative comments often couched as questions, such as: What is the rationale for change? Are PE and/or sport in schools valued? Is the link between the quality of PE, school sport and other policy agendas not recognised? In contrast, and whisper it quietly, it was naïve to think that funding had to continue unabated and SSPs could have done more to embed their positions into local infrastructure. Such a highly charged policy process means that to maintain the profile of PE and school sport on the political agenda, one should have an awareness of the micro-dynamics not just of the evidence but of 'policy entrepreneurship' requiring champions to make the case and fight the cause (Talbot 2011). The next fight for the PE profession is the slimmed down revision of the National Curriculum. There is no indication, at the beginning of 2012, of what the curriculum will look like and little likelihood, let alone indication, that free schools will not be exempt from guidelines adopting a basic provision of PE and school sport. If PE professionals needed any further persuasion about the need to demonstrate the value of their subject and, indeed, profession, two excerpts from the Culture, Media and Sport Questions in Parliament in December 2011, should energise them to be involved with one view or the other.

> *Ms Harriet Harman (Lab)*: Is not school sport the bedrock of participation, and should it not be a priority? If so, why have the Minister's Government cut spending on school sports by 64%? Is that not sending the message that school sport no longer matters?
>
> *Hugh Robertson (Minister for Sport, Con)*: The first point is that ... this Department is not responsible for school sport, which is funded by the Department for Education. The Secretary of State [for the DCMS] has championed personally a school games competition that is intended to drive up participation.
>
> *Ms Harman*: The Minister talks about driving up participation, but will he tell us how he will monitor how much sport young people are doing in schools when he has scrapped the school sports survey? As his Government have cut the school sports partnership (network), it is even more important that we know what the effect on participation in sport is. Is it not remarkable that Ministers are sitting there saying, 'It's nothing to do with u'"? They really should be making an impact on Ministers in other Departments to ensure that they support school sport across the whole of Government.

Mr Robertson: I am afraid the right Hon. and learned Lady is mistaken. The policy responsibility for school sport lies with the Department for Education, and she should know that all too well. This Department is playing its part by introducing a new school games competition. That has been extraordinarily successful, with 11,000 schools now signed up. We will also produce a new measure for those aged 16–24 – precisely the point at which we take responsibility for young people - among whom participation has been falling year on year for most of the last 10 years.

(Hansard 2011b, column 907)

Clive Efford (Lab and shadow minister for sport): The person who launched School Games was the Secretary of State for the Department of Culture, Media and Sport, not the Department of Education, now they have been using a figure of one-in-five children involved in inter-school competitive sport and they will know that that figure comes from the PE Sports Survey carried out of schools every year and that that figure is measured on the basis of children taking part in nine competitive sport events against other schools in a school year. Now we know from the Under Secretary of State for Education in the Westminster Hall debate that he says that that's not an ambitious target, so can the minister tell us how is he going to measure the increase, the impact of School Games, on increasing participation in competitive sport, and is the benchmark nine times in the school year, or is it more?

Mr Robertson: Let me answer in two parts, by the number of schools that want to sign up, and I'm delighted to say we've got 11,000 schools signed up, which I'm sure he would welcome, and the part of the equation for which this department is responsible, which is the cadre of people from 16–25, where we will be making the announcement in the New Year.

(Hansard 2011c, cols 912–13)

A(nother) strategy for youth sport – 2012 and the future

There is nothing inherently wrong with competitive sport in schools for many young people; nor is there any clear reason to predicate competitive sport over the development of physical literacy. As early as 1987, the Thatcher government commissioned an inquiry which found no evidence of any philosophy that is against competition. *If* there has been a decline in competitive sport (and if so, it has been greatly exaggerated) it has little to do with ideology and much more to do with the entrepreneurship of often ill-informed politicians. Competitive school sport alone does not constitute a holistic government policy, especially when less than 60 per cent of schools are signed up, according to the parliamentary reply given by the Sports Minister, to the flagship policy. The Secretaries of State for Education and the DCMS must comprehend that successful participation in competitive sport can be achieved only by first mastering the basics of sport and PE. High quality PE is essential for developing the necessary skills and confidenceto participate effectively in competitive sport. But prioritising pupils into competitive sport, without first building physical literacy is, at best, unrealistic and at worst disasterous. That prompts some immediate questions about how more competition relates to PE, and to issues of health and obesity; and to whether competition is likely to be inclusive and what effect these competitions will have on existing school resources and programmes. Another underlying theme, perhaps based more on instinct than ideology, is the Conservative-led preference/prejudice for competition. There seems to be no underlying rationale for the preference/prejudice in favour of competitive team sports and no explanation of how competitions relate to participation and Olympic legacy for the vast majority of young people. Is the instinct of politicians and policymakers actually one which is bounded by the discourse frameworks which have developed their own personal ideologies? Only by changing a system that in the past has focused too closely on the able and the willing, can the government's ambitions be met. Competition does not increase participation *per se*; rather, it is regular participation that engenders entering the competitive arena (Keech 2012).

Sport England and NGBs have been identified as being primarily responsible for legacy but it is uncertain about with what and whom they will work. With schools being given the option to structure curriculum and invest in subjects as they see fit, will PE and school sport remain priority areas? The ongoing challenge to address the issue of sustainability will always be at the forefront of local practice. With approximately 20,000 schools in England alone, and just over eight million pupils, the School Games could reach out extensively to many young people. But they won't. In January 2012, the Coalition government published the latest strategy for youth and community sport in England, *Creating a Sporting Habit for Life* (DCMS 2012). In a departure from Labour policy, and in a return to policies first articulated in 1982 (Sports Council 1982), the focus has returned almost entirely to those aged 14–25.

> Since London won the right to stage the Games in 2005, participation rates amongst young people have fallen, with many of our major sports – including Football, Tennis and Swimming – seeing declines in the proportion of 16-25 year olds regularly taking part. Whilst participation rates remain relatively high in school (where curriculum Physical Education (PE) is compulsory), when young people leave school the proportion who continue to play sport falls dramatically. The problem is starker for girls, with around only a third participating in sport at 18 compared to two-thirds of boys.
>
> (DCMS 2012: 3)

Amongst other vaguely defined promises, every secondary school in England,will be offered a community sport club on its site with a direct link to one or more NGBs, depending on the local clubs in its area, county sports partnerships will be given new resources to create effective links locally between schools and sport in the community and all secondary schools who wish to do so will be supported to open up, or keep open, their sports facilities for local community use, and at least a third of these will receive additional funding to make this happen. Further education colleges and universities will also be given revised resources to help meet policy targets. There is nothing new here other than the rhetoric of discourse, unsubstantiated by exactly how policy will work out in practice. NGB Whole Sport Plan investment is being asked to focus on growth in participation in the 14–25 age range and across the adult population; the quality of sporting experience to keep people playing sport; high quality talent development to create a better talent pool and help those with real potential to make the grade; growth in participation by people who have disabilities, including the most talented. The strategy has £1 billion of funding, but other than the Sainsbury's funding for the School Games, all of the money had already been allocated in previous public or quasi-private announcements. What is different, according to the Culture Secretary Jeremy Hunt, is the refocusing of the available resources – away from adults (a group which has seen an increase in participation since London won the right to stage the Games in 2005) towards teenagers and young people (Bond 2012). The difference, unfortunately, only relates to the previous government and not to the ideas of 30 years ago.

Conclusion

The elements of continuity and change in PE and sport are evident in the new youth sport policy. The continuity is provided by the need to continue to address the same key issues as 10, 20 or even 30 years ago. The language, the rhetoric and the emerging discourse of the current government provide both a point of analysis and of concern and confusion, not just because, through no fault of their own many involved in community sport and physical activity fail to grasp the key issues. If policy is predicated on the dedication of volunteers there should never be surprise that volunteers fail to grasp the nuances of the professionalised world of developing PE and school sport. Dedicated PE and sports staff in schools are often asked to demonstrate innovation, but such practice is often guided by one or more of four key principles which shape policy in practice; access, equity, opportunity and sustainability – nothing has changed there and nothing has changed from 30 years ago when the national sports strategy barely mentioned PE. A lack of a centralised structure will simply mean that some of the networks created by the previous government will continue; and continue to ensure that the progress of the last ten years is not lost. In some schools and communities, school sport will cease to be a priority because there are other, more urgent priorities. There should be no doubt that present cuts are hitting PE and sport hard and disproportionately, with the most disadvantaged groups suffering the most. The changes in recent policy have not been thought through or planned properly and there was little understanding of both short- and longer-term consequences. It is argued that the negative effects of this ideologically or instinctively driven approach will be exacerbated by Sport England's strategy for improving sports participation, which is chasing the wrong targets and relying too heavily on a national governing body approach, which traditionally and in the main only has expertise in performance-based sport. The weakness of the PE and sports lobby as a whole means that understanding the 'needs' of young people have been an increasing policy priority but the preliminary ideas for the new national curriculum illustrate that a 'needs'-based approach may be more common in the future, reflecting the words of Roberts (1996) who first noticed the development of broader activity-related participation. Physical education, sports development and the sports coaching profession as a whole have been told repeatedly of the need to embrace and develop innovation and creativity to respond to political change, and to accusations, real or imagined, about the lack of sustainability, and the survival-at-all-costs mentality. In the build up to the next incarnation of the physical education National Curriculum, now scheduled to be implemented in 2014, the buzzwords and messages centre upon understanding in much more detail and with greater sensitivity the motivations for participation and the specific types of activities that young people wish to participate in. Sadly, and once again, there's nothing new in this and the sooner we can all recognise the point, a consensus about the meaning, purpose and actual achievements of PE and school sport can be established.

Note

1   Parkour is a form of urban gymnastics originating from an activity otherwise known as 'free running'.

References

Bacchi, C. (2000) 'Policy as discourse: what does it mean? Where does it get us?', *Discourse: Studies in the Cultural Politics of Education*, 21(1), 45–57.

Bloyce, D. and Smith, A. (2010) *Sport policy and development: an introduction*, London: Routledge.

Bond, D. (2012) Securing Olympic legacy proves tricky task, www.bbc.co.uk/blogs/davidbond/2012/01/securing_the_olympic_legacy_pr.html#more (accessed 11 January 2012).

DCMS (2000) *A Sporting Future for All*, London: DCMS.

DCMS (2001) *A Sporting Future for All, the Government's Plan for Sport*, London: DCMS.

DCMS (2012) *Creating a Sporting Habit for Life*, London: DCMS.

DCSF (2008) 'School Sport Survey 2007/08', London, Department for Children, Schools, and Families, RR DCSF – RW063.

DfES (2003) *Learning through PE and Sport, A guide to the physical education, school sport and club links strategy*, London, DfES.

Department of National Heritage (1995) *Sport: raising the game*, London: Department of National Heritage.

DoE (2010) Refocusing sport in schools to build a lasting legacy of the 2012 Games, Press Release, 20 October, www.education.gov.uk/inthenews/inthenews/a0065473/refocusing-sport-in-schools-to-build-a-lasting-legacy-of-the-2012-games (accessed 11 January 2011).

England, K. (1994) 'Getting personal: Reflexivity, positionality, and feminist research', *The Professional Geographer*, 46(1), 80–9.

Flintoff, A. (2003) 'The school sport co-ordinator programme: changing the role of the physical education teacher? *Sport, education and society*, 8(2), 231–50.

Griffiths, M. and Armour, K. (2010) 'Physical education and youth sport in England: conceptual and practical foundations for an Olympic legacy?', *Paper presented to the one day conference: Fit for London, 2012? An Assessment of UK Sport Policy in Comparative Contexts*, University of Birmingham, 19 July 2010.

Hansard (2011a) WH, col. 203 (13 December).

Hansard (2011b) HC vol. 537, col. 907 (15 December).

Hansard (2011c) HC vol. 537, cols. 912-3 (15 December).

Houlihan, B. (2000) 'Sporting excellence, schools and sports development: the politics of crowded policy spaces', *European Physical Education Review*, 6(2), 171–93.

Houlihan, B. and Green, M. (2006) 'The changing status of school sport and physical education: explaining policy change', *Sport, Education and Society*, 11 (1), 73–92.

IYS (2008a) School Sport Partnerships: *Annual Monitoring and Evaluation Report for 2007: School Sport Coordinator Survey*, Loughborough: Institute of Youth Sport/ Loughborough University.

IYS (2008b) School Sport Partnerships: *Annual Monitoring and Evaluation Report for 2007: Primary Link Teacher Survey*, Loughborough: Institute of Youth Sport/ Loughborough University.

Keech, M. (2003) 'Sport Through Education? Issues for Schools and Sports development', in: Hayes, S. and Stidder, G. (eds) *Equity and Inclusion in Physical Education*, London: Routledge, 211–31.

Keech, M. (2012) 'Youth Sport and London's 2012 Olympic Legacy', in Sugden, J. and Tomlinson, A. (eds) *Watching the Olympics: politics, power and representation*, London: Routledge, 82–96.

Quick, S., Simon, A. and Thornton, A. (2010) *PE and Sport Survey*, London: Department of Education, Research Report DFE-RR302.

Roberts, K. (1996) 'Young people, schools, sport and government policy', *Sport, Education and Society*, 1(1) 47–57.

Rowe, N. and Champion, R. (2000) *Young People and Sport National Survey, 1999*, London: Sport England.

Sport England/Youth Sport Trust (2009) *The PE and sport strategy for young people: a guide to delivering the five-hour offer*, London: Sport England/Youth Sport Trust.

Sports Council (1982) *Sport in the community: the next ten years*, London: The Sports Council.

Talbot, M. (2011) 'Power plays in sport and physical education', keynote address to the 5th annual conference of the PSA Sport and Politics sub-group, *Sport under Pressure: the sustainability of sport in times of austerity*, University of Birmingham, 18 March.

Vasager, J. (2010) School sport is growing but not fast enough, say Ministers', *The Guardian*, 24 September, 3.

12 Healthism and the obesity discourse

Approaches to inclusive health education through alternative physical education

Gary Stidder and Gerald Griggs

Reference to freezing little kiddies in t-shirts, says Peter. When I was at school we had a teacher in our primary school who took the games lesson. We were all, one freezing day, in shorts, and flimsy short sleeved football shirts. The teacher turned out wearing a deerstalker, gloves, a scarf and a sheepskin coat full length. He spent the entire lesson shouting to us 'don't be wimps. Run around and get warm!' Games teachers. Didn't you love them?

Ken Bruce
BBC Radio 2
8 December 2011

If you always think what you've always thought,
you will always do what you've always done.
If you always do what you've always done,
you will always get what you've always got.
If you always get what you've always got,
you will always think what you've always thought.

(Russian Proverb)

Introduction

It seems fitting that the final chapter of this book should draw together a number of important issues raised by other contributing authors and put this into the context of health as this cuts across all socio-demographic groups such as class, ability, gender, race and ethnicity. It is an issue for all pupils irrespective of who they are or what they are! Before doing so, we believe that we need to consider a number of critical questions regarding opportunities for all pupils to engage in purposeful physical and health education programmes that are not reserved exclusively for those who can afford the membership fees of trendy health clubs or have access to state-of-the-art fitness suites. So what contribution can physical education make to improving the nation's health? Are physical education teachers best equipped to tackle the obesity epidemic amongst young people? Is it a naïve aspiration for the physical education profession to expect the poor eating habits and weight management of young people to be solved in the gymnasium or on the playing field? Can we expect physical education teachers to influence lifestyle changes and combat over-eating and sedentariness amongst young people? This chapter attempts to answer these questions and considers the role of physical education teachers as an ever-increasing obesity crisis sweeps across the UK. In doing so, we propose ways to engage all pupils in health-promoting physical activities that could potentially provide an incentive to pursue the types of physical activities further and thus contribute to the health and wellbeing of each individual pupil.

Healthism and physical education

Physical education in the UK finds itself, as a curriculum subject in something of a unique position, in a 'crowded and contested policy space' (Penney 2008: 35) with pressures exerted from multiple competing discourses and policy areas, namely education, sport and health (Houlihan and Green 2006). For example, the sport discourse competes with discourses surrounding the purpose of physical education within schools, such as physical activity for the purposes of health and issues surrounding the discourse of 'healthism' (Evans *et al.* 2008) as well as competing with discourses of education surrounding issues related to the content of physical education in the school curriculum and their educational objectives (Capel 2007). Consequently, as important policy areas, education, sport and health have served as powerful vehicles that have influenced and shaped what physical education has become over time. Though issues of commonality may be found across the world it is the movement culture within which physical education is located that serves to highlight specific areas for critical discussion (Crum 1993).

Within UK movement culture, of the three competing discourses, it is 'sport' that has occupied a dominant position, traditionally conceived of as highly competitive in which the achievement motive has remained uppermost. As a consequence, a skills and performance-focused approach has been pervasive for generations within both coaching and teaching structures. Thus based upon pseudo sporting practices, physical education has continued to be delivered using a limited range of teaching approaches, the most prevalent of which are formal, didactic and teacher-centred (Kirk 2010). However the diet of physical education taught in UK schools consistently fails to engage many young people and consequently fails to prepare them to become active consumers of the varied forms of physical activity available outside school and beyond (Sandford and Rich 2006). This problem is exacerbated by the cycle of reproduction of curriculum and practice within physical education which has proven to be enduring and surprisingly resistant to change (Tsangaridou 2006) and is indicative of the opening Russian proverb at the beginning of this chapter.

Solving the obesity crisis

It is claimed that physical education and sport in schools is the best environment as well as the magic answer to the overweight 'crisis' amongst young people (Green 2010: 127). Likewise, it is commonly argued that the inclusion of physical education as a curriculum subject in schools is based on the perceived health benefits that can be accrued from taking part in compulsory physical activity (Harris 2009). Other contributors to this book have also shown that government policy can influence the promotion of health-related learning and behaviours through physical activity. And yet, despite the fact that health-related exercise is an integral part of the National Curriculum for Physical Education in England, some schools fall short in promoting lifelong healthy, active lifestyles for pupils due to an over-emphasis on competitive team games (Ofsted 2009). It seems that whilst the national curriculum for physical education in England has promoted the inclusion of different physical activities so that pupils can learn about the value of healthy, active lifestyles, the actual day-to-day content of the physical education curriculum has remained relatively unchanged and has limited appeal to a significant proportion of pupils with particular consequences for future participation. As Kirk (2005) highlighted, traditional physical education teaching methods are accountable for the decline in physical activity later in life:

> The adult participation data since the 1970s tells a consistent story, which is that only small numbers of adults participate in activities they experienced as part of secondary school PE. Even if we include exercise activities such as jogging, cycling, swimming, aerobics, weight training and so on, the introduction of health-related exercise (HRE) since the early 1980s seems to have had only a limited impact on adult activity.
>
> Kirk (2005: 247)

Competitive sport in schools, in particular, has been put back into the heart of physical education as a type of preventative medicine as part of the UK coalition government's quest to save the nation from a looming obesity epidemic whilst ensuring that talented athletes might achieve their full potential at international sporting events. This could be seen as problematic in respect to health promotion. For example, as Harris (2009) suggests:

> Some responses by schools to combat sedentary lifestyles and rising obesity figures may be misguided and could consequently dissuade some young people from being more active.
>
> Harris (2009: 96)

This has prompted us to consider whether an increased focus on competitive sport is simply viewed by politicians as a means to an end. Green (2010: 43) maintains that the assumptions about the health benefits of competitive sport for young people are, to say the least, contentious and pervasive as it ignores socially constructed advantages gained for example from being male and/or middle class. Indeed, Evans and Bairner point out in Chapter 9 that being middle class offers significant advantages if the goal is to achieve health longevity or to perform in elite level sport. Whilst there has been a groundswell of interest amongst those who are teaching and learning physical education in secondary schools to consider the health benefits of *'alternative'* activities within the formal physical education curriculum (Stidder and Binney 2011; Quick *et al.* 2009; Ofsted 2009; Griggs 2008) there also appears to be an anomaly. Green (2010: 145), for example, suggests that physical education teachers in schools continue to teach sport and sports skills which are often competitive and this is how most young people experience physical education. Unsurprisingly, there remain a significant proportion of pupils in schools who dislike physical education and tend to lead very sedentary lifestyles. With this in mind, and as pointed out in the introduction to this book, if competitive sport is putting children off exercising, then how could more of it possibly address the increasing number of sedentary young people?

The concern for physical educators is how to engage more pupils in physical activities that have universal appeal. According to Sport England's (2003) typology of young people one in four pupils actively dislike physical education lessons, referred to as 'the reluctant participants'. In a poll commissioned by the Cricket Foundation (2009) it was found that:

- physical education lessons provide the unhappiest memories of school days amongst 1253 55 year-olds
- the misery of struggling up ropes in the gym and jogging through freezing fields in shorts and vests leaves its mark on many pupils
- a third of those polled about their school day memories cited Physical Education as their most horrid experience.
- women were more likely to have bad memories than men (34% compared to 21.3%).

www.chancetoshine.org
accessed 17 April 2012

We would like to think that the situation has changed but the Cricket Foundation also found that 20 per cent of 15–16 year-old pupils actively *'hate'* physical education at school which may account for the fact that one third of parents admitted to writing a note requesting permission for their child to be excused from physical education lessons without a genuine reason. Four-in-ten children admitted to asking their parents to lie and come up with an excuse on their behalf, nearly a quarter resorted to faking a problem to fool their parents and 15 per cent admitted to forging a sick note. This is compounded by the fact there are even websites for children to find out the top ten excuses for getting out physical education lessons at school:

www.kidzworld.com/article/4886-top-ten-excuses-for-getting-out-of-pe-pg-2
accessed 17 April 2012

Similarly, the Football Forum asked people to post their views on their website and asked: So, what are your fondest memories of school physical education, and what are the worst? Below is one example of what people found particularly negative about their school PE lessons:

> PE at school was very traumatic for me, as the teachers clearly weren't interested in me at all. Eventually I made sure all my instrument lessons were scheduled for PE so I could avoid it.
>
> www.thefootballforum.net/forums/lofiversion/index.php?t169928.html
> accessed 15 August 2009

The BBC children's television programme 'Newsround' asked young people about their views of school physical education lessons using the following questions on their website offering a chatroom forum to post responses.

> The government will tell schools to double the amount of physical education lessons according to a report out today. But what are YOUR views on this?
>
> Are you well pleased that you'll get to do more sport in school?
> Or are you thinking that you're going to have to come up with more excuses?!
> But do you also see it is a good thing if it helps tackle the problem of child obesity?

Many of the responses from these young people were positive but a significant number of responses highlighted the negative perceptions of some young people, one of which is listed below:

> I think PE is the only lesson where most public humiliation comes about. It can be very daunting for some and a lot of bullying goes on in this particular subject. It is a dreadful idea to double the lessons, if kids want to keep fit they can do it in their own time, it's a choice not something kids should be pushed to do.
>
> http://news.bbc.co.uk/cbbcnews/hi/newsid_4040000/
> newsid_4042000/4042097.stm
> Retrieved 17 April 2012

If these types of experiences and feelings are representative of a significant proportion of young people is it any wonder that the percentage of sedentary young people has been steadily increasing resulting in an obesity epidemic in the UK? Whilst the answer might seem to be obvious in the form of alternative physical activities and improving diet it is not necessarily a straightforward task nor is it necessarily the sole responsibility of physical education departments. Green (2008) has concluded that several processes, trends and developments in physical education have been prominent themes which may suggest a major change to and overhaul of the way physical education is taught in many countries is required. In this respect, Green (2008) refers to the '*sportization*', '*healthization*' and '*academicization*' of physical education as part of a continuum from professional stability – to fragmentation – to transformation in the UK. Green suggests that because of these developments in the UK, traditional physical education has been moving towards a process of re-branding itself as 'school sport' and moving towards the margins of the curriculum. Penney and Evans (2005: 26) observed that 'the overlap between physical education and sport is no longer incidental and nor are those in authority content for it to be left to chance'. One of the reasons behind this is that competitive school sport rather than physical education has become a marketing tool and a source of power, as it is in North America, where the economic and symbolic value of extra-curricular sport forces physical education departments to 'sell themselves' to their pupils and parents, and in doing so, to their schools (Green 2008: 228). This lends credence to Green's (2008) claim that the use of sport within physical education departments is an increasingly common feature of a marketised education system in the UK which has served as a power resource for many physical education teachers and their respective departments. Consequently, many governing bodies and headteachers are now more dependent on physical education departments to provide sport, whilst there is an expectation of physical education teachers to achieve sporting success amongst their pupils and contribute to the school's standing within the educational marketplace. In many cases this has often resulted in a paradox between physical education teachers, educationalists and politicians as well as the national governing bodies of sport. Many physical education teachers claim that the promotion of health, citizenship, and academic development for all pupils is a central aim of the physical education profession whilst the development of talent within élite sport is often viewed by politicians, school governors, and headteachers as the responsibility of physical education teachers. One might ask whether politicians would be hard pressed to distinguish between physical education and sport. In terms of health there seems to be an anomaly between the policymakers and the policy implementers.

Whilst we acknowledge that there has always been a long-established tendency for the routine of physical education to be wedded to the practice of sport (Green 2010: 144) there is increasing evidence that some physical education teachers are responding to the changing interests of pupils and have incorporated more diverse activities other than a staple diet of sport and competitive team games. There is also increasing acceptance within the profession that competitive sport is an intimidating experience for some pupils as it often exacerbates feelings of self-consciousness and embarrassment (Griggs 2008). Rather than being viewed as 'trendy', politically left-leaning teachers portrayed as abandoning 'traditional' physical education and school sport (Green 2010: 118) we believe that there are some physical education teachers at the 'cutting edge' – young practitioners who are beginning to embrace the revised national curriculum for physical education and taking the opportunity to provide innovative and relevant programmes of activity suited to a broader population of pupils promoting a more holistic approach to teaching and learning in schools. Likewise, we are also aware that a commitment to equity and inclusion through a common, broad and balanced curriculum in physical education is often dependent and reliant on the aspirations, interpretations and actions of individual teachers and teacher educators as others have pointed out 20 years previously (Evans and Davies 1993). This leads us to the question as to whether physical fitness testing in schools should be part of the overall physical education curriculum and what contribution, if any, this can make to improving the health and well-being of young people. This is a question that has no universal answer and opinion remains divided amongst the physical education profession. Wallis and Harley (2010) suggest, however, that less time should be spent assessing and testing children's fitness in schools and more time exposing them to a broad range of physical activities that are available to them.

The revised version of the national curriculum for physical education (QCA 2007) has encouraged an increase of interest amongst teachers and pupils to explore alternative types of activities within the formal physical education curriculum. Evidence of this has been emerging as more schools and physical education teacher training institutions in England are continuing to broaden their physical education curricular to include newer alternative games and lifestyle activities such as handball, ultimate Frisbee, cycling and cheerleading (Ofsted 2009, 2011; Stidder and Binney 2011; Quick *et al.* 2009; Griggs 2008). Elsewhere in the UK a similar picture has been apparent as reported by the Scottish Executive (2004) which showed a distinct lack of interest amongst pupils in what was being offered in physical education lessons who were often left out of the decision-making process. In this respect, there appears to be little or no acknowledgement amongst politicians that participation rates, including those of *'reluctant girls'*, were sustained and often improved when they could choose activities that were non-competitive and social in nature (HMI for Wales 2007). If motivation to participate in physical education lessons is essentially enhanced when pupils are given a choice in the content and style of their physical lessons then we believe that it makes sense to listen their 'voice' rather than impose central government policies that have the potential to deter many pupils and subsequently result in an increase in excuse notes, failure to bring kit and higher numbers of pupils withdrawing altogether from their physical education lessons – a consequence that we had witnessed ourselves during our years of teaching physical education in schools.

Trends in youth sport and physical activity suggest that there is increasing appeal to young people of less formal, more casual and recreational types of activity and an increasing popularity of more individual and informal leisure and sporting activities over the past four decades (Green 2010: 194). Green (2010: 140) suggests that if only a small minority of young people continue to play competitive sports in their adult lives it begs the question as to whether current trends are signalling the terminal decline of sport – and competitive games in particular – among young people and concludes that this reflects a broadening and diversification in participation and a shift towards lifestyle sports and activities rather than a wholesale rejection of sport per se.

The National Curriculum for Physical Education highlights a number of key concepts that underpin the study of physical education in schools. It states that pupils need to understand these concepts in order to broaden and deepen their knowledge, skills and understanding. With regards to health the national curriculum provides the following advice to teachers:

> Understanding that physical activity contributes to the healthy functioning of the body and mind and is an essential component of a healthy lifestyle. Recognising that regular physical activity that is fit for purpose, safe and enjoyable has the greatest impact on physical, mental and social wellbeing.
>
> (QCA 2007: 190)

Armstrong (1998: 9) suggested, however, that 'physical activity is a complex behaviour and the accurate assessment of young people's physical activity patterns is extremely difficult' whilst Kolle *et al.* (2009: 1368) maintained that 'children's physical activity has provided serious measurement challenges for researchers'. Oliver *et al.* (2007: 47) stated 'the types of activities that are important are yet to be determined'. However the findings placed value upon both family and early years' learning settings such as parental encouragement, motivation to get the children to be physically active and the parents' own levels of physical activity as important factors in influencing both the physical activity and health of young children. The implication here is that early years and primary educators need to be supported to promote physical activity, in particular the importance of physical activity and health with their children, and also the social promotion of physical activity. Trudeau *et al.* (1999) emphasised the importance of daily physical education for primary school children and suggested that this had long-term effect on physical activity throughout not only the school day but also later on in life (Howells 2011). Suffice to say that *'If we always do what we've always done, we'll always get what we've always got'*. In other words, the problem will persist and get worse so unless alternative solutions are considered, the potential for further dissatisfaction and disengagement from physical education therefore remains extremely high.

Reflecting on an alternative

When one concludes that an alternative must be found the inevitable question remains as to 'what should it be?' Reflection in this way can often lead to some interesting places as to which values one holds dear and others than are reacted against, as Gerald Griggs' thoughts on his school PE indicate.

> Upon reflection my physical education experiences were largely centred around participation and little else. Primary PE as a pupil for me was football for every outdoor games lesson and for indoor lessons we appeared to alternate between the dubious game of 'crab' football and following instructions on a dance tape. The only reprieve to this was being taught by a

Scottish lady in Year 6 who did her own version of country dancing instead of following the tape. However this variation carried its own special social awkwardness as we were to discover as this either required us to dance with a member of the opposite sex (not cool aged 11) or a member of the same sex (also not cool aged 11) – a real Catch 22. Passing the 11 Plus saw the move to an all boys grammar school where my grounding in football, crab football and questionable dancing left me unprepared for participation in the school's holy trinity of hockey, cricket and rugby. I was only ever any good at rugby out of the three but as I seemed to go through the growth spurt later than most, after the age of 14 my appearances for the school ceased as I was considered 'not big enough' to be selected. More accurately I was not a 'favourite' of the teacher picking the team.

Similarly Gary Stidder's recollections of training to teach physical education in secondary schools indicates ways in which reflexivity can provide thought-provoking insights into the ways things were done in the past and how they might be done in the future:

When I began to train as a physical education teacher in the 1980s I had no idea that the four year Bachelor of Education (BEd) degree course would cover so many different types of activities. My previous experiences certainly did not prepare me for what was to come. I had never played basketball, netball or hockey nor had I been taught any of the rules; I had never danced nor had I any experience of gymnastics. I did not learn to swim at school either. Instead, I did football, cross-country running, athletics and cricket which I enjoyed partly due to the enthusiasm of my physical education teacher. Fortunately, I had plenty of opportunity outside of school to do different things thanks to my parents and was physically active throughout my teenage years. Looking back, my physical education lessons at secondary school were at best adequate whilst at Sixth Form College they were practically non-existent. So why did I become a physical education teacher?

In writing such reflections, the sharing of such stories becomes inevitable and also becomes a revealing practice with conversation after conversation revealing for many a narrative that begins with how they did not like physical education at school and a list of reasons to illustrate. Such conversations are typically ended with the justification as to why as an adult they have continued to do little physical activity or how in later life they have taken up a particular activity that they love, in spite of physical education and not be because of it. In light of such thoughts a possible way forward here might be to embrace Crum's (1994: 116) proposal that 'Physical Education should be arranged in view of learning with utility value for the movement culture outside the school [maximising] its potential to qualify youngsters for an emancipated, satisfying and lasting participation.' The viewpoint of emancipation for young people has a resonance with the ideals of 'second modernity' in which we currently live (Beck *et al.* 2003; Beck 2011). This might, therefore, see physical education take its place within movement culture which allows growing children opportunities to not only support their progress through a multitude of activities, a narrow range of which may be found in a physical education curriculum, but to support experiences they need in later life for lifelong health and wellbeing. Examples could therefore include such aspects as learning to swim, even paced walking and riding a bike. Further examination of this issue led Crum (1992) to consider that the breadth of the preparation that physical education might need to offer children preparation for Élite Sport, Competitive Club Sport, Recreation Sport, Fitness Sport, Risk and Adventure, Lust Sport and Cosmetic Sport. Though the use of this and other classifications may be debated, what is clear is a need to make physical education relevant to more young people and reconnect it to the wider movement culture so that there is less 'drop out' amongst pupils.

Towards an alternative physical education curriculum

To achieve a vision of a credible alternative a vital aspect to have in place is an overarching concept that spans all age phases. This may at face value appear obvious but it is something that the physical education curriculum in England has been lacking for some time. An appreciation of this can be gained by examining the review and implementation of the revised National Curriculum for all subjects including physical education for all Key Stage 3 pupils (pupils aged 12–14; QCDA 2008). In this iteration, the areas of focus were completely changed whilst the structure of the curriculum in Key Stage 1 and 2 (pupils aged 11 or under) did not. Such disconnections were further exacerbated by the clear 'top-down' models of the Physical Education, School Sport, Club Links (PESSCL) and Physical Education Sport Strategy for Young People strategies where a large majority of the time, money and resources were being put into the secondary sector via the Specialist Sports Colleges.

Again visiting the thoughts of Crum (1993) one can extract the following five concepts which may provide a useful place to start:

- competence in performing technomotor skills
- competence in dealing with sociomotor problems and in performing sociomotor skills
- increased knowledge and reflective capacity to master problems in rule-governed contexts
- development of a positive affective bond
- enrichment and connection with wider school life.

Without being too prescriptive, in terms of a range of content, schools need to deliver a broad range but have a flexibility to choose what is best for their pupils concerning their needs and facilities. If we insist schools complete prescribed certain activities, the realities are they may not be able to deliver on this.

However, given the cycle of reproduction seen earlier and given the chance physical education teachers will *always do what they've always done* a concern to be further addressed is to offset the continued pursuit of a traditional programme of physical education. We do not mean in any way to deskill or disempower professionals, far from it. We merely seek a reappreciation of what the subject is for and more thought about how it might be operationalised. In light of this drawing on the work of Davies (1999) (and developing this further) we would like to propose that all activities are framed with four broad areas being namely Expressive, Acrobatic, Competitive and Athletic.

Given the importance that should be placed on confidence that is drawn from familiarity from different environments and the variety of environments that can be found within and around schools, we would like to put these at the heart of the range of content, grouped under natural and artificial. Thus schools could then choose from activities within this matrix of areas and environments (see Figure 12.1).

The activity choices can be made by schools putting an activity in each box and then obeying the choices permitted in each Key Stage/Age Phase (see each relevant Key Stage section). An activity may not appear in two boxes and equal time must be given to each box.

To develop progression between Key Stages/Age phases we would recommend the following guidelines based on combined recommendations from Gallahue and Ozmun (1995) and Almond (1997) dovetailed with the suggestions above.

AQ
1996
new ▮

Key Stage 1

- activities should take place on at least one natural surface and one artificial surface
- activities should cover each of the expressive, acrobatic, competitive and athletic areas activities should concern themselves with the development of generic movements
- activities should be performed alone or in small groups
- activities should use modified equipment.

Area/ Environment	Expressive	Acrobatic	Competitive	Athletic
Artificial - Indoor				
Artificial - Outdoor				
Natural – Grass or Woodland				
Natural – Water/Ice				

Figure 12.1 Matrix of areas and environments

Key Stage 2

- activities should take place on both natural surfaces and both artificial surfaces
- activities should cover all of the expressive, acrobatic, competitive and athletic areas
- activities should concern themselves with the development of combined movements
- activities should be performed in small groups
- activities should use modified equipment.

Key Stage 3

- activities should take place on $3/4$ of the natural surfaces and artificial surfaces
- activities should cover $3/4$ of the Expressive, Acrobatic, Competitive and Athletic areas
- activities should concern themselves with the development of combined movements
- activities should be performed in both small and large groups
- activities should use both modified and specialised equipment

Key Stage 4

- activities should take place on any $2/4$ of the natural surfaces and artificial surfaces
- activities should cover $2/4$ of the Expressive, Acrobatic, Competitive and Athletic areas
- activities should concern themselves with the development of specialised movements
- activities should be performed in all/any group sizes
- activities should use specialised equipment.

All teaching sessions at every Key Stage school include all the Key Concepts and should not be reduced to mere activity. A further point to make here highlights the importance of future teacher training being focused at the subject level of planning and not get drawn down into content knowledge training or debates. This will allow trainees to have knowledge and understanding that can be portable to different situations and environments. Continued professional development (CPD) can address specific content knowledge needs and outside agencies could serve as a further tool here but not as a replacement.

The importance and focus of the 'primary' age phase

One of the most serious concerns of any disconnected curriculum is the inhibiting of children to pass through movement 'proficiency barriers'. This is caused by the absence of progressive steps that allow children to move from experiencing simple activities in the early years of education to the more complex activities of later childhood and beyond (Jess *et al.* 2004). Put simply, if children are unable to efficiently perform basic physical competencies such as throwing and catching a ball, they will find it difficult to participate successfully in physical activities that require these skills at a later time. This is underpinned by ecological approaches to studying the motor development of children which have revealed that mature movement patterns are influenced not only by maturation but also by environmental factors including equipment, cue information and feedback, 'thus refuting the "it happens naturally" misconception' (Bailey 2009 *et al.* 8). With the most significant periods of development take place almost entirely within the primary age range (Gallahue and Ozmun 1995) putting the right building blocks in place from the bottom-up is key and builds a much stronger and sustainable curriculum model (Jess *et al.* 2004; Haydn-Davies 2005; Griggs 2007).

Ensuring that these primary experiences are positive and inclusive should lie at the heart of the delivery within the primary classroom. If pupils begin to experience Expressive, Acrobatic, Competitive and Athletic activities delivered in this way in a range of environments this should provide them with a wonderful freedom to explore movement wherever it may occur. Furthermore if activities first concern themselves with the development of generic (fundamental) movements, performed alone or in small groups and using modified equipment individual competence and confidence of movement will inevitably grow. As pupils move through the primary age phase the development of carefully selected combined movements should then come to the fore. However these should be as a built on progression from generic movements and not ill thought-through ideas which lead the idle practitioner in repeating watered down versions of secondary or adult practices. If these building blocks are in place pupils would be more than well-equipped to move on to secondary experiences.

Implications for teachers of secondary physical education

Wallis and Harley (2010) maintain that if the ultimate goal of health-related education is to encourage lifelong health enhancing physical activity patterns then getting pupils to reflect on their current activity patterns can be a very powerful tool in this process. In this respect, the national curriculum for physical education in England states that there are essential skills and processes that pupils need to learn to make progress which should involve them identifying the types of activity and role they are best suited to in order for them to make choices about their involvement in healthy physical activity (QCA 2007: 192). Within the range and content that national curriculum for physical education advises teachers that pupils should be:

> … exercising safely and effectively to improve health and wellbeing, as in fitness and health activities.Exercising safely and effectively: This includes activities such as aqua aerobics, weight training, jogging and power walking, in which success is related to improving feelings of health, fitness and wellbeing. Goals might include emotional wellbeing, healthy weight management, toned muscles, healthy skin and a healthy heart.
>
> (QCA 2007: 194)

Moreover, teachers are provided with guidance on how to promote further curriculum opportunities for pupils to:

> ... get involved in a broad range of different activities that, in combination, develop the whole body ...

(QCA 2007: 195)

What works for one age group, one community or one ethnic group might not work for others. Asking pupils what they want to do, rather than assuming that politicians or teachers know what they want is a significant strategy in raising levels of participation. To this end, exposing pupils to a range of physical activities that are available to them other than the ones that are typically on offer can provide teachers of physical education with potential strategies for increasing participation rates. In the UK, as it is in North America, the participation of pupils in physical education and school sport continues to decline sharply as they grow older and become adolescents and is most significant in the upper years of the secondary and high school. The lack of choice is particularly important to consider when examining the reasons for apathy amongst adolescent girls (Olafson 2002). Bailey *et al.* (2004) reported that as girls moved through secondary school there tended to be a progressive decline in their sporting activity and in particular girls of 14 and 15 years of age. Sykes (2008) revealed that whilst 56 per cent of girls aged 11 to 12 were meeting the UK government's national recommendation for physical activity of one hour most days per week this figure drops to just 41 per cent by the time girls are aged 13–15 years. Likewise Sport Scotland (2005) found that the adolescent years of 11–16 have particular implications for girls with regards to physical activity as they tend to be affected by puberty much earlier than boys. In the USA, O'Sullivan *et al.* (2002) alludes to the fact that adolescent girls are twice as likely to be inactive compared to boys in physical activities and physical education. The issue of choice and personalised learning was, therefore, considered to be important.

Stidder (2009) found that over a third of girls suggested that different activities should be included within the physical education curriculum including activities such as boxing, yoga, lacrosse, rollerblading, baseball, break dancing, hip hop dancing, fitness training, horse-riding, softball, water polo, martial arts, skating, bowling and ballet. Sport Scotland (2005) has shown that self-confidence is linked to competition. Although most girls enjoy the competitive element of physical education and sport, many girls are turned off physical education and school sport because it is too competitive. This is one of the reasons why activities such as aerobics, gymnastics and yoga are increasingly popular amongst girls, and why some traditional team sports are less popular. To cater for all pupils, they have suggested that teachers need to provide a wide variety of both competitive and non-competitive sporting opportunities.

Stidder and Binney (2011) provide a detailed analysis of the physical education curriculum and suggest that there is an overwhelming rationale for changes to the formal provision of physical education in secondary schools. When seen in the context of the seventy six hours of formal curriculum provision each pupils receives in an academic year there are many alternative activities that have health-promoting advantages such as Zumba dance, multi-stage fitness activities, alternative games, cheerleading, street-surfing and combat activities. Breadth, depth and balance are an important aspect of inclusive practice in physical education as it contributes to the development of the whole person. However, this is often inhibited by teacher attitudes; staff expertise; school ethos; physical education department ethos; facilities; finance; resources; and pupils' previous experiences. Nonetheless, teachers might consider ways that pupils can engage in health-promoting activities other than the standardised version of physical education dividing the percentage of curriculum time equally across the range and content of activities.

Linked to Figure 12.1, it is feasible to embed a series of alternative activities within the framework proposed. Using Expressive, Acrobatic, Competitive and Athletic activities in a variety of different settings would provide breadth depth and balance of experience and potentially reach a much higher target audience. For example, pupils can work to achieve maximum performance; engage in activities that promote expression and artistic development; develop tactical/strategic contests; enable agility and personal control; involve pupils in challenging the environment and themselves; promoting the leading of active, healthy lifestyles through alternative physical education programmes. Rather than view physical education as a series of distinct components (games, gymnastics, dance, swimming, track and field athletics, outdoor pursuits) teachers might think more abstractly: for example, looking at headings like those noted below and highlighting what an alternative curriculum might look like over an academic year – perhaps creating one which might have greater appeal to a much broader population of pupils in schools:

- aesthetic activities (trampolining, cheerleading, rhythmic gymnastics)
- artistic activities (street dance, hip hop, Ti-Bo, Zumba)
- athletic activities (skateboarding, street-surfing, in-line skating,)
- adventurous activities (orienteering, climbing, mountain biking)
- aquatic activities (water polo, life-saving, personal survival)
- aerobic activities (Boxercise, double-dutch skipping)
- alternative games activities (Korfball, Kinball, Tchoukball, handball, Kronum, ultimate frisbee).

Conclusion

As we bring this chapter, and indeed this book, to a conclusion, it is still evident that a significant proportion of schools remain out of touch with the interests of young people and their preferred activity choices. The extent to which teachers can address the problem of pupil disengagement and disaffection with the provision of physical education must be based upon making changes to very traditional and prescriptive programmes. Rather than looking at physical education as a series of isolated activities teachers should consider the extent to which the curriculum meets the needs of all pupils and how developments in professional practice respond to those needs in terms of participation rates and improving the health and wellbeing of all pupils. In this respect it seems appropriate to consider the old adage that 'as one chapter closes another chapter begins'.

If physical education is seen as a vehicle for health promotion and for addressing the national obesity epidemic then one might ask whether it is actually the antidote to physical and mental illnesses it often claims to be. What is certain is that physical education is fast becoming more fragmented, diverse and unstable. This has prompted Green (2008) to ask whether the contribution of physical education to a pupil's health and wellbeing will be reduced and less influential? Are we, as Green suggests, experiencing a significant occupational shift where physical education teachers remain in the classroom, sports coaches and development officers are on the field and in the sports hall, health and fitness instructors are in the gymnasium, dance teachers are in the dance studio, outdoor education instructors are on the mountain or lake? Or are we about to witness alternative approaches to the teaching and learning of physical education in schools through a more diverse health-related curriculum that might make a small, but nonetheless, significant contribution to the health and wellbeing of every pupil in schools? Certainly, the increased focus on competitive sport in schools will only serve to provide more intimidating experiences for pupils as it often exacerbates feelings of self-consciousness and embarrassment. Consequently, this has the potential to marginalise those pupils who are disaffected and unmotivated by what is on offer within the school physical education curriculum and could be deterred from physical education altogether when they perceive it to be a substitute for competitive sport. The politicians had better be careful what they wish for!!

> *If you always think what you've always thought,*
> *you will always do what you've always done.*
> *If you always do what you've always done,*
> *you will always get what you've always got.*
> *If you always get what you've always got,*
> *you will always think what you've always thought.*

(Russian Proverb)

References

Almond, L. (1997) *Physical Education in Schools*, 2nd edn, London: Kogan Page.

Armstrong, N. (1998) 'Young people's physical activity patterns as assessed by heart rate monitoring', *Journal of Sports Sciences*, 16: 9–16.

Bailey, R., Armour, K., Kirk, D., Jess, M., Pickup, I., Sandford, R. and BERA Physical Education and Sport Pedagogy Special Interest Group (2009) 'The educational benefits claimed for physical education and school sport: an academic review', *Research Papers in Education*, 24(1), 1–27.

Bailey R., Wellard I. and Dismore, H. (2004) 'Girls' participation in physical activities and sports; Benefits, pattern, influences and ways forward', *World Health Organization Report*, www.icsspe.org/documente/Girls.pdf

Beck, U. (2011) 'The Cosmopolitan Manifesto', in Held, D. and Brown, G. (eds) *The Cosmopolitanism Reader*, Cambridge: Polity Press.

Beck, U., Bonss, W., and Lau, C. (2003) 'The Theory of Reflexive Modernization: Problematic, hypotheses and research programme', *Theory Culture Society*, 20(2), 1–33.

Capel, S. (2007) 'Moving beyond physical education subject knowledge to develop knowledgeable teachers of the subject', *Curriculum Journal*, 18(4), 493–507.

Cricket Foundation (2009) 'Sick Note School Kids Avoid PE with a little Help from Mum and Dad', www.chancetoshine.org/mediacentre, accessed April 17th 2012.

Crum, B. (1992) *Over de Versporting van de Samenleving*, Haarlem: De Vrieseborch.

Crum, B. (1993) 'Conventional Thought and Practice in Physical Education: Problems of teaching and implications for change', *Quest*, 45: 339–56.

Crum, B. (1994) 'Changes in Movement Culture: Challenges for Sport Pedagogy. Proceedings from the AISEP conference', 2, *Sport Leisure and Physical Education, Trends and Developments.*

Davies, M. (1995) *Helping Children Learn through a Movement Perspective*, London, Hodder Stoughton.

Evans, J. and Davies, B. (1993) Equality, Equity and Physical Education, in Evans, J. (Ed.) (1993) *Equality, Education and Physical Education*, London: Falmer Press, 11 - 27.

Evans, J., Rich, E., and Davies, B. (2008) 'Health Education or Weight Management in Schools?', *Physical Education Matters* (official journal of the AfPE), 3(1), 28–33.

Gallahue, D. and Ozmun, J. (1995) *Understanding Motor Development: infants, children, adolescents, adults* (3rd edn), Madison, WI: Brown & Benchmark.

Green, K. (2008) *Understanding Physical Education*, London, Sage.

Green, K. (2010) *Key Themes in Youth Sport*, London, Routledge.

Griggs, G. (2007) 'Physical Education: Primary matters, secondary importance', *Education 3–13*, 35, 1: 59–69.

Griggs, G. (2008) 'A new curriculum for girls' Physical Education', *PE and School Sport Today*, October 2008 available online at: http://www.teachingexpertise.com/articles/new-curriculum-girls-pe-496

Harris, J. (2009) 'Health-Related Exercise and Physical Education' in Bailey, R. and Kirk, D. (eds) (2009) *The Routledge Physical Education Reader*, London, Routledge: 83 –101.

Haydn-Davies, D. (2005.) 'How does the concept of physical literacy relate to what is and what could be the practice of physical education?', *British Journal of Teaching Physical Education*, 36(3), 45–8.

Her Majesty's Inspectorate for Education and Training in Wales (2007) *Girls' Participation in Physical Activity in Schools*, July, www.estyn.gov.uk

Houlihan, B. and Green, M. (2006) 'The changing status of school sport and physical education: explaining policy change', *Sport, Education and Society*, 11(1), 73–92.

Howells K. (2011) 'An Introduction to Physical Education', in Driscoll P., Lambirth A. and Roden J. (eds) (2011) *The Primary Curriculum: A Creative Approach*. London: Sage.

Jess, M., Dewar, K. and Fraser, G. (2004) 'Basic moves: Developing a foundation for lifelong physical activity', *British Journal of Teaching in Physical Education* 35(2), 23–7.

Kirk, D. (2005) 'Physical education, youth sport and lifelong participation: the importance of early learning experiences', *European Physical Education Review*, 11(3), 239–55.

Kirk, D. (2010) *Physical Education Futures*, London: Routledge.

Kolle, E., Steene-Johannessen, J., Klasson-Heggebö, L., Andersen, L. B. and Anderssen, S. A. (2009), 'A 5-yr Change in Norwegian 9-yr Olds' Objectively Assessed Physical Activity Level', *Medicine and Science in Sports and Exercise*, 41(7), 1368–73.

O'Sullivan M., Bush, K. and Gehring, M. (2002) 'Gender Equity and Physical Education: a USA perspective', in Penney, D. (ed.) *Gender and Physical Education: Contemporary Issues and Future Directions*, London: Routledge, 163–89.

Ofsted (2009) *Physical Education in Schools 2005/08: Working towards 2012 and beyond*, April, Reference No. 080249, www.ofsted.gov.uk

Ofsted (2011) *School Sport Partnerships: A Survey of good practice*, June 2011, Reference No: 100237.

Olafson, L. (2002) 'I Hate Phys. Ed: Adolescent girls talk about physical education', *The Physical Educator*, 59, 2: 67–74.

Oliver M. O., Scholfield G. M., Kolt G. S. and McLachlan C. (2007) 'Physical Activity in Early Childhood: Current state of knowledge', *New Zealand Research in Early Childhood Education Journal*, 10: 47–68.

Penney, D. (2008) 'Playing a political game and play for position: policy and curriculum development in health and PE', *European PE Review*, 4, 1: 33–49.

Penney, D. and Evans, J. (2005) 'Policy, Power and Politics in Physical Education', in Green, K. and Hardman, K. (eds) (2005) *Physical Education: Essential Issues*, London, Sage: 21–38.

QCA (2008) *The National Curriculum for Physical Education at Key Stages 3 and 4*, accessed 10 November 2009 from http://curriculum.qcda.gov.uk

Quick, S., Dalziel, D., Thornton, A. and Simon, A. (2009) *PE and School Sport Survey 2008–2009*, Department for Children, Schools and Families, Research Report DCSF-RR168.

Sandford, R. and Rich, E. (2006) 'Learners and popular culture', in Kirk, D., Macdonald, D. and O'Sullivan, M. (eds) *The Handbook of Physical Education*: London: Sage: 275–91.

Scottish Executive (2004) *The Report of the Review Group on Physical Education*, Scottish Executive, June.

Sport England (2003) *Young People and Sport in England 2002: A survey of young people and PE teachers*, London, Sport England.

Sport Scotland (2005) *Making Women and Girls More Active: A good practice guide*, Sport Scotland, www.sportscotland.org.uk

Stidder, G. (2009) *'A comparative analysis of Secondary and High School Physical Education policy and practice for girls in the United Kingdom and the United States of America'*, Unpublished PhD Thesis, University of Brighton.

Stidder, G. and Binney, J. (2011) 'Alternative Approaches to Teaching and Learning Physical Education in Secondary Schools', *Physical Education Matters*, 6(2), 27–32.

Sykes, F. (2008) 'Change blows through PE departments', *Future Fitness*, Wharncliffe Publishing, April: 23.

Trudeau, F., Laurencelle, L., Tremblay, J., Rajic, M. and Shepherd, R. J. (1999) 'Daily primary school physical education: effects on physical activity during adult life', *Medicine and Science in Sports and Exercise*, 31(1), 111–17.

Tsangaridou, N. (2006) 'Teachers' beliefs', in Kirk, D., Macdonald, D. and O'Sullivan, M. (eds) *The Handbook of Physical Education*, London: Sage: 486–501.

Wallis, J. and Harley, R. (2010) 'Learning and teaching through fitness and health activities', in Stidder, G. and Hayes, S. (eds) (2010) *The Really Useful Physical Education Book; Learning and Teaching Across the 7–14 Age Range*, London, Routledge.

Index